ROWAND ANDERSON

'The Premier Architect of Scotland'

'He was ... by general admission, the premier architect of Scotland. ... As a great Scot ... we honour him; as a great educationlist also, but most of all as a great architect.'

A.N. PATERSON
President of the Institute of Scottish Architects
21 June, 1921

ROWAND ANDERSON

'The Premier Architect of Scotland'

Sam McKinstry

EDINBURGH UNIVERSITY PRESS

© S. McKinstry 1991
Edinburgh University Press
22 George Square, Edinburgh

Set in Linotron Baskerville 2
by Photoprint, Torquay
and printed in Great Britain by
Cambridge University Press

British Library Cataloguing
   in Publication Data
McKinstry, Sam
Rowand Anderson : the premier
   architect of Scotland.
1. Scotland. Architecture, history
I. Title
720.9411

ISBN 0 7486 0252 6 (cased)

The publisher acknowledges subsidy
from the Scottish Arts Council
towards the publication of this
volume

Contents

Foreword

BY CHARLES MCKEAN
Secretary of the Royal Incorporation of Architects in Scotland

The ethos of 'Victorianism' has always seemed somehow less applicable to Scotland than to England: and the broad generality of what used to be called Victorian architecture, as an adequate description of what was constructed in 19th Century Scotland, has already been sundered. To date, however, published information of the underlying realities, and particularly on the two self-conscious attempts to revivify a Scottish architecture for contemporary use, has been scant.

By choosing the career of Robert Rowand Anderson, Dr McKinstry's biography focusses admirably the conflict between the first, picturesquely-based, revival of the mid century, and the Anderson-led, practically-based revival of the *fin-de-siècle*. The intent to create a truly national architecture appropriate to a technology-driven Scotland was common to both; but first time round the 'Scottishness' was only turret-deep. When it later reappeared under the hand of Anderson's admonitions, it was consistently thorough. For it was Rowand Anderson himself who created the conditions and provided the leadership for that second Scottish Revival, whose most brilliant exponents were Sir Robert Lorimer and Charles Rennie Mackintosh. Anderson's own achievements have suffered somewhat by comparison to such brilliant progeny, and this book should redress the balance. Yet he still proves elusive, lacking Lorimer's gush and Mackintosh's temperament.

His bust and portrait in the Headquarters of the Royal Incorporation of Architects in Scotland embody the impression given by his books, his folios of press cuttings, his journals and, indeed, his erotica: the impression of a commanding architectural statesman of a truly European breadth of vision. From this book, we can make a tentative stab at approaching the man beneath. From the very beginning, his driving ambition is clear. One of the few student drawings to appear at all in the entire run of the *Building Chronicle* is his, and his published folio of drawings of mediaeval France and Italy is scarcely more reticent with its dedication to Sir George Gilbert Scott. He clearly enjoyed taking on the establishment, particularly the Royal Scottish Academy, and then circumventing it with, first, the foundation of a new School of Architecture, and latterly the creation of the RIAS itself. These actions proclaim the single-mindedness of an outsider. Instead of changing the system from within, he established a new one of his own. Something of that flavour informs the activities of the Royal Incorporation today.

1990 was the 150th Jubilee of the founding of the Institute of the Architects of Scotland in 1840. It was as a deliberate recreation of that body that Sir Robert Rowand Anderson proposed the creation of what became the RIAS in 1916. He not only founded it, but provided it with funds, his town house in Rutland Square, and his lesser furniture. It is wholly appropriate that funds from the prize commemorating Anderson's esteemed colleague Dr Thomas Ross were able to assist Dr McKinstry to travel to Northern Africa in pursuit of this study. The Incorporation was delighted to assist in the development of a biography of its founder, and will be greatly satisfied by its completion and publication.

The time is apt. We are once again at a *fin-de-siècle*. Questions as to the nature of a truly Scots architecture in a high-technology age are again to the fore. Once again, the re-integration of applied art and craft with architecture is under scrutiny. Once again, a study of the past may well provide a clue to where to go in the future. Many of the arguments explored in this book are as relevant today as they were 100 years ago and as much merit study now as they did then.

1

An Edinburgh Childhood

On 5 April 1834 a child destined to become one of Scotland's greatest architects was born in the parish of Liberton, Edinburgh, the son of James Anderson, a solicitor, and Margaret Rowand, his wife. The exact place of his birth cannot be pinpointed with certainty, but it is known that the Andersons, whose home was on the southern margins of the spreading city, owned a cottage near Fernieside on the Drum estate, where Margaret may have chosen to spend her confinement.[1] The boy was called Robert and was the third of the Anderson children. Seven years earlier, Margaret had borne a daughter, Catherine, and had also in the interim given birth to a second child, George.

James Anderson's motives in pursuing a legal career were doubtless affected by a desire for social improvement. His father, George, had been an Edinburgh haberdasher and must have provided the membership fees required of James by the Society of Solicitors at Law, the small profess- ional body he had joined on completion of his law apprenticeship in 1818. The omens for a successful legal career were propitious. Scotland was in the throes of industrialisation, and her population and its commerce were increasing rapidly. The prestige of the law, centred on Edinburgh, had lately been enhanced by the reputations of Lord Cockburn and Sir Walter Scott himself. By the beginning of Queen Victoria's reign, however, a fourth child, Janet, had been born to the Andersons and it was apparent that James' career was proceeding at no more than a modest pace. The 1841 Census reveals that the family was living in rented tenemented housing at 2 Hay Street, the name then given to the tiny thoroughfare at the north-west corner of Nicholson Square. The block in which the family lived also had among its occupants a carver and gilder, a coachbuilder, and a Mrs Schultz, who ran a ladies' school. While the district was unable to vie with the fashionable expanses of the growing New Town, it was clearly respectable enough. At this stage in his career, James Anderson operated his law practice from his home address, perhaps from an office

on the ground floor. At the same time, a twelve-year-old servant, Mary
Black, helped Margaret Anderson with the heavier domestic chores, her
presence also denoting the conventional Victorian desire for respectability,
as well as the absence of sufficient means to achieve it on a conspicuous
scale. Nevertheless, it is apparent that Robert Anderson's early family life
was lived in a stable and supportive atmosphere.

On 4 October 1841 he was admitted to one of Edinburgh's most famous
schools, George Watson's Hospital, following his elder brother, who had
joined a year and a half previously.[2] The school was a charitable
foundation and had been endowed by George Watson, the wealthy banker
and philanthropist. When he died in 1723, Watson left 144 000 pounds
Scots to create an institution 'for entertaining and educating of the male
children and grandchildren of decayed merchants in Edinburgh'.[3] The
'Hospital', so called because of its residential facilities, was administered
by the Company of Merchants through a board of governors. James
Anderson's boys were eligible for admission since their grandfather,
George, had himself been a member of the Merchant Company. While
George Watson's had been set up by its founder as a charity, in reality
'decayed merchants' were a rarity and therefore very few of the children
attending were there out of genuine need. Indeed, the majority of its
pupils were the sons of bankers, solicitors, successful tradesmen or small
businessmen. Although the school was situated a mere few hundred yards
to the west of Nicholson Square, the Anderson boys were obliged to 'live
in'. Pupils were, however, allowed to dine at home on Saturdays. The
school building had been completed by William Adam in a restrained
classical style in 1741, and its location and architectural features must
have had some impact on an impressionable and sensitive young mind
such as Robert Anderson's. Long, symmetrical and rather plain, old
illustrations reveal that it was nevertheless nicely proportioned and sat
well in its wide expanses of tree-studded parkland. Generous balustraded
steps in the centre of the frontage led the pupils to the school's second
storey, where the main teaching rooms, chapel and dining room were
situated along a straight axial corridor. The top floor housed the sleeping
accommodation while the basement was given over to the kitchen,
pantries, storerooms and laundry.[4] When Edinburgh Royal Infirmary
was rebuilt on the school's grounds in the 1870s, it had to be demolished.
All that remains is its west bay, preserved by David Bryce in the heart of
his new Baronial hospital complex; here it is still possible to savour the
atmosphere of the very rooms once frequented by the youthful Anderson.

The value of an education at George Watson's during these years was
considerable; everything was geared to the boys' physical, mental and
spiritual development. Pupils were given health examinations before
admission and thereafter were well fed and clothed. The diet included

'butcher meat', oatmeal, 'sweet milk' and bread, and, even by today's standards, appears to have been carefully balanced. Old pictures reveal that the school uniform consisted of jacket, long trousers and flat-topped cap in 'green and drab', worn with shirt and tie. When the boys outgrew these clothes, they were given to the poorer children of the neighbourhood, reinforcing in their young minds the Christian ethos which pervaded every aspect of the school's life. Each day's activities began at six or seven o'clock, depending on the time of year, with devotions prior to breakfast. Thereafter, the boys were taught the basic skills of reading, writing and arithmetic before moving on in senior classes to the study of Latin, Greek, French, geography and bookkeeping, a curriculum reflecting Edinburgh's classical heritage as well as the commercial interests of the school's founder and the Company of Merchants.

Meals punctuated the teaching periods at one o'clock and four o'clock, and afterwards, before supper, opportunities were provided for instruction in singing, Scottish country dancing and drawing. Anderson is known to have acquired a fondness for sketching early in life and this is likely to have emerged or at least to have been cultivated at school. While the timetable regulated the day there is no indication that discipline was unduly severe; scholastic rigour was mixed with play and physical exercise. A contemporary illustration shows young Watsonians flying kites, playing with bows and arrows and strolling with parents on the parkland in front of the school. As well as being allowed occasional access to relatives, the boys were under the general superintendence of a matron, a Miss McFarlane, succeeded in 1844 by a Miss Orwin. The school's complement of pupils, limited by the constraints of accommodation, seldom exceeded seventy and the high ratio of teaching staff to students made possible the development of close relations with tutors and permitted detailed attention to individual interests and problems. The Governors, too, emerge from the Hospital's minute books as benevolent and pious men, imbued with the spirit of George Watson himself. The teaching of the Christian faith, as formulated by the Established Church, lay at the heart of the educational process and the boys were taken regularly to religious services in the nearby Greyfriars Church. Shortly after Robert Anderson's arrival at Watson's, a new headmaster, the Rev. Adam Thorburn, himself a minister, took charge of the school. As an expression of sympathy with the Seceders, who had just recently made their dignified exit from the Kirk to found the Free Church, Thorburn and his two assistant headmasters Whyte and Smith resigned in June 1843. A fire gutted Greyfriars Church in 1845. These events and the illness and death of several boarders are sure to have disrupted the happiness and equilibrium of school life.[5]

Anderson's schooldays were enacted against a backdrop of change, both religious and social; while Britain was at peace with her traditional enemies abroad and expanding her empire, Edinburgh, the centre of Scotland's religious, cultural and political life, was in its throes. Its architectural manifestation was the spreading New Town, whose apartments were being taken up by the burgeoning professional classes, the inward thrust of the railways, which by 1846 stretched along the front of the castle rock, while on the outskirts the occasional factory chimney punctuated the skyline. By the late 1840s, a wave of church building was in progress to house the Seceders, the newly emancipated but still unpopular Roman Catholics and the expanding congregations of Episcopalians. If these developments expressed the shape of things to come, they also expressed the power of the past; the stylistic trappings of Greece and Rome were still much in evidence in many of the new buildings. As late as 1850, W.H. Playfair produced a Greek temple design for the new National Gallery on the Mound, a style outmoded nationally but very much in keeping with the slightly older edifices which brooded over the city from the summit of Calton Hill. Further along Princes Street, Kemp's Scott Monument was gradually taking shape, signifying the growing influence of the Gothic style as well as the posthumous thrall in which the Bard of Waverley still held his public. The *Heart of Midlothian, Old Mortality* and their sister novels still spun a web of late Romantic nostalgia for things Scottish, a love for the medieval period and its remains, while imparting to the city's ancient precincts a sense of history, half imagined, half real. These factors must, however subconsciously, have helped shape Robert Anderson's spatial and historical awareness. So too must the proximity of Adam and Playfair's Old College, Wallace and Ayton's George Heriot's Hospital and the intoxicating historical ambience of Greyfriars cemetery, the Grassmarket or Edinburgh Castle.

Anderson left George Watson's in 1848, taking up a five-year legal apprenticeship with John Keegan of David Street, just off Queen Street in the New Town. During this period Robert received an annual allowance of ten pounds from George Watson's Trust.[6] His legal apprenticeship was perfunctory: on 12 October 1849 he enrolled as a part-time student of art and design at the Trustees' Academy in the Royal Institution, abandoning classes on 20 May 1850.[7] By 1851, he had joined his father's firm, and it is likely that these changes of direction came about as a result of parental exhortation, perhaps associated with an upturn in James' business fortunes. Certainly the family had by this time moved across Nicholson Street to 4 Hill Square, tenemented ashlar property erected some forty years previously, and close to the new Roxburgh Free Church. All four children were still living at home. George was serving an apprenticeship with a silk mercer, a liaison doubtless arising from his grandfather's connections. The presence of a female servant,

Mary Morgan, aged nineteen in 1851, confirms the general impression of a slight improvement in the family's circumstances. Much of James Anderson's work was based on the local Sheriff Court. It was not, however, work which Robert Anderson found stimulating, a fact increasingly obvious to his parents and certain to lead to a change of direction.

During these years, architecture and design were never far from public consciousness; the Great Exhibition of 1851 received voluminous press coverage, on a daily basis in the build up to the official opening on 1 May. The various steps and vicissitudes in the erection of Joseph Paxton's vast 'Crystal Palace' were faithfully reported as it took shape in Hyde Park. The names of Owen Jones, responsible for its interior decoration, and Matthew Digby Wyatt, Secretary of the Executive Committee, were household words. The personal involvement of Prince Albert and of Queen Victoria herself fuelled the general enthusiasm. Daily bulletins gave details of the number of visitors to the Exhibition, which sometimes exceeded 60 000 per day, and of the merits of the various exhibits, both national and international.[8] At the same time Barry and Pugin's work on the Houses of Parliament was in an advanced state, with the heart of the complex, the House of Commons, coming into use in 1850. The creation of these two gigantic buildings had vast and immediate implications for British design. Early in 1851 John Ruskin further increased the British public's awareness of architecture and design with the publication of *The Stones of Venice*. These developments and the architectural activity on every hand in his native city accelerated Anderson's progress in the direction of his true vocation.

2

Architectural Training

Robert Anderson's transfer to the architectural profession can be dated
to late 1852 or early 1853. The register of the Trustees' Academy records
that he restarted classes there on 7 February 1853 on the recommendation
of Robert Deuchar, a solicitor and family friend from Nicholson Square,
enrolling himself as an 'architect'. Also enrolling that same day was John,
the son and namesake of John Lessels, Anderson's new employer. Lessels
was architect to the governors of George Watson's Hospital and although
not as fashionable as David Bryce, who by this time was building country
house after country house in the Scots Baronial style, was a highly competent and respected practitioner. Like Bryce, he had trained under
William Burn, thus gaining vast experience of all kinds of commissions in
a wide variety of styles ranging from neo-classical to Perpendicular
Gothic. Lessels was a brilliant draughtsman and a painter of pictures with
titles such as *Landscape With Fine Old Ruins of an Abbey*.[1] These and his
collection of works by Grecian Williams and J.M.W. Turner confirm that
he was immersed in the Romanticism of the times and the lore of Scott.
The evidence suggests that Lessels may have imbibed this spirit as early
as his schooldays: he was educated in Kirkcaldy under two teachers who
had subsequently risen to national eminence, Thomas Carlyle and
Edward Irving, the latter the theological draughtsman of the Catholic
Apostolic Church. A devotee of Coleridge, Irving's theology and outlook
were permeated by mysticism and the pursuit of the numinous. His
personal piety may also have rubbed off on Lessels, who was renowned
as a man of high integrity and Christian principle.[2]

During these years formal architectural apprenticeships were by no
means mandatory; it was still possible to rise through the ranks on the
basis of hard work and competence. After training on the more menial
tasks, a good pupil could become a draughtsman leading to assistantship
and perhaps eventually partnership, the route now being taken by
Anderson. The opportunities given in the Lessels office to build the

knowledge and experience he required were neither spectacularly large nor particularly opulent, but they were nevertheless challenging and interesting. The commissions in hand included the alteration of a farm-house, Turtleton House, in Berwickshire, and the remodelling and extension of Blackadder, in the same county. The first of these involved the addition of dormer heads and bay windows to a small 'Tudorbethan' building, this style having been popularised in Scotland by Burn in the opening decades of the century.[3] The dormers were given the high triangular pediments favoured by Scots builders of the late sixteenth and early seventeenth centuries and recently revived by the Baronial special-ists, Bryce and his followers. At Blackadder, an eighteenth century classical house situated on rising ground was impressively rebuilt with balustraded terraces and wall heads, a large asymmetrical wing, the addition of strapwork patterning suggesting a transitional style.[4] In 1855, the architect was busy designing terraced housing for Melville Street in the western New Town, constrained by costs and the classical conventions of New Town architecture, under the aegis of the Walker Trust. The result again underscores his competence and versatility and points to the range of experience being acquired by his young employee, who was also busying himself with his design education at the Trustees' Academy.

This remarkable institution had a distinguished past. Its inauguration in 1760 was almost an accident of history. The Board of Trustees for Fisheries, Manufactures and Improvements in Scotland had been estab-lished by an Act of Parliament in 1726 to fulfil three main functions, the encouragement and regulation of linen and hemp manufacture, the encouragement of herring fisheries, and the encouragement of the manu-facture of coarse wool, activities arising in the wake of the Treaty of Union partly as a means of resolving fiscal inequalities. The Trustees' Academy, founded in Edinburgh, was created out of these initiatives: good design increased trade. The Academy, Britain's first school of design, did however have very modest beginnings, starting with no more than twenty pupils, drawn from trades such as house painting and pattern making, under the guidance of William Delacour, the French landscape painter and muralist. It quickly grew from strength to strength so that by 1798 painting was introduced into its curriculum by the gifted artist John Graham, and during these years Sir David Wilkie, Sir William Allan and Sir John Watson Gordon trained there. Throughout the first forty years of the nineteenth century it continued to grow, attracting leading artists as teachers and building up its educational resources, among which was a large and very fine collection of classical sculpture casts which included copies of the Elgin Marbles and the Ghiberti Baptistery doors. In 1837 the teaching of 'ornament and design' was for the first time entrusted to a separate master, Charles Heath Wilson, with William Dyce taking over the fine art side of the Academy from William Allan, who had been elected President of the new Royal Scottish Academy.[5]

During Anderson's studentship, the Academy was still divided into two functions, with Alexander Christie in charge of the department of ornament and design, and Robert Scott Lauder in charge of the fine art areas. Christie, a former student of William Allan, had studied in London before assuming Directorship of the Trustees' Academy in 1845. At that point he was also personally responsible for the architecture and design section of the Academy, while its fine art training came under the supervision of a subordinate, John Ballantyne. In 1852 a reorganisation had taken place. Ballantyne had not handled his duties satisfactorily and responsibility for fine art education had been given to Scott Lauder, with Christie relinquishing overall control of the Academy. The change was for the better. Both departments flourished under the new arrangements. Together these talented teachers instructed some one hundred and fifty students in cramped conditions in the Royal Institution, part of their studies taking place in the morning and part in the evening, by gaslight. The composition of the classes provides insight into the school's potential and aims. In session 1853/4, there were one hundred and forty-two students, which included thirteen painters, three sculptors, eighteen architects and designers, the balance being 'artisans'. The programme available under Christie consisted of 'Elementary' and 'Architectural' classes, the latter including 'Ornamental' and 'Fresco'. Students completing these studies would then progress to Lauder's classes, where 'The Antique', 'Life' and 'Colour' could be studied.

Christie, like Anderson, had started out on a legal career before turning to art and design. He was an Associate of the Royal Scottish Academy, exhibiting throughout the 1840s and 1850s a number of paintings depicting a range of historical, literary, religious and landscape themes. In 1889, Robert Brydall ventured the opinion that 'he drew well and painted with considerable vigour, but was rather rough, hard and strong in his manner'. In 1846 Christie had, with the help of his pupils, carried out the decoration of a new chapel at Murthly, Perthshire, the seat of Sir William Drummond Stewart. This had been done in collaboration with the architect James Gillespie Graham and involved a powerful fresco by Christie depicting *The Vision of Constantine* and the decoration of the roof and walls with stars and gilding. Christie's use of field trips also extended to his architectural pupils: Anderson was involved in sketching outings to St Anthony's Chapel, Edinburgh, Holyrood, Melrose and Dryburgh Abbeys, all popularised in Scott's novels, and also to the nearby Duddingston Church. The students, stimulated by their experiences, also arranged trips on their own account to the ancient churches of Dalmeny and Kirkliston, and to Falkland Palace.[6] These activities supplemented

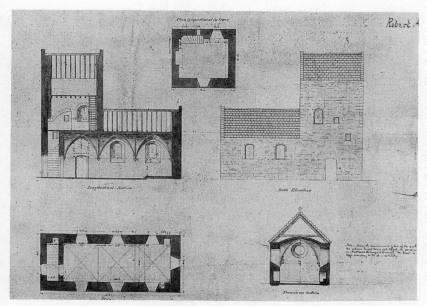

Plate 1. St Anthony's Chapel, Edinburgh, conjectural restoration. Prizewinning drawing by R. Anderson c. 1855 (Anderson Office Drawings, Edinburgh University).

the more prosaic but necessary study of styles, exercises in perspective and composition and geometrical and three-dimensional drawing. Added to this interesting and pleasurable range of activities were visits from distinguished figures such as Sir Noel Paton the painter, and Professor Millar, who explained the construction of the human frame, 'using a well built soldier as his model'.

It is clear that the course of study was much more than a training in the sketching of historical ruins. The architectural students worked up their alfresco notes, prepared with the help of measuring rods purchased by Christie, into fully developed measured drawings. The object of the exercise was 'pictorial anatomy', the analysis of the relationship between form and function, as well as the acquisition of accurate stylistic syntax. The Board of Manufactures awarded prizes for the best measured drawings; on at least two occasions, Anderson's came first. His prize-winning illustrations of St Anthony's Chapel and of the Norman chancel arch of Duddingston Church still survive (Plates 1 and 2). Drawings made on other trips to Falkland, Melrose and Dryburgh also survive. As further evidence of Anderson's immense commitment to his new career, he was also taking additional classes in architectural drawing from a private teacher, of whom there were a number in Edinburgh.

Plate 2. Chancel arch, Duddingston Kirk. Prizewinning drawing by
R. Anderson c. 1855 (Anderson Office Drawings, Edinburgh University).

Study at the Trustees' School of Design was occasionally enlivened by
visits from Robert William Billings, the English illustrator and architect,
who between 1845 and 1852 had published his magisterial work, *The
Baronial and Ecclesiastical Antiquities of Scotland* in four volumes. This work
consolidated Billings' reputation as a master of draughtsmanship while
at the same time making tangible Sir Walter Scott's Romantic visions of
ancient Scottish architecture. Billings' drawings were at that point the
most accurate representations of historic Scottish buildings yet published,
but were still full of atmosphere. His illustrations were a constant source

of reference for David Bryce and his followers, who were building imitations of Baronial castles for landowners erecting new mansions or extending old ones and wishing to do so in the 'old Scotch' style.[7] Billings clearly enjoyed his visits to the Trustees' School of Design and was friendly and approachable. In 1855 each student was given a copy of his 1851 book *The Power of Form Applied to Geometric Tracery* in which he advocated a free approach to the design of Gothic details, using geometry as a starting point, rather than the slavish reproduction of historical examples. Quite obviously, studentship in such a school was a fascinating experience.

When, by the middle 1850s, Anderson left Christie's classes and came under the jurisdiction of Robert Scott Lauder, he found that this master was also at the height of his powers. Lauder had himself studied at the Trustees' Academy and had worked as an artist in London and on the continent before rejoining his old school in 1852. His father-in-law was the Rev. John Thomson of Duddingston, clergyman and artist, who may have influenced his style of painting, which was characterised by 'breadth of effect and flow of line'. Lauder was an immensely gifted teacher, a charismatic figure; during these years he taught Orchardson, McWhirter, McTaggart, Pettie and others who also rose to fame. His technique was not to mould but to inspire, evident from the range of approaches seen in his most eminent pupils, many of whom became Anderson's friends.[8] By the time Anderson left the Trustees' Academy in 1856 he owed an immense debt to Alexander Christie; in later years his architecture would also be admired for its 'breadth of treatment', a quality that may also have owed something to Robert Scott Lauder's teaching.

As well as learning his profession in the Lessels practice and at the Trustees' Academy, Anderson was able to absorb and evaluate the architectural theories of leading practitioners, who frequently gave papers at the Architectural Institute of Scotland, the meetings of which were held in Edinburgh. The Institute was founded in 1850, marking both the upsurge of interest in architecture and the increased building activity on every hand. An earlier organisation, the Institute of Architects in Scotland, had been founded in the 1840s, but had collapsed within a few years. Its successor had wider support, welcoming not only practising architects but all other lovers of art. The Architectural Institute's membership included most of the leading Edinburgh architects, together with the cream of the Glasgow profession, men such as John Honeyman, Alexander 'Greek' Thomson, John T. Rochead, James Salmon, John Burnet Senior and John Carrick. The problems of travelling from Glasgow to Edinburgh undoubtedly affected the ability of the Glasgow membership to present papers and to attend, giving the Institute an unfortunate if unintentional geographical bias. The figures delivering lectures in the 1850s, while

Anderson was in membership, do however provide a cross section of national architectural opinion, even if geographically skewed; moreover, most of them were his personal and professional acquaintances, men whose views helped shape his own.

In 1851, a paper 'On the Architectural Features of Edinburgh' was presented to the Institute by John Dick Peddie. Peddie, in his twenty-seventh year, was the son of a solicitor, a former pupil of the distinguished architect David Rhind, and had already begun to display in his expanding practice a preference for classical styles. His purpose was to celebrate the picturesque beauty of Edinburgh, to identify some of the factors that had contributed to it, and to exhort his audience to ensure that it was pre-served. He began by emphasising the great variety and 'marked character' of the city's natural features and the 'singularly happy adaptation to these of the buildings which cover them'. Among its architectural delights were the 'broken, picturesque and tumultuous piles of the Old Town . . . the baronial castellated buildings of the jails . . . the classic monuments of the Calton Hill [and the] . . . elaborately ornamental spire of the Scott Monument'.[9] Since the preservation of such beautiful vistas was a matter of the highest importance it was necessary that architects should 'design everything, not as a member of an architectural group only, but of a great natural scene'. Some mistakes had been made. Nelson's monument ought to be replaced by a lofty and broad classical building rising to an apex to finish the outline of the hill, culminating in a low dome, perhaps of the type found in Turkish mosques. This would ensure that it would be 'assimilated in character to the Observatory'. Peddie concluded by praising the Parthenon, expressing the hope that it would soon have its Edinburgh counterpart upon the completion of Playfair's edifice on Calton Hill.[10] As well as showing a fair degree of oratorical skill, Peddie had laid bare his architectural preoccupations. The dominance of visual values, the importance of shaping buildings into broad architectural groups or into a wide landscape scene, all locate Peddie in the picturesque tradition, a fact underscored by his frequent use of that term. Peddie's aesthetics had roots as far back as Gilpin, extending through the previous generation of architects and possibly even Sir Walter Scott. Nor was he by any means alone in his pursuit of these ideals.

The next year, R.W. Billings presented a paper to the Institute 'On Certain Features of the Ancient Architecture of Scotland'. He began by expressing his basic assumption, that Scotland's ancient architecture was created by clever artists, whose works never failed. Their buildings were designed to show to advantage on their sites and were beautifully composed to harmonise with the surrounding scenery. In churches the 'spire crowns the valley' contrasting with the low undulating lines of flat

country on every side. The designers of such buildings 'invariably placed
the point of effect in exactly the right place', emphasising in his mind that
there were 'laws for the amalgamation of scenery and building which
should be observed'. Surely, he argued, contemporary architects ought to
follow the same principles.[11] In fact, many were already heeding his
advice: those who plundered *The Baronial and Ecclesiastical Antiquities of
Scotland* for design ideas, including David Bryce himself, were preoccupied
with the effects their buildings would create and their interaction with the
landscape.

Billings next emphasised that old buildings should not just be used as
a source of ideas for architectural enrichment, but as whole compositions
in their own right. Nevertheless, the details were delightful, and these he
proceeded to extol: the beauty and peculiarity of turret shapes and sizes,
newel stairs and the quaint texts which adorned the entrance to many an
old Scots mansion. Failing to countenance even the possibility that non-
visual considerations had played a part in their design, Billings next con-
ceded that he did not understand 'the jutting lines breaking out all over
a building' nor the fact that at times 'you can hardly tell whether the
perpendicular or horizontal line of composition prevails'. Nevertheless, he
contented himself that this apparent confusion of axes was 'often exceed-
ingly picturesque' and perhaps related to irregular sites.[12]

The papers given by Billings and Peddie show quite clearly the extent
to which picturesque considerations had permeated Scottish architecture
at this time. During the session 1853/4, however, it was made apparent
that there were other quite different theoretical perspectives. No less a
figure than Alexander Christie, Anderson's own teacher at the Trustees'
School of Design, himself presented a paper 'On the Adaptation of
Previous Styles of Architecture to Our Present Wants'. In November 1853
John Ruskin had delivered his Edinburgh lectures, which on his own
admission 'excited . . . considerable indignation among the architects who
happened to hear them'.[13] Christie's paper was quite clearly inspired by
Ruskin's controversial remark that 'the Greek system of construction was
weak and barbarous', a view almost certainly owing its origins to A.W.N.
Pugin, who had just died in 1852. With this Christie did not agree, and
he sought to demonstrate in his own lecture that most of the historical
architectural styles, Greek included, were suitable for contemporary use.
He began by posing a question often aired.

> Why adopt any previous style whatever — why not invent a new
> one? Why should we, who boast increased intelligence and comforts,
> be housed in imitation of our benighted ancestors? . . . The answer
> to all this is very simple. We do not require any new style of building.[14]

The reasoning behind this bold assertion was twofold. Firstly, style was

a by-product of constructional technique. The Etruscan arch had been
'found in the granaries of Egypt, as a piece of hidden construction before
it became the feature of a style'. Moreover, Christie felt,

> of the three great principles of architectural construction, the Beam,
> the Arch and the Tie, we have added to the second, and we may
> fairly claim the third. A stray skew arch or two may be found in old
> Gothic buildings (I think there is one at Oxford); but it was only
> when the rigid railways required rivers and roads to be bridged over
> at all angles, that its power and convenience caused it to rise into
> importance.[15]

It therefore followed that, if the existing repertoire of constructional
principles still sufficed for man's needs, then their by-products, the
historical styles, were quite sufficient, all the more so since the full
potential of ancient constructional principles was only beginning to be
exploited. As examples of that fact, he cited Telford's bridge over the
Menai Straits and the Crystal Palace, which he believed rivalled 'the
mightiest structures in stone and lime'. Christie was also impressed with
the 'tapering line' and 'faultless construction' of factory chimneys.

He next turned to the central theme of his paper, concentrating on
Greek architecture, which was said to be 'unfit for our purposes'. This
Christie denied, reminding his audience that, while Greek architecture
was based on symmetrical form, it seldom relied on symmetrical plan.
The proof was the group of buildings on the Acropolis, which was
irregularly planned, asymmetrically laid out, varied in mass and wholly
splendid. However, he had to admit that 'the greatest difficulty with
regard to the Greek seems . . . to be in the fenestral arrangements and in
provision for the chimneys' but he was hopeful that ingenuity and
technology combined would 'render Greek forms as plastic in our hands
as Romanesque or Gothic'. The allegation that Greek was 'barbarous'
was completely ill-founded. Architects should therefore seek 'good in
every thing', stylistically speaking, a logical conclusion for a theorist who
had also stated in his paper that all European styles 'sprang from our
wants'.

In attributing architectural evolution to the changing practical needs
of society and in aligning historical styles with constructive principles,
Christie showed himself to be both functionalist and rationalist in his
approach. He was not, of course, oblivious to the aesthetic dimension,
even using the term 'picturesque' in his speech. Unlike the two speakers
previously cited, however, he had not advocated the deliberate manu-
facture of picturesque effects in architecture. As well as demonstrating his
ability to construct and present a witty and rational argument, Christie's
speech displayed considerable erudition; it was spiced with quotations
from Hume, Scott, Fielding, Johnson and the Bible. Not surprisingly,

perhaps, it also showed that he was familiar with the writings of Francesco Milizia, the eighteenth century Italian neo-classical theorist and function- alist. Christie emerges from the mists of the past as an urbane and entertaining lecturer, qualities which must have appealed to the young man destined to become his most distinguished pupil.

John Lessels, Anderson's first employer, also gave a paper at the Architectural Institute, albeit a little later, in 1860. The survival of his speech in some ways makes up for the disappointing lack of evidence concerning Anderson's early training, providing as it does valuable insights into the architectural thinking to which he was exposed during this period. Lessels' paper was entitled 'An Enquiry as to the True Principles for Our Guidance in the Restoration of Old Buildings'. In dealing with a controversial subject, Lessels let slip his Romantic leanings in a passage very reminiscent of Scott:

> many [old buildings] also, from the lapse of time and other accidental causes, present to the eye objects of such picturesque beauty, that poets and painters find in them a constant theme for the exercise of their talents, and they have now become so enhanced in value by the associations that surround them, that one feels it to be desecration to interfere with a single stone, or even to remove one single stem of the ivy which threatens, in the luxuriance of its growth, to overthrow the very pinnacle to which it has clung in its aspirations.[16]

These sensitive remarks betrayed Lessels' painterly instincts and were wholly consistent with his liking for the art of Turner and Grecian Williams. He was, however, a realist, and concluded somewhat reluctantly that restoration was 'the order of the day' and that some principles were therefore necessary. In a church where 'the walls . . . have in many places got dilapidated, and there are portions of them slightly displaced' would it be right to apply new stone? Should window tracery adjacent to any such new work be altered to suit that new work? 'I think I can anticipate a negative to both of my questions, and am afraid you think me very fool- ish to have asked them'. Lessels' plea was for a careful and conservative approach to restoration; his audience hardly needed to be reminded of the evil committed at St Giles by Burn, his own master some years earlier, when he had encased the ancient structure in new stone.

He proceeded to clarify his position on secular buildings. When carrying out the restoration or alteration of old dwelling houses, their architectural character ought to be preserved, but only in so far as the client's requirements permitted. It would be entirely incorrect to sacrifice 'fitness', identified by Lessels as the 'groundwork of all good architecture' in order to adhere to a particular style. He next amplified his views on the use of styles:

> I cannot conceive a greater absurdity than for a man, in the erection

of a new mansion, to confine the size of its windows to the dimensions
of pigeon holes, to the exclusion of all the glorious benefits of sunlight,
in the silly idea that he was carrying out the pure Scotch style,
overlooking altogether its progressive character.[17]

In the High Victorian period, many architects spoke of 'fitness' or
'fitness for purpose', their thinking influenced by the exhortations of
Owen Jones and others associated with the Great Exhibition. The
Baronial specialists, particularly Bryce, had in any event always been
conscious of the need to plan new country houses sensibly even if,
externally, they were gorged with historical details. In the circumstances,
they felt quite justified in claiming that their buildings met the 'fitness'
criterion. When they spoke of the 'progressive' character of any historical
style, they referred to its adaptability to modern purposes in this manner.
In this way they attempted to reconcile visual Romanticism and practical
utility, two aims that were frequently in conflict. Lessels therefore
provides a useful insight into the mental processes of many architects for
whom 'the picturesque' was a paramount consideration.

The vitality of Scottish architecture during the 1850s had another
manifestation quite apart from the Architectural Institute: the *Building
Chronicle*, a monthly journal edited and in large part written by James
MacLaren of Dundee. MacLaren had worked for David Bryce and was
himself an architect. While the *Chronicle* only lasted from 1854 to 1857, it
survives as evidence of architectural opinion and debate during these
years. If the speeches at the Architectural Institute give insights into the
theories being advanced by leading practitioners, the *Building Chronicle*
provides a more comprehensive national picture. In addition, it involved
itself in criticism, an activity less appropriate at the Institute, where
architects presented papers before their professional colleagues. The
Chronicle was required reading for aspiring architects and, indeed, Anderson took it.

MacLaren's editorials, written in a somewhat heavy style, provided the
journal's analytical and critical meat. These would cover issues of British
significance, such as the battle between the classical and Gothic styles,
an area in which MacLaren declared himself neutral, disagreeing with
the chauvinistic pro-Gothic arguments raised in the publications written
by A.W.N. Pugin during the previous decade.[18] A reasoned firmness characterised the *Chronicle*'s critical approach. This extended to MacLaren's
1854 critique of Scottish architecture entitled *On the Principles of Design*, in
which he noted a complete absence of 'catholicity of principle' in critics,
architects and the public alike. Architects, he felt, simply selected from a
wide range of historical styles without having any theoretical principles
to guide them. Moreover, their use of styles was often downright
indiscriminate, exemplified in a classical building known to MacLaren,

which, in contrast with its rich exterior, had a bare whitewashed interior. Sometimes the fault was sheer inappropriateness, as in the case of prisons in the form of 'mimic castles' with 'little round towers and battlements, and cross slots for imagined archers'.[19] Castles were for keeping people out; prisons were places for keeping people in. As a final example, MacLaren cited a building with a massive Doric portico, solid and severe. Was it an academy, library or the museum of a 'learned incorporate society'? No: it was a theatre.

In the May 1854 edition of the *Chronicle*, there appeared an article innocuously entitled *Amateur Criticism of Architectural Works*, but which contained critical dynamite. The criticism was as vehement as its origin was strange. Patrick Allan Fraser was a man of property from Arbroath who had started off as a house painter. He then became an artist, marrying well in the process.[20] Fraser was not loath to publicise his views on the wide range of topics which occupied his enquiring mind, and the *Chronicle* was reporting on his recent lecture on 'Architecture, with Special Reference to Local Buildings', delivered to the Arbroath Literary and Scientific Association. While deploring Fraser's 'penchant for dwelling on points of difference rather than points of agreement', the *Chronicle* found 'much to approve in the good taste and intelligent acumen evinced'. But, apart from his amateur status, a major obstacle lay in the path of his critical credibility — he had earlier remodelled his house, Hospitalfield, in a manner of which the Chronicle did not approve:

the traveller from Dundee northward, may, as he nears Arbroath, catch a glimpse of the conical turrets of an old Scotch mansion on his left, designed, we should say, in close imitation of that particular style. Presently the train whisks past the lodge and gateway — an orthodox Tudor subject — the archway of which has been manufactured into a ruin. You may also be informed of a Corinthian picture gallery attached to the castle.[21]

Although Fraser had opened his speech by admitting, in relation to Hospitalfield, that 'those who live in glass houses should not throw stones', the *Chronicle* found it difficult to square his mordant criticism and his expectation of being forgiven for errors committed 'in his chrysalis state'.

Fraser came immediately to the point at the start of his lecture:

During all my examinations of ancient buildings . . . I have ever found strong proofs that one great principle, that of usefulness, had suggested and controlled their original construction, and however quaintly picturesque in some of their lesser features, even they clearly indicate the fact of their having grown out of the requirements of the individuals or bodies for whom they were erected, and that invariably their exterior forms correspond in character with their interior arrangements, and with the end and object for which they were designed. But I have failed in my attempts to discover any such leading principle as usefulness regulating the construction of modern buildings. I see Police Offices, Infirmaries, Railway Stations, Clergymen's Manses, Jails, Country Mansions, Villas and farm houses, all possessing pretty nearly the same external features, and all bearing evidence of a want of consistency or harmony between their exterior and interior arrangements, and the requirements of those for whom they have been erected.[22]

He continued with a criticism of Arbroath Infirmary, a building in the 'Elizabethan' style: its geometrically exact gables had no function, except, apparently, to make the building look Elizabethan. The hospital had undergone alterations at the hands of several architects, a fact which Fraser appears to have overlooked, but the *Chronicle* was in general agreement with his critique of Dundee Infirmary, which he described as 'merely an imitation of an English baronial residence of the sixteenth century, and not intended to be carried out in the interior consistently with its interior form'. Fraser particularly objected to its two 'large pretentious towers' as well as the usual profusion of pointless gables. In old Elizabethan houses, towers were never just ornamental. 'To the shrewd good sense of this we have nothing to add', commented the *Chronicle*.

Next, new wings at Forfar County Jail came in for criticism. These had been built in a castellated style, and rejoiced in 'battlemented parapets, flat roofs and a bartizan turret at each corner in imitation of an old feudal castle'. On visiting the building the *Chronicle* found a 'strange conglomeration of style outside, and most erratic arrangements internally — such indeed as to make us emphasise Mr. Fraser's opinions on it'. Fraser next attacked disguised chimneys, which sometimes came

> in the shape of a black iron pipe peeping up at the back of the battlemented parapet, ashamed to own that it is a chimney, and unwilling to lessen the dignity of the castle by admitting the existence of a fireplace.[23]

As well as receiving the *Chronicle*'s slightly qualified blessing, Fraser's views were credible enough to warrant a hearing at the Architectural Institute. On 4 February 1856 he delivered a lecture in the same vein, with illustrations of the faults just mentioned based, rather tactlessly, on an Arbroath building designed by John Henderson, a resident of Edinburgh and himself a member of the Architectural Institute.

Robert Anderson, therefore, was exposed to two polarities of approach in Scottish architecture during the period of his training, firstly a bias towards picturesque and visual qualities, represented by a range of architects working in a variety of styles, but notably the Scots Baronial

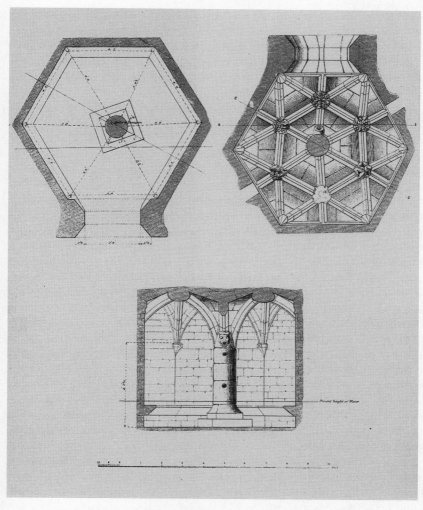

Plate 3. St Margaret's Well, Restalrig. Measured Drawing by R. Anderson, 1855 (*Building Chronicle*, January 1856).

style. Sometimes this expressed itself in modified form: architects such as David Cousin or the designer D.R. Hay, both Edinburgh men and well known to Anderson, were interested in achieving visual effects through geometrical proportion.[24] Those less reflective and scrupulous earned the opprobrium of the *Building Chronicle*, which was increasingly siding with the other camp, the champions of a more 'ethical' approach, concerned with the expression of function, the primacy of utility and other aspects of architectural 'morality'. During this period, they came not from the ranks of architectural practitioners, but from those on the margins, such as Patrick Allan Fraser or Alexander Christie. The source of their inspiration is not hard to find. Fraser quite obviously borrowed from Pugin, as did most of the theorists advocating this 'new' approach elsewhere in the United Kingdom.

In the meantime the young architect was beginning to come to the attention of the public: on 1 January 1856 his measured drawings of St Margaret's Well, Restalrig were published in the *Building Chronicle*, together with an explanatory article which described him as a 'young and promising student of architecture'[25] (Plate 3). At this stage his growing experience led to his being made responsible for supervising the erection of the new roof given to Old Greyfriars Church. Greyfriars had a complicated history. It had been built in the second decade of the seventeenth century, a church of six arcaded bays with a west tower, which had blown up in 1718 while being used as Edinburgh's powder magazine. The four eastmost bays were enclosed by a wall and this portion was then called Old Greyfriars. The western section of the church was rebuilt by Alexander McGill in 1722 and was retitled New Greyfriars, becoming a separate church. At the time of the 1845 fire, Old Greyfriars had been gutted and the roof and some of the furniture in New Greyfriars were seriously damaged. The repairs to New Greyfriars had been undertaken almost immediately by David Bryce, but Old Greyfriars was left to languish. Responsibility for its rebuilding under Scots law rested with the city council, dominated by Free Church men, who seem to have been in no hurry to repair or replace it. The plans for its rebuilding were at last produced in the mid 1850s by David Cousin the city architect, to the specifications of Dr Lee the minister.[26] Lee did not want the arcades rebuilt, and a large single span open timber roof was substituted. The Y tracery of the windows was converted to Gothic lancets and filled with stained glass, perhaps the first use of stained glass in the Established Church. A later commentator regretted that a seventeenth century Scots church had been converted to a thirteenth century English one. Some contemporary comments were, however, quite favourable.[27] Lee, with his progressive inclinations towards a less austere form of worship and more beautiful surroundings, was following contemporary English trends. While Anderson in later years came to have qualms about restorations of this kind, it was through these events that he gained first hand experience of working with an archaeologically accurate open timber roof, described as a 'creditable piece of work'. His involvement may well have come about as a result of the close personal friendship between Lessels and Cousin. In any case, it signalled his readiness for greater responsibilities.

3

A Rising Man

During the period 1857 to 1860, Robert Anderson took decisive steps in furtherance of his career. For all but a year of that time he worked as an assistant to the country's most successful architect, the Gothic revivalist George Gilbert Scott, whose office was situated in Spring Gardens, London, just off Trafalgar Square. Exactly when and how he joined the Scott office has not yet come to light. His involvement at Greyfriars is unlikely to have detained him in his native city beyond the early part of 1857, however, and from time to time in the late 1850s Scott was in Edinburgh in connection with several Scottish commissions. The opportunity for personal or vicarious approaches was certainly there. Although little direct evidence of Anderson's experiences in the Scott office survives, two things are absolutely clear: Anderson came to hold Scott in deep esteem, and Scott for his part quickly recognised Anderson's great potential. Thus, a lasting friendship was born.

At the time Anderson joined Scott, he had just published his *Remarks on Secular and Domestic Architecture*. In this book, Scott fully explained his architectural philosophy. He had originally been excited 'almost to fury' by Pugin's claims that the Gothic style was based on rational construction allied to functional requirements and by the argument that each apparently decorative element had a practical use. As an evangelical, Scott naturally disowned the more fanatical aspects of Pugin's Roman Catholicism and his almost fetishistic interest in the full panoply of ritualistic worship. At the same time, he was entirely convinced of Pugin's central thesis, that the lessons of accurate Gothic archaeology were applicable in modern society and that the style was capable of 'development' to meet contemporary needs. In *Remarks*, Scott made it plain that a building need not, indeed, should not, simply be a reproduction.

As the champion of the Gothic Revival at this point, Scott was admired by clergy and public alike. At, or about, the time of Anderson's joining his staff, however, the building of the Government Offices in Whitehall was fast becoming a matter of national controversy, one in which parties inimical both to Scott and the Gothic style would emerge. In 1856, three competitions had been held for the offices, one for the Foreign Office, one for the War Office, and one for the general treatment of the Whitehall area. In 1857, winners were announced. Scott had come third in the Foreign Office competition with a Gothic design, failing to make an impact in the other two. To his amazement and to the amazement of the whole architectural profession, the results were set aside by Lord Palmerston, who appointed a non-contestant, James Pennethorne, as architect. At this stage both Scott and his architectural colleagues began a campaign of lobbying and protest at this unwarranted interference. The question was temporarily resolved when, in 1858, a Tory government was elected. A Select Committee was created to look at the matter and appointed Scott architect, whereupon a new Gothic design was prepared. In May 1859 the Tory Government fell and was succeeded by the Liberals under Palmerston. The new Prime Minister summoned Scott and instructed him that the design was to be classical.[1] During these years, therefore, prior to the final episodes of this 'battle of the styles', Anderson was exposed to one of the largest and most exciting projects of the times, and must have pondered afresh the conflicting claims of classicists and Gothicists. At the same time the detailed attention and research which Scott devoted to the planning of the giant complex would have made a deep impression.

Over against this great architectural and political saga, the routine work of the Scott office had to carry on. The exact nature of this work can be visualised quite readily from T.G. Jackson's contemporary account of the practice's organisation and operation.[2] Below Scott there was a three-tier hierarchy, beginning with pupils, senior pupils, then salaried assistants. The salaried assistants, Anderson included, transformed Scott's expressive sketches and loose instructions, often delivered at breakneck speed, into fully developed drawings. Counting the clerks and the various technical specialists, the staff numbered some twenty-seven at the time. In an atmosphere that was frequently hectic, a vast volume of work was put out. This related to ecclesiastical commissions such as Exeter College Chapel, Oxford (1857–9), Woolwich Dockyard Chapel (1858–9), St Michael's, Crewe Hill, Cheshire (1858), St James, Doncaster (1958), or All Souls, Haley Hill, Halifax (1856–9). The latter, for the industrialist Akroyd, was considered by Scott to be his finest church. The ecclesiastical work also consisted of major long-term restoration programmes at Gloucester and Lichfield Cathedrals. By this point, the most controversial phase of Scott's career as a restorer was over, and he had become much less destructive and much more respectful of the past than in earlier days. A diverse selection of secular commissions was also passing through the office, including the large country house, Kelham Hall. Scott, in short, was at the height of his career, and the experience gained by Anderson was invaluable.[3] The style in vogue in the office in the late 1850s was 'the most severe geometrical Gothic'. This was thought by the Ecclesiological Society, the High Church–dominated arbiters of ecclesiastical design and taste, to be the purest form of Gothic, since it incorporated beautiful embellishment without falling into excess. The Society, like Scott, had formulated its views in the wake of Pugin's publications, although its members would have been somewhat reluctant to acknowledge the source of their inspiration. Over the years Scott had been influenced by this body whose journal, the *Ecclesiologist*, often reviewed his new churches, mostly very favourably. It is certain, therefore, that Anderson heard views expressed in the Scott office similar to those he had heard aired in Edinburgh by Patrick Allan Fraser and Alexander Christie. Spring Gardens was, after all, the very seat of High Victorian architectural morality, the headquarters of its chief apologist. In due course it would become clear that Anderson was persuaded by much of what he heard, although like Christie and Fraser, and like many of his fellow pupils in the Scott office, he would not restrict his allegiance to the Gothic style.

As a man, Scott was impulsive, extrovert, kind, energetic, with powers of intellect that have frequently been underrated, but which are apparent from his books and published papers. He has, with justification, been described as a man of the 'via media', which is true both of his personal religious beliefs and of his architecture. While on friendly terms with the High Church clergy and, indeed, the designer of some of their buildings, he did not wholly share their views. Architecturally, Scott's Gothic never approached the bluntness and severity of his fellow Gothic revivalists Butterfield, Brooks or Street, the latter a former pupil. It tended, on the whole, to be archaeologically more accurate, and much more palatable therefore, to the general public. Even in its more 'severe' phases, it seldom departed from historical precedent, nor was Scott's fondness for rich detailing ever completely submerged.

For a man so deeply immersed in work, Scott was surprisingly committed to encouraging and developing the young men to whom he delegated so much and who toiled so hard in his office. In the midst of a frequently chaotic schedule of client meetings, site visits and professional engagements, Scott took time to counsel and to pass on advice. This genuine concern for education was also reflected in his speeches and his published works, and indeed, the Scott office had acted and would continue to act as the training ground for the nation's leading architects. Those graduating from the Scott school included his sons John Oldrid Scott and George Gilbert Scott Junior, as well as Street, William White, George Frederick Bodley, John James Stevenson, E.R. Robson and Thomas Garner, not to mention a host of lesser known but important architects.[4]

It is fairly clear that Anderson was acting on Scott's advice when he embarked on his continental tour of 1859. Scott himself had undertaken such a tour and had learned much from it. So too had Alfred Waterhouse, William Burges, and Richard Norman Shaw, who had in due course published his continental sketches in book form. The tour was very much regarded as part of the finishing process expected of the aspiring architect. T.G. Jackson himself was also advised by Scott, through his father, to undertake such a tour, and the counsel he was given must have been similar to that given to Anderson, his colleague in the office. 'If he travels . . . I would strongly recommend his directing his sketches chiefly to architecture especially to that of the 13th century'.[5] Anderson's itinerary began in France, and involved visits to Bayeux and Caen, where he was particularly taken with the robustly constructed Abbey Barn, as well as a visit to Provins, near Paris. His travels also took him southwards to Bourges, and to Limoges, at the west end of the Massif Central. Many sketches and photographs were taken in the towns and villages skirting this vast area, as well as some in the vicinity of Lyons. Anderson next travelled to Italy where, in the north, he visited a mixture of well-known and less well-known places before journeying southwards to Florence, Pisa, Siena, Perugia and Viterbo. It is likely that the young architect would take the opportunity to visit Paris, Rome or Venice, although there is no proof that he did so.

In all these places, with camera, sketchboard and measuring rod, Anderson recorded secular and domestic Gothic architecture, most of which was little known outside France and Italy. It was his intention to publish selections from his tour in a book. His strategy was obvious: to concentrate on secular and domestic Gothic would impress the influential Scott, and a book containing illustrations of good, little-known, Gothic buildings would be more likely to make an impact than studies of familiar structures. Another motive lay behind his thinking: his drawings would also provide a fund of ancient examples for incorporation in future designs. Featuring prominently in his studies were elevations of buildings in early and Geometric Gothic, in particular those where wide expanses of wall plane had been preserved, and the detail carefully rationed out. The most striking examples in this style, eventually illustrated in book form, were the Maison du Grand Veneur at Cordes, and a house in Place Champollion at Figeac (Plates 4 and 5). Supplementing his observations of facades, both Italian and French, were sketches of tracery details, sections of mouldings, roof timbers and particulars of chimneys. At some time towards the close of 1859, while making his way homewards, Anderson spent a short period of time working in the office of P.J.H. Cuijpers in Roermond, Holland.[6] This architect's reputation was rising both locally and internationally, and although his most famous buildings, the Rijksmuseum and the Central Station, both in Amsterdam, still lay in the

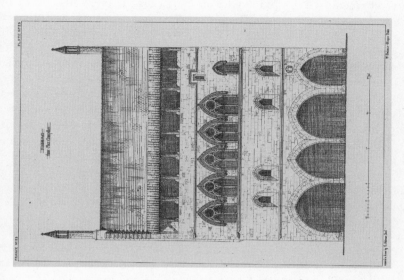

Plate 4. Maison du Grand Veneur, Cordes (R. Anderson, *The Domestic and Street Architecture of France and Italy*, 1868).

Plate 5. Place Champollion, Figeac (R. Anderson, *The Domestic and Street Architecture of France and Italy*, 1868).

future, his church work had come to the notice of London architects. This was characterised by 'triple decker' arcading in nave, triforium and clerestory. It would appear, though, that Cuijpers, as well as reading the French Gothic scholar Viollet le Duc, was returning the compliment and looking to England for inspiration. An unexecuted design for a picture gallery, illustrated a few years later in the *Ecclesiologist*, is strongly redolent of Deane and Cole's Oxford University Museum of 1855–60.[7] Cuijpers' church designs in later years, some of which featured canted naves, may also have owed something to G.E. Street. While Anderson would note with interest his use of brick and his restrained constructional polychromy, so typical of the Scott office, there was little that was new. Nevertheless, a brief spell in such a prestigious practice could do nothing but good.

By 1860, Anderson, then in his twenty-sixth year, was back in Edinburgh. His family had moved to the New Town, where his father was then practising. On his return, he advertised his services as an architect, working out of his father's address at 8 Dundas Street.[8] Nothing is known of his activities during this period. In the spring of that year, however, Anderson reminded the city of his prowess and recent experiences by exhibiting three drawings at the Royal Scottish Academy, *Town Hall in Twelfth Century, St. Antonin, France*; *Palazzo Pubblico, Perugia, Front Facing the Cathedral* and a *Design for a Fountain*.[9] That same year, he presented a paper on his recent tour to the Architectural Institute of Scotland. His talk was didactic. A further meeting was called to discuss its 'implications'. All that is known of these meetings is that the latter was judged a success.[10] It is very probable, though, that the architecture studied in France and Italy appeared to Anderson to bear out the theories of Scott and Pugin, that structure and function were the prime concerns of the ancient architects, and that the 'implications' related to the reprehensible overemphasis on 'the picturesque' seen in the work of their Scottish successors.

At around this time Anderson joined the staff of the Royal Engineers, who worked in an office at 42 Northumberland Street. Although its records have disappeared, it is clear that the office dealt with Scotland's coastal fortifications, and it is known that during the 1860s the staff numbered around nine, made up of three army officers, three 'clerks of works', and three clerks. All but the officers were civilians.[11] The Engineers had already made an impact on Edinburgh itself. Not far away, Captain Francis Fowke had designed the iron-framed Royal Scottish Museum, which was just completing, and a few years earlier Lieutenant Colonel Moody, also of the Engineers, had prepared a proposal, brilliantly illustrated by Francis Dollmann, for new barracks, six storeys high, at Edinburgh Castle. These were to be in the Baronial style, and would have drastically altered its north and west elevations.[12]

Plate 6. Broughty Castle, Broughty Ferry (National Monuments Record of Scotland).

The work done by Anderson and his fellow architects was less exciting than these two projects. In 1859, Lord Lyndhurst had made a speech on national defences, prompted by suspicions that the French were mobilising for war. This called for work on coastal fortifications. Anderson was made responsible for upgrading the ruinous Broughty Castle, Broughty Ferry, into a serviceable fort to stand alongside several batteries of guns facing out to sea, and intended to defend Dundee from naval threats. The castle's central keep was roofless, with the wall heads exposed to the elements. The facing stones had long since fallen off large areas of the structure, exposing the rubble at the hearts of the walls. An accurate restoration of the building in a careful and archaeological fashion was out of the question. What was required was sound, practical building.

In spite of these constraints Anderson, who was clearly given full responsibility for design as well as construction, performed with distinction. In addition to producing a building which today still bears his unmistakeable personal stamp, he managed to incorporate a few accurate restorative touches, such as the stepped gables to the cap house, assumed to have been removed in prior centuries, as well as some keyhole-shaped gunports (Plate 6). The keep was rebuilt with a rectangular extension on the north-west side, roofs were supplied and all walls made sound. To meet the fort's military requirements, windows were formed or enlarged within the keep, and the vaults were adapted as a magazine. Around the castle itself, landward- and seaward-facing fortifications, designed to provide enfilading fire in the event of land-based attack, were built. Within this complex, between the keep and the Tay, two sixty-eight pounders and six ten-inch shell guns were mounted on earthwork emplacements.[13] In the wake of rapid developments in military technology, Broughty Castle soon became very vulnerable, and as a consequence no real deterrent to maritime invaders. Today, it survives as a monument to High Victorian military thinking as well as proof that, by 1860–1, Anderson was capable of producing buildings of real presence and quality.

Not many miles away from Northumberland Street, at Leith, a project that would soon call for Anderson's architectural intervention had been in progress since 1859. By the end of that year, sufficient monies had been provided through legacies to build a new church for the Episcopalian congregation of St James the Less at Leith, and George Gilbert Scott had been selected as architect. His discussions with the Episcopal Bishop of Edinburgh, Charles Hughes Terrot, and with the incumbent, John Alexander White, involved a Brechin-based design, but by 1860 Scott had written to confirm that this would have cost more than the funds available. Instead, it was decided to build a church loosely based on the much less elaborate Dunblane Cathedral. Scott had a fondness for east or west elevations based on Scottish models. By November 1860, the drawings, much delayed, were forwarded to the church after an increasingly heated and illegible correspondence between Scott's 'head man', John Burlison, and the incumbent. Tempers had become frayed on both sides as accusations of incompetence and broken promises flew back and forth.[14] The immense workload of the Scott office and the desire of a clergyman to see his new church rise up quickly were quite clearly proving to be irreconcilable.

By 20 November Scott had been asked to name a clerk of works, to which he replied that

> I have a strong objection to local architects in that capacity. A clerk of the works is best selected from among plain, practical men and one who devotes all his time to the work.[15]

The job was by this point developing into a fiasco. Local tenderers were unable to understand Burlison's bills of quantities, which precipitated another spate of half legible but plainly vituperative notes between Leith and Spring Gardens. This situation prevailed for the best part of 1861, with relations between the architect's staff and the client at an unprecedented low, and many of the contractors pondering their financial position. Exactly one year after the initial request had been made, on 20 November 1861, a clerk of works was appointed: Robert Anderson. The circumstances surrounding his appointment are not clear, but he was in many ways the obvious choice. As well as having assisted Scott, he was known to Terrot, who was a member of the Architectural Institute, and

Plate 7. St James the Less Church, Leith (Grant's *Old and New Edinburgh*, Vol.III, 1883).

he had lately been immersing himself in the practicalities of building at the Engineers' Office.

Anderson's timely arrival at St James' marked a turning point. His presence on the spot and his personal knowledge of the operation of the Scott office soon combined to good effect. The young architect quickly assumed command, taking charge of drawings and supervising the work. On 4 December 1862, J.T. Moubray, W.S. was able to write to Scott that

Mr. Anderson the clerk of works called here last evening and stated that he wished me to desire Mr. Johnston the surveyor, immediately to measure the work already executed.[15]

Matters were at last under control, a conclusion obvious not only from the tone of the correspondence, but from the reduction in its volume. Receipts for salary from Anderson still survive, and these show that he earned two guineas a week from 20 November 1861 to 20 February 1864, some two hundred and forty pounds. Scott himself gave a receipt for two hundred and fifty pounds on 13 August that same year. Another receipt dated 20 February 1864 shows that Anderson took a cab from Leith to Northumberland Street on a Saturday night, confirming that the young architect was working in a dual role throughout. The design of St James' (now vacated and ruinous) owes nothing to Anderson (Plate 7). At the same time its building was a testimony to the young architect's single mindedness, energy and managerial skill.

While working for the Engineers and at Leith, Anderson had also been carrying out other commissions. The earliest of these was small: the design of a monument to the 78th Ross-shire Highlanders who had fallen in the Indian Mutiny in 1857–8.[16] This was erected in 1861 on the esplanade of Edinburgh Castle, and consisted of a Celtic cross in black stone mounted on a plinth and decorated with cable work (Plate 8). By the close of the St James the Less commission negotiations were in hand for a similar monument, on a grander scale, which was to be erected on a hillock at Logierait, four miles south of Pitlochry, in memory of the late Sixth Duke of Atholl. David Bryce had been involved in initial discussions with the memorial committee, but the commission was passed to Anderson, perhaps on Bryce's recommendation.[17] It was erected in 1866 (Plate 9). Against this background of growing demand for his professional services, Anderson on 23 July 1863 married Mary Ross, daughter of Henry Ross, a tenant farmer of Kinnahaird, near Strathpeffer in Ross-shire. The wedding took place in Contin Parish Church, 'according to the forms of the Established Church', and the young couple set up house at 11 Duncan Street (now Dundonald Street), off Drummond Place in the New Town.[18]

The St James' commission at Leith was a sign of new life in the Scottish Episcopal Church, which for some years to come would provide Anderson with a great deal of work. The Episcopal Church had been in a state of revival since the beginning of the Victorian period. The Church was not, contrary to popular belief, an English implant. It had arisen from a movement, present within the post-Reformation Scottish church, inclined towards an Episcopal rather than a Presbyterian order and commanding the support of the royal government intermittently in the 1570s and 1580s, and for two prolonged periods in the seventeenth century, from 1600 to 1638 and again from 1661 to 1690. Thereafter, however, a Presbyterian establishment prevailed and Episcopalians, through their continued association with the exiled House of Stuart, were suspected of disloyalty. After

Plate 8. 78th Highlanders Memorial, Edinburgh Castle (Grant's *Old and New Edinburgh*, Vol. I, 1883).

the Jacobite rising of 1745–6, restrictions were placed on their activities and the indigenous Episcopal body had also to face competition from the 'qualified chapels' which operated in association with the Church of England. In 1792, however, constraints on the Episcopal Church had been lifted with the repeal of the oppressive Penal Acts.

The Church had traditionally been strong north of the Tay. Between 1838 and 1858, though, the number of congregations had risen from 75 to 150 and the Church was in a state of revival nationwide, for which several reasons can be ascribed. The country's population was expanding, providing a greater target for the Church's missions. Secondly, the general barrenness of Presbyterian worship, where church music and decoration

Plate 9. Atholl Memorial, Logierait (Author).

were still kept under strict control, was causing disenchantment among an increasingly educated and growing middle class. This trend was fomented by the upper classes, who, from the post-Union period onwards, were more closely associated with their English counterparts. At the same time, the Oxford Movement was spreading its influence. It is difficult to dissociate these developments from the Romanticism of the times.

In the High Victorian period, the Church had in its ranks a number of clergymen whose personalities were vastly influential in increasing membership. Perhaps the most notable of these was Alexander Penrose Forbes, Bishop of Brechin from 1847 to 1875, a distinguished scholar with a reputation for selfless charity and personal piety. Forbes was educated

at Oxford, and came from the Forbes family of Pitsligo, eminent Episcopalians. During his episcopate he consolidated a large number of small
churches into larger units, and carried out mission work leading to the
creation of a number of new congregations in Dundee. A friend of Pusey,
Forbes was deeply influenced by the Oxford Movement. When he decided
to erect a large new church, St Paul's, in Dundee, he chose Scott as
architect, hoping that he would design 'a builded prayer in stone and
lime, a standing creed'.[19] In the event, he was not disappointed.

It would be a mistake to regard the Scottish Episcopal Church at this
time as being unanimous either doctrinally or liturgically. It had a history
of internal disagreement on liturgy, arising in part from its diverse origins
and from the historical difficulties it had experienced. As a rough guide,
those portions of the Church north of the Tay were to prove more disposed
to the Oxford Movement than those south of it. In Edinburgh, two distinguished churchmen were presiding over a revival of a different character
to that taking place at Dundee. Charles Hughes Terrot, already mentioned
in connection with the Leith church project, was a mathematician with a
logician's approach to Christianity. Terrot had been Bishop of Edinburgh
since 1841. E.B. Ramsay was Dean of Edinburgh and had been the
incumbent of St John's, Princes Street, since 1830. Although Terrot was
an Englishman and Ramsay, while Scots, had received an English
education, both men were extremely fond of Scotland, its culture and
traditions.[20] Theologically they were moderates, suspicious of the Oxford
Movement. Both men had emerged from a tradition where friendship and
co-operation with senior clergy of the Established Church was perfectly
acceptable. At one stage Terrot had gone so far as to say that 'every
conspicuous perversion of a lay member of the Episcopal Church in
Scotland has occurred under the baneful influence of some English
clergyman'.[21] Under Terrot and Ramsay, large congregations built up in
St John's, and in the churches in and around the New Town. On the city's
south side, working class congregations were also expanding and prosper-
ing. One exception to the moderate approach prevailing in the Diocese
was the new church, St Columba's by the Castle, where the congregation
reinstated the Scottish Liturgy in 1848. This involved a movement
towards ritualism, and was carried into effect in spite of opposition from
Ramsay and Terrot.

It was not unusual for senior Episcopalian clergymen to participate
actively in learned societies, and in the intellectual debates of the day. In
1854 Forbes invited Alexander Christie to deliver a lecture on industrial
design to a Dundee audience, subsequently reported in the *Building
Chronicle*.[22] Christie roundly condemned shoddy design and associated
quick profits, and brought with him ancient locks as examples of what
could be achieved. Both Ramsay and Terrot were active members of the

Architectural Institute. In Session 1850/1, the former gave a paper on
'The Method by which the Members May Practically Follow Out the
Architectural Purposes of the Institute'.[23] Having declared himself an
amateur, Ramsay refrained from practical advice, turning his paper into
a treatise on the revival of Gothic, followed by an exhortation to avoid
contention over stylistic issues, which, he argued, 'was inconsistent with
the liberal spirit of the times'. In the course of his lecture he revealed that
he had once known Rickman, which may in part have explained the
obvious command of Gothic syntax displayed in his talk.

On 13 January 1857, Bishop Terrot in turn delivered a paper 'On the
Elements of Architectural Beauty, in Reference Specially to the Recent
Structures in Paris'. After protesting his lack of expertise, Terrot prefaced
his visual experiences of Haussman's Paris with characteristically incisive
comment:

> The beauty . . . of the human form, depends upon its apparent
> adaptation to its purpose. We need not, indeed, deny all truth to the
> systems which profess to define beauty by certain combinations of
> different angles and proportional length of parts; but it is very
> certain, that the sentiment of admiration is excited, not by the
> perception of mathematical relationship, but by the perception of
> fitness for a desirable purpose.[24]

This startling defence of functional beauty was exactly in line with the
teachings of Scott and Pugin. It was little wonder then that Terrot had
an affinity with Scott and that he had once expressed the desire to discuss
'dulce et utile' in correspondence relating to the design of St James', Leith.
Terrot provides yet another example of rationalist and functionalist views
among Edinburgh's non-architectural intelligentsia in the 1850s.

In train with the expansion in Episcopalian congregations, a movement
towards church design inspired by the Ecclesiological Society was clearly
visible in this denomination's new buildings. It would be mistaken,
however, to assume that new churches in this style always reflected
ritualistic churchmanship. While this was true of Butterfield's St Ninian's
Cathedral in Perth, it seldom applied elsewhere. From the 1840s onwards,
Episcopalian congregations started to introduce new furnishings and the
occasional new, ecclesiologically 'correct' church, usually as a result of
the preferences of the clergyman or the architect, or both. At this stage,
there was no great demand from congregations for a distinct nave and
chancel, stepped ascents to altars and the other historically accurate
details preferred by the Oxford Movement and the *Ecclesiologist*.[25]

By 1843, however, two churches in this style were in the course of
erection, one at Cruden, Aberdeenshire, by William Hay, and the other
at Dunblane, by John Henderson, under whom Hay had trained. Both
churches had chancels, raised Holy tables and other 'correct' details. For

most of the next two decades, Henderson was busy designing new
Episcopal churches in the same vein. It is clear from the visual evidence
that by 1843, Henderson was a man transformed. His St Catherine's,
Blairgowrie is a plain rubble box with some Y tracery, showing little trace
of architectural aptitude, far less Ecclesiological influence. That same
year, his Dunblane church was taking shape in fashionable early Gothic,
quite plainly following Pugin and the Ecclesiologists, as did all the
subsequent commissions. While Henderson was awarded most Episcopal
Church commissions from the 1840s until his death in 1862, leading
English architects were occasionally involved in Scottish commissions.
Scott himself was responsible for St Mary's, Broughty Ferry (1848), an
undistinguished if cheap design. A decade later he was in much better
form at Hawick, where he designed a fine 400 seater, or at St James the
Less in Leith. Other architects, such as Slater and Carpenter, who
designed the beautiful St Peter's, Lutton Place, Edinburgh (1860),
deepened the current of ideas flowing from England to Scotland.

There is no denying, though, that Henderson, while the main indigen-
ous proponent of these ideas until 1862, was not a great architect. The
Ecclesiologist at one point reported on his magnum opus, Trinity College,
Glenalmond, an institution founded by W.E. Gladstone, J.R. Hope and
Dean Ramsay, in the following terms:

> the design of the building was in due time entrusted to Mr.
> Henderson, who as a Scotsman, and belonging to the [Scottish
> Episcopal] Church, was employed at that time for most of its
> ecclesiastical structures . . . The rich red sandstone of which the pile
> is built warms the landscape, otherwise there is little to remark in
> the architecture, which is a sort of conventional Gothic, not exactly
> Middle or Third Pointed, with heavy labels, and other features likely
> to occur in the building of a second rate architect of that epoch.

Relenting slightly it continued:

> Still we are unwilling to be severe on Mr. Henderson for this
> treatment; for when he was designing, S. Augustine's was only being
> contemplated, and Hurstpierpoint not dreamed of.[26]

Henderson's biggest weakness was, however, in his massing of churches,
where the proportions of chancels, viewed externally, are mismatched to
those of naves, examples being St Mary's, Dunblane itself, or St Mary's,
Hamilton.

Towards the end of 1862, the year Henderson died, it was to Robert
Anderson that the Episcopal Church turned for its next building, Christ
Church, Falkirk. The precise details of Anderson's appointment do not
survive, but Terrot and Ramsay were deeply involved in the project.
Earlier that year, Terrot had issued a fund-raising circular which explained
the need for a new church. Upwards of two hundred Episcopalians in the

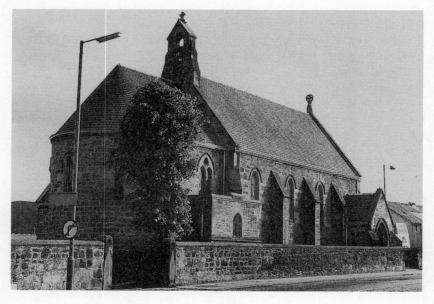

Plate 10. Christ Church, Falkirk (Author).

Falkirk area were worshipping in a room on Sunday evenings, and were dependent on the incumbent of Dunmore for services.[27] On 8 May 1863 Dean Ramsay officiated at the foundation stone ceremony, informing his congregation that the new church would be in the Gothic style, since that style, through the 'association of ideas', was synonymous with church building and was conducive to the thinking of solemn thoughts; the 'skill of the intelligent architect' would make sure this was so. Anderson's initial efforts at Leith, coupled with his growing reputation, were already beginning to pay dividends. As well as confirming Anderson's rising status, Ramsay's remarks underscored his own churchmanship. No reference at all was made to the liturgical potential of the new church's design.[28]

By April 1864, the building was complete. It was constructed as a two-cell chapel, with provision for a south transept, very much in the 'vigorous' tradition established by Brooks, Butterfield and Street. The nave was of four bays, the chancel terminated in a semicircular apse, and the style was transitional early Gothic, visible in the change from lancets to plate traceried windows, moving from west to east (Plate 10). While this style was fashionable enough, it may to some extent have resulted from the low budget. A mere £1300 was all that was available. A schedule of disbursements discloses how the money was spent:

James Law, Mason   £718 – 2 – 3½d

James Black, Carpenter	£350 – 0 – 0
James Miller, Plasterer	£26 – 10 – 1
R. King, Plumber	£39 – 0 – 5½d
W. Fairbairn, Surveyor	£18 – 0 – 0
John Meiklejohn, Heating Apparatus	£43 – 0 – 0
James Milne, Gasfittings	£30 – 18 – 0
D. Draper, Slater	£54 – 19 – 8
Ferguson and Bell, Painters	£10 – 13 – 6

Anderson himself was paid £79–1–8, representing the customary five per cent, plus expenses and extras. The constraints of finance prevented Anderson from providing a more elaborate west gable. This was to have featured a double bellcote, supported by two full-length buttresses, a design closely related to the architect's studies of the Abbey Barn, Caen, which would eventually be illustrated in his forthcoming book.

Inside the building, Anderson's skill was equally apparent. A contemporary newspaper report advised that the chancel arch was 'of dressed and moulded stone, and springs from moulded and carved corbelled shafts'.[29] These were modelled on historic precedent, owing nothing to the Ruskinian notion that the craftsman should be allowed free rein. In this area, Anderson stuck closely to the Scott practice of archaeological verisimilitude. His debt to Scott is also visible in the constructional polychromy of the building's exterior. Built of cream sandstone rubble, the church was finished off with red stone banding carried round the walls at the window bases, hood moulding terminations and cornice. Christ Church, Falkirk was no apprentice piece — it was the work of an architect already fully formed, a building, if small, of real gravitas and power. At a stroke it lifted indigenous Scottish achievement in this genre to a higher plane.

The year 1864, as well as seeing the completion of the Falkirk and Leith commissions, was a particularly happy one for the Andersons. On 5 June a daughter, Annie Ross Anderson, was born. Just prior to this, the architect had been approached regarding designs for a new Episcopal Church at Brougham Street, Edinburgh. For some years before this date a congregation had developed under the care of the Rev. Alexander Dimmie Murdoch, a missionary based at St John's, Princes Street. The congregation then worshipped in a building in Earl Grey Street. On this occasion Anderson had competition: no less a figure than William Hay, and also W.L. Moffat. After studying the three sets of designs, Dean Ramsay and the Building Committee resolved that 'Mr. Robert Anderson should be the architect'. The matter was decided on 3 June, just two days before the birth of his daughter.[30] As usual, though, the initial plans were more grandiose than funds eventually allowed. It was intended that the new church should seat 600, and a rough cost of £4000 was established.

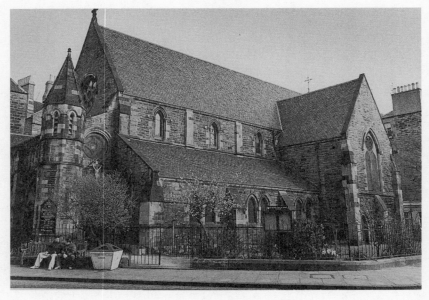

Plate 11. All Saints Church, Edinburgh (Author).

An undated drawing of a church larger than that eventually built still survives.[31] It depicts an austere but impressive building of nave, aisles and chancel in Geometric Gothic, rising high out of the ground. Its height and a bell fleche over the crossing suggest French inspiration.

By 20 March 1866, a new design featuring a smaller church of nave, aisles and chancel had been produced, with an elegant saddleback tower at its west end. This design, too, was cut down, the new church, dedicated to 'All Saints', opening without a tower on 20 June 1867, with seating capacity for 450. The small corner site had posed problems, but in spite of this the church was correctly oriented and well massed. The group of buildings now visible (Plate 11) results from several additions, all by Anderson. A narthex and a small-scale tower were added in 1876, the *Builder* commenting that while a massive tower was contemplated 'this feature has been abandoned in the meantime, and the church is complete without it'. The *Building News* was able to report on 22 June 1877 that a school and hall, able to seat 500–600 people had been completed in Glen Street at a cost of £4000, the mason being Mr A. Angus. In addition, a rectory was built alongside the church in 1878, linked to it by the vestry and narthex, and finally, in July 1888, plans leading to the completion of the Lady Chapel were produced.

The design, as executed, retained the French character of its predecessor. This was accentuated by the squat yet lofty proportions of the

Plate 12. Waddell's house, Portobello, contract drawings (Anderson Office Drawings, Edinburgh University).

interior, and also by the rose window on the west gable and the vigorous stiff leaf carving on the capitals of the columns, which were given squared abaci. Ecclesiological and archaeological correctness were visible on every hand. The chancel, which terminated in a polygonal apse, culminated in an altar, approached by seven steps. It was furnished with several aumbries and was floored in encaustic tiles. The church was not provided with a distinct chancel arch; instead, the entrance to the chancel was denoted by cylindrical wall shafts raised from the piers of the last bay. The roof was superbly judged; in order to give loftiness to the interior and avoid the spatial interference caused by tie beams, a wagon roof, its collar beams and rafters clinging to the surface, was chosen. As well as consolidating his reputation, All Saints Church again brought Anderson into contact with David Bryce, with whom he had to deal over the questions of plot shape and feu duty.

Anderson's career had taken off. By 1866 he was extremely busy, still working at the Engineers' office, still refining the drawings from his continental tour for publication, and at the same time dealing with new commissions. That year he designed a house in Portobello for a Mr Waddell, which no longer survives. The drawings (Plate 12) indicate that it was a house of two storeys plus attic, asymmetrically planned, with Gothic touches. There was nothing innovative about the house, although the planning was sensible and interior layout was expressed on the

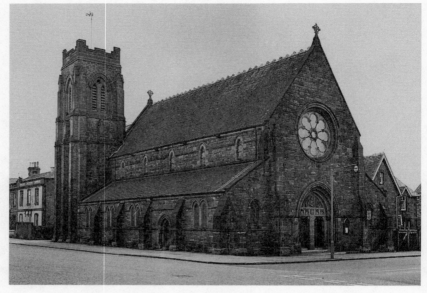

Plate 13. St Michael and All Angels Church, Helensburgh (National
Monuments Record of Scotland).

exterior. The design bore some resemblance to the plain Gothic house
designed by Scott for the incumbent of St James' at Leith some years
earlier. Towards the autumn of 1866, a number of Episcopal church
commissions came up almost concurrently. The first of these concerned
a new church for the Helensburgh congregation, who since 1843 had been
housed in Holy Trinity Chapel, described as a 'small, plain edifice in the
Tudor style of architecture'. The congregation's growth, assisted by the
arrival of the railway in 1857, necessitated a larger building. On 1 August
1866, Anderson's design was approved by the vestry. Once again, he had
been commissioned outright.

   The following February, the foundation stone was laid by the bishop
of the diocese, and with architect and Building Committee in attendance,
the church was dedicated to St Michael and All Angels. Situated on a
good corner site, the Helensburgh church is broader, squatter and more
'muscular' than his earlier churches (Plate 13). Its short but lofty proportions, western wheel window and rough-faced red sandstone construction
combine to suggest an early French derivation. This is confirmed by the
interior, where the red and cream voussoirs of the nave arcades sit on
squared abaci and the capitals are again vigorously carved. A pointed
wagon roof, planked over, with surface ribs, is continued in the chancel.
The rafters are exposed on the aisle ceilings and separated by white
plaster. The chancel, lit by three lancets and a vesica on the east gable,

is paved and walled in encaustic tiles, which become progressively more ornate as the altar is approached. The church cost £2500 in its initial state, and was built by James McKinnon of Helensburgh. The subscribers to the church included Gladstone and the Earl of Glasgow.

The architect's punctilious care over every detail can be detected from his specification.[32] It reveals that he called for some of the stones to be 'scabbled . . . in the manner of old work' and carefully matched for colour. The stone to be used for internal dressings was to be 'the best riven rock from Dumbarton Quarry, uniform in colour'. The wagon roof was to be of fir, 'from Riga or Dantzic', and the slates of the previous church, where possible, were to be used to keep costs down. Anderson designed screen, pulpit and choir stalls, and made special drawings for the gargoyles. The church was consecrated and opened for worship early in 1868.

While the Helensburgh church was in hand, the Earl of Mar and Kellie was planning to upgrade the accommodation of the Episcopalians of Alloa. On 13 October 1866, he wrote to the Rev. A.W. Hallen, the rector, advising him of his intention to endow a new church at the foot of his park.[33] This was near the heart of Alloa, and contained Alloa Tower, a fourteenth century keep which the family still used, as well as a more modern house. His letter called for a swift reply as he expected an architect 'in a few days'. Naturally, his offer was accepted, although his proposed site turned out to be unsuitable. A site was eventually purchased at Broad Street, at the western edge of his park. For the first time in his career, Anderson had an absolutely free hand, with no competition, and a wealthy landed aristocrat prepared to meet all costs. The church was, however, to be small, in its initial phase having to accommodate only 155 people.

Building operations began with the laying of the foundation stone on St John's Day, 27 December 1867, marking the church's dedication to that saint. The congregation was in no rush to vacate its old quarters, which had been sold to the Roman Catholics for £600 on the condition that the old building would not be handed over until the new church was ready. This was opened and consecrated with immense ceremony on 4 August 1869, in the presence of civic and ecclesiastical dignitaries which included Bishop Forbes of Brechin and the Primus of the Episcopal Church, the Bishop of Moray and Ross.

The new building (Plate 14) originally consisted of a nave and chancel, the south aisle not being added until later, although it was provided for in the original drawings and plans. In spite of the church's severely blackened condition today, its initial glories can easily be imagined. Its Geometric tracery and general massing strongly evoke Pugin's own illustrations in *True Principles*, and the tower, powerfully composed with broach spire and prominent louvres, is faintly reminiscent of St James',

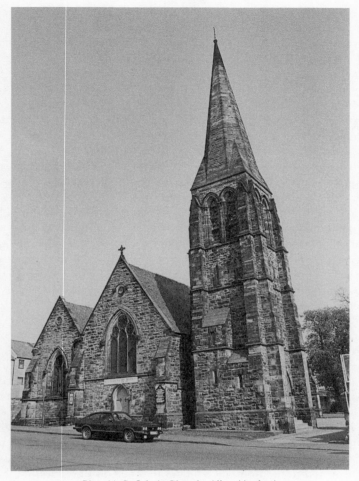

Plate 14. St John's Church, Alloa (Author).

Leith. In the *Alloa Advertiser* of 7 August, a six thousand-word article on the church's opening appeared. As usual, the reporter had relied on the architect for descriptive detail, and in so doing gave Anderson's own rationale for the building's design. Its exterior, 'severely treated', was 'utterly devoid of unnecessary decoration', a description confirming the visually obvious, that the church owed much to the functionalist principles of Pugin and Scott.

In contrast with the exterior, the interior was a blaze of High Victorian colour, now lost, but described in detail in the *Advertiser*, from which the undernoted passage has been taken:

The decorations of the church are profuse in the extreme, and indeed superb. No expense has been spared to make them completely and handsomely beautiful. The passages between the low-backed and comfortable seats have been laid with encaustic tiles in the nave; the walls round the nave are for several feet coloured with deep India red; from thence to their heads they are of a vellum tint, with diaperings of chocolate, ochre, and Indian red, and then to the wall plates are powderings of stars, fleur-de-lis, etc. Between the windows are circular medallions, each one bearing a bust of an apostle, with his emblem and name. Over the entrance is to be a rich canopy covering a figure of St. John . . . Inside the chancel the decorations are profuse and brilliant. The leading decorations of the chancel vault are a choir of angels, painted on blue grounds and medallions bearing the emblems of the Passion.[34]

In addition there was a pulpit of alabaster and marble, and a triptych reredos in Venetian mosaic by Salviati. Overhead, a pointed wagon roof sprung from 'richly coloured mouldings'.

Among the many toasts given later at a celebratory luncheon at the Earl of Mar and Kellie's residence was one to the architect, proposed by the Earl himself. He praised Anderson's 'exquisite and classical' taste, noted that 'in no instance whatever have we had a dispute', finally expressing the hope that his obvious success with the new church 'may lead to his being the acknowledged best ecclesiastical architect in Scotland'.[35] Anderson replied that he was a man 'more of deeds than words', that he could not express the happiness he felt at the opening of the church, and that his only regret was that 'its very success was a signal of the closing of his connection with a work in which he had ever taken great pleasure'. The *Ecclesiologist*, in its only review of an Anderson building, stated that a 'poor Episcopal chapel' was about to be replaced with 'an excellent church', noting that 'the ritual arrangements are thoroughly good, except that the rise is of six, instead of seven steps'. Not given to unreserved praise, it continued that 'the vestry has a transverse gable, which we do not like' and thought the two doors at the west end unnecessary. While the tower was 'a good composition', the belfry stage 'ought to be a few feet higher, so as to clear the ridge of the nave roof'. The journal, which obviously prided itself on detailed exactitude, rather carelessly attributed the design to a 'Mr. Willis'.[36]

The church's final cost, taken from a record kept by the Earl, was as follows:[37]

	£
Purchase of old houses	850 – 0 – 0
Mason	2,504 – 13 – 7½d
Carpenter	490 – 18 – 5
Slater	75 – 10 – 8

Plasterer	104 – 14 – 0
Plumber	83 – 14 – 9
Smith	215 – 13 – 9½d
Sculptor (Farmer and Brindley)	304 – 14 – 0
Decorator	276 – 0 – 0
Gas Brackets	254 – 16 – 0
Godwin (Tiles)	71 – 6 – 2
Salviati (Reredos)	125 – 0 – 0
Gibbs for 3 windows	252 – 0 – 0
Organ	330 – 0 – 0
Architect	294 – 10 – 0
Curtains and Hassocks	8 – 0 – 0
East Window	120 – 0 – 0
Misc.	30 – 0 – 0
	6,391 – 11 – 5½d

The church's south aisle, the gift of the Earl and Countess, was built in 1872, the year the Earl died. In 1874 his recumbent effigy, in alabaster, was placed on its north side. It too was designed by Anderson.

While working on the designs for the Alloa church, Anderson had been commissioned to build a new church for the Episcopalians of Cupar, who were worshipping in a chapel designed by Burn in 1817, on an ancient site. The congregation was quite small and not wealthy, but on 11 December 1866 the vestry were perusing 'plans and schedules of measurement and two communications . . . received from Mr. Anderson the architect'.[38] The vestrymen, however, were not at this stage totally happy with the designs, the minutes stating a little belligerently that the architect 'had not attended to the suggestions as to the construction of the seats' and were of the opinion that the 'side aisle will be much too dark and request the architect to provide for sky lights in the roof of the aisle'. Anderson resolved this problem without committing the solecism suggested: it was recorded at a later meeting that 'the architect has changed his plan from the one submitted . . . by removing altogether the windows in the aisle and substituting six small clerestory windows in the nave'. The vestry minutes also bear witness to the fact that, during the early stages of negotiation with the architect, whom clearly they not did not know, attitudes had become a little high handed. After a timely and unannounced appearance by Anderson off the Edinburgh train, however, tensions were defused and confidence restored, obvious from the deferential tone of the minutes thereafter. Building began in the spring of 1867, on a very cramped site which only just permitted a full gable to be presented to the street. The result in these very constrained circumstances is laudable

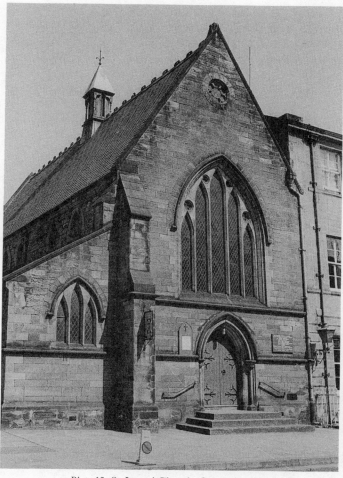

Plate 15. St James' Church, Cupar (Author).

(Plate 15). The overall effect owes much to the low springing points of the lancets, which were perhaps inspired by the lower choir of Glasgow Cathedral. Inside, the nave has a pointed wagon roof, and is separated from the single aisle by a three-bay arcade of simple dignity. Five steps, floored in Godwin's encaustic tiles, ascend through the chancel to the altar, and an aumbry has been provided in the chancel wall.

Meanwhile, at nearby St Andrews, the Episcopalians were well advanced in their fund raising for a new church, Bishop Wordsworth having issued an appeal circular on 28 June 1865. The existing church could only house 220, and had already been enlarged. Wordsworth was keen that, in St Andrews, 'for many centuries the Ecclesiastical Metropolis of our land', the Episcopalians should be worthily housed. The new church should be both 'spacious' and 'handsome'. It was decided that no less a figure than G.E. Street should act as adjudicator in a limited competition in which the participants were Anderson and John Milne, the local architect. On 22 October 1866 the vestrymen examined one plan from Milne and two from Anderson, together with Street's report, which favoured an Anderson design. The incumbent, Robert Skinner, was asked to convey the decision to the successful competitor, inviting him to confer with the Building Committee. In due course, Milne's account was paid and the relevant section of Street's report was sent to him.

Thereafter, communications began to flow between Anderson and Skinner, written in the architect's bold, clear and neat hand, and tersely expressed. One of these, dated 19 January 1867, reveals an important and surprising turn of events:

> If you are going to develope [sic] into a Cathedral I think the position of the tower and spire should be altered, it ought to be central, at present the design is of the parish church type — there is nothing about it that would indicate its being a cathedral. The removal of the tower and spire to the centre would of course . . . involve greater expense so that it may be useless to make the suggestion but if you thought it would be entertained I have a design that I sketched roughly since I got your note that would eclipse all my former efforts and which I would get put into proper shape for submission to the vestry.[39]

Although nothing came of this plan to make the new church a cathedral, it appears to be related to the disputes between Bishop Wordsworth and the clergy and congregation at St Ninian's, Perth, over Tractarian-inspired ritual. This so repelled the prelate that since 1859 he had officiated at St John's Church, Perth rather than St Ninian's. Certainly, the building of a new church and the presence of the cathedral ruins nearby would have provided an opportunity to resolve the problem.

Subsequent correspondence, as well as communicating something of Anderson's increasingly powerful character, records his deep interest in practical matters and his concern for cost reduction. This was expressed in his suggestion that the good timber resulting from site clearance should be sold and that the clerk of works, T. Wilson, should alternate between the St Andrews and Cupar churches, with his wage being shared by the two congregations in the proportions two-thirds and one-third, respectively. Further letters record that Anderson had sent a short note to the editor of the *Dundee Advertiser*, expressing his displeasure at the 'gross ignorance of medieval art' shown by its reporter in a recent article on the new church, and that he intended taking the drawings of 'the Cathedral' to the Ecclesiological Society. The letters go on to reveal that, by July

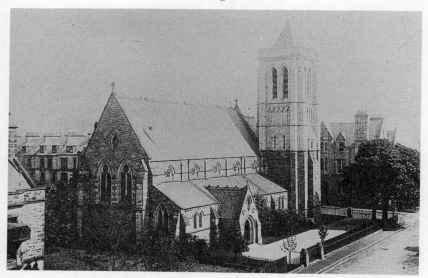

Plate 16. St Andrew's Church, St Andrews, c. 1900 (J.H. Scott).

1867, work on the new building was well advanced. At the end of this month the Foundation Stone ceremony took place with full Masonic honours. The stone was laid by John Whyte-Melville, who, as well as being a vestryman of the new church, was also Grand Master Mason of Scotland. The notice advertising the ceremony lists the contractors, J. McIntosh, Mason; J.R. Swann, Carpenter; J. Hart, Plumber; and J. McPherson, Plasterer. The clerk of works, T. Wilson, was also mentioned, as well as 'Brother Robert Anderson'. During the year which followed, the project moved smoothly towards completion, the architect as ever immersing himself with equal enthusiasm in the practicalities of building as well as the aesthetic issues, epitomised in a letter sent with an estimate for oiling all the red pillars in the church's interior: 'The oil will bring out the colour of the stone as well as tend to harden it'.

Although the church was opened in 1868, some twenty years were to elapse before it received its tower, (Plate 16), which was taken down again in 1938. As built, it accommodated 600 in ecclesiologically correct surroundings, extending to credence table and sediliae in the chancel, fine views of which are afforded from the nave. Externally, it is not difficult to see why the design met with Street's approval. Its economical thirteenth century styling, reliant on the subtle interplay of delicate and crisply cut mouldings with broad passages of wall plane, creates an effect of understated elegance. Shortly afterwards, Street would himself create Gothic buildings in a similar vein at Haddo House and at the Law Courts in·the Strand.

Over at Falkirk, Anderson had suffered a minor setback. In spite of his preparing at least nineteen design drawings for the new parsonage house there, the commission was given to Wardrop and Reid, whose house, with prominent barge boards, steeply raked roofs and false pantry window, was very much in the picturesque tradition. Anderson's plainer parsonage would have harmonised better with the new church, although it was undoubtedly one of his less inspired designs. Meanwhile, at Kelso, Anderson had been asked in 1867 to design another Episcopal church. The congregation had become too large for the old St Andrew's Chapel, which was in any case thought to be structurally unsound. As usual, Anderson was constrained by the funds available, one of the surviving design drawings showing what might have been achieved (Plate 17). Nevertheless, the end result was extremely good (Plate 18). Built by local craftsmen in red sandstone with cream dressings, the church combined 'elegance and utility in an unusual degree'. The interior, like the exterior, is austere but well proportioned, with a splendid view eastwards. The roof consisted of a multitude of scissor beams, and the chancel ceiling was originally decorated with a pattern of sacred symbols executed in distemper. Unusually, Anderson was permitted to design the stained glass of the east window, the theme of which was 'the humiliation and exaltation of the Redeemer, the principal subjects being the Crucifixion, the transfiguration and the Ascension'.[40] This window was made by Burlison and Grylls, and attempted, with some success, to emulate medieval work. The church cost over £4000.

While these commissions were proceeding, Anderson had been making good progress with his continental tour drawings, and with a little help from Axel Hermann Haig, the London-based artist and draughtsman, the book was complete and ready for publication in 1868. Of the 103 plates it contained, Haig was responsible for seven relating to Italian locations, having worked them up from photographs, sketches or drawings by Anderson, with the architect responsible for the rest. It is obvious from the best of these that Anderson was a very competent and careful draughtsman. Certainly, little attempt was made to produce artistic effects. Anderson would subsequently make it clear that he saw drawing as a means to an end, not an end in itself.[41] The book was published as *Examples of the Municipal Commercial and Street Architecture of France and Italy from the 12th to the 15th Century*, and ran to two editions, the first bearing the inscription

> To Professor G.G. Scott, R.A., This Work is, by Permission, Most Respectfully Dedicated, with Feelings of Most Profound Esteem and Admiration for his Great Achievements in Art, by the Author.

Relieved from the task of preparing his book, and facing an ever

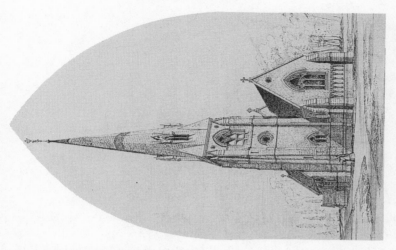

Plate 17. St Andrew's Church, Kelso, design drawing (Anderson Office Drawings, Edinburgh University).

Plate 18. St Andrew's Church, Kelso (Author).

increasing flow of new commissions, Anderson in 1868 made the final break with the Royal Engineers' Office, opening up in independent practice at 43 George Street.

4

Into the Public Eye

The early days of independent practice were characterised by Episcopal Church work carried over from previous years and also by some low budget, utilitarian buildings, the first of which was erected for John M. Balfour, at the street which bears his name on the north side of Leith Walk. Here, Anderson built a four-storey block of tenemented flats (now demolished), the drawings indicating that the building was symmetrical, with a central stair well culminating in a Gothic gablet at attic level.[1] The chimney breasts were carried up the two side walls, and inside the planning was standardised, working on the 'mirror image' principle on opposite sides of the stair. The flats, clearly built for working people, consisted of a lobby, coal cellar, room, kitchen and water closet. Each kitchen was also provided with a bed recess. The designs were approved by Balfour on 8 October 1868 and the building was erected during 1869.

There next followed a new school built under the aegis of St Patrick's Roman Catholic Church, in Edinburgh's Cowgate. The church was in the classical style, and it was therefore logical that the school, which was to sit in front of it, should harmonise. Thus, Anderson's first non-Gothic commission came about. The funds available, however, were limited, amounting to just £1600. Over and above this constraint, the ground sloped downwards from north to south, with a sudden drop in levels from west to east. Anderson's school (long since demolished) amounted to a single-storey rectangular box divided into two bays by shallow pitched roofs resting on a central cast iron colonnade, and running from west to east, parallel to the Cowgate.[2] The drop in levels from west to east was handled by arching the sunken area and using the space thus created for storage and coal. The fenestration consisted of roof lights, with a lofty circular window illuminating each bay on the west and east gables. The school presented a blank masonry wall to the Cowgate. An extra classroom, quite small, was tacked on to the north-east corner in a rectangular extension, and was lit by a west-facing Venetian window. The

Plate 19. Houses at Inverleith, design drawing (Anderson Office Drawings, Edinburgh University).

school was briefly reviewed in the *Builder*, the reporter dwelling mainly on the heating arrangements, which consisted of a fire supplied with air from beneath. During 1869, while St Patrick's School was still under discussion, Anderson designed and built the tiny St Mungo's Episcopal Church at the nearby village of Balerno. The church, now encrusted in harl, was given four buttressed bays and lancet windows. Inside, a roof of tiny scissor beams, dark stained, complements painted brick walls.[3]

The year 1870 brought a commission for three blocks of flatted terraced housing at Inverleith Terrace, on the north side of Edinburgh and close to the Botanic Gardens. The houses, designed with bay windows and sunken basement, were sensibly planned with dining rooms at street level and drawing rooms above, and were given classical elevations (Plate 19). The detailing was altered in the course of building. Adjacent to this development, a splayed block of tenements, straddling Inverleith Terrace and Inverleith Row, was built at approximately the same time. Four storeys high, this block boasted special sanitary arrangements. A twelve-foot square ventilating shaft communicated with open air at top and bottom, and bore an individual soil pipe from each flat. The intention was to obviate smells on the stairway and to make repairs inobtrusive.[4] David Bryce, as feuing architect, was again involved in approving the plans.

In 1871, two further Episcopalian commissions came in. At Pittenweem, Fife, a new rector, P.H. Moneypenny, had taken office, and asked for designs for a new church. Anderson drew up two separate plans for a small-scale chapel, both ecclesiologically correct, as ever, one with a tower, the other with a bellcote at the crossing.[5] The congregation made do with alterations. The second commission was for a large new Episcopal church at Dumbarton, to seat 550. Anderson submitted three alternative

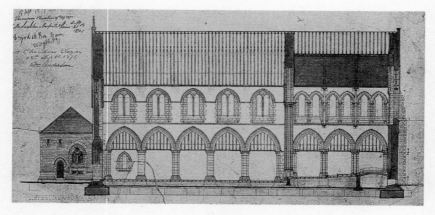

Plate 20. St Augustine's (formerly St Luke's) Church, Dumbarton
(Anderson Office Drawings, Edinburgh University).

plans and a rough estimate in April 1871.[6] The site was difficult, affording
a narrow frontage to the street, and the buildings on either side caused
problems with lighting. The design executed overcame these difficulties
with distinction. Large east and west windows, filled with Geometric
tracery, provide plenty of light, its supply supplemented by a clerestory
of double lancets. The interior of the church is one of Anderson's finest
(Plate 20), and yet of the utmost simplicity. Here, the beautifully
proportioned structural elements, arcades, chancel arch and scissor beam
roof combine in a most satisfying fashion. A magnificent stone reredos,
also designed by Anderson, was added in later years. This splendid result
was only achieved after practical difficulties and delays, however. The
building contractor became insolvent at an early stage of construction.
When the church was finally opened on 27 November 1873, its cost had
risen from an anticipated £7000 to £9000. In the circumstances, it was
impossible to complete the intended tower. At the rear of the church,
Anderson also provided a parsonage house in 'vigorous' plate traceried
Gothic. Even in its current dilapidated state its original quality can easily
be imagined.

Although the Scottish Episcopal Church's requirement for new buildings was beginning to reduce by the early 1870s, the downturn came too
late to affect Anderson's already considerable reputation. This served him
well in the negotiations for his next commission, the rebuilding of St
Vigean's Church, Arbroath, which as well as being his first restoration,
was to prove pivotal in his advancing career. The church is situated in
open countryside two miles north of Arbroath, and sits on a smooth green
hillock some forty feet high, past which the Brothock burn flows. While
Christianity may have come to the district as early as the seventh century,

the church was not consecrated until 1242. A tower was added later, with little alteration to the fabric until the Reformation, when the position of the pulpit was changed and a west gallery was added. By 1720, repairs to the walls were needed and towards the end of the eighteenth century the roof was replaced, an east gallery was built, and the belfry was repaired. In 1827 a second north aisle was built, and roof repairs were carried out, the latter poorly executed. By 1871 the building needed urgent attention. Over and above the roof problems, the south aisle arcade was well out of plumb, while externally the accumulation of shoddy alterations in different styles was not visually coherent. That being the case, the incumbent, the Rev. Dr. William Duke, decided to go ahead with a major restoration.

Duke, an antiquary, was well aware of the need for a sensitive restoration on such an historic and beautiful site, and decided to seek opinion from ecclesiastical colleagues as to who might be a suitable architect. Early in 1871 three letters were sent out, one to the Rev. George Jamieson, incumbent of St Machar's Cathedral, Aberdeen, one to the Rev. George Alexander at the Church of the Holy Rude, Stirling, and one to A.P. Forbes, the Episcopalian Bishop of Brechin.[7] Jamieson replied that his church's recent employment of 'Mr. Mathews' of Aberdeen had resulted in disappointment, and that notwithstanding the presence of several 'fair' architects in that city, his personal preference was for George Gilbert Scott. He doubted, though, that the St Vigeans heritors would entertain the expense of bringing Scott from London. Under Scots law the heritors, the local men of property, were responsible for providing and maintaining an adequate parish church, but there was no obligation upon these men to spend any more than the minimum. In any case, he observed, Scott was in poor health. Alexander's reply was more positive. He had recently used James Collie of Bridge of Allan at his own church, where he had 'overcome unexpected problems successfully' as well as pleasing Stirling of Keir 'the great man of taste in this neighbourhood'. The Bishop of Brechin's reply came in, with his congratulations on the proposed restoration, which he observed 'is a delicate operation and should be in fac simile'. He went on to warn Duke that many historic Churches had been ruined by poor restoration, finally passing on the following advice:

> Before you commit yourself to any architect I would make enquiries about Mr. Robert Anderson of George St. He is a pupil of Gilbert Scott's & has published some interesting plates on Continental Gothic. He has also done some good work in Scotland.[8]

Both Collie and Anderson were therefore contacted early in January 1871. Anderson arranged to come on 5 January, while Collie, some three weeks later, indicated his willingness to be involved.

A letter from Anderson dated 31 January suggests that he had been commissioned, and reveals that he was about to start. His immediate intention was to 'measure and draw all the existing church', after which he proposed to 'visit some of the old churches in the district' in order to shed light on some of the stylistic problems that were bound to arise. The impression of energy and commitment emerging from the correspondence is compounded by his request to Duke for access to the nave roof, and to have the harling removed from the bottom of the tower, the corners, and some of the aisle windows prior to his arrival. A letter written towards the end of February informs that his plans were well advanced and that, rather than 'terrify the heritors with ornament', he had 'not added a single superfluous feature or detail'. To do otherwise, he felt, would in any case 'put the old work out of countenance'. He next expressed himself satisfied with his design for the open timber roof, which he felt was 'very plain, but thoroughly characteristic'. The constraints of providing maximum accommodation at minimum cost to the heritors were next shown in his statement that, in spite of having retained a small western gallery and having put the new north aisle further eastward, he still could not 'screw up the accommodation much beyond the 500'. Early in March Anderson advised that the alterations were to cost at least £1500 plus an additional £500 for the intended new chancel.

Matters, however, were not as clear cut as they appeared. Shortly after Anderson had written these letters to Duke, a deputation from St Vigeans had called at his office, ostensibly to examine his plans, their clumsy remarks making it obvious that an alternative set of designs and estimates was in existence, requisitioned by a faction within the church. On 11 March Anderson wrote to Duke describing the visit, and expressing his relief that Duke's party had 'carried the day' as well as his hope that there would be no further disruptions. The project was soon back on course, with Anderson recommending a hypocaust for heating to avoid the disfigurement and expense of hot water pipes, as well as the use of English slates, which, he believed, were more resistant to sea air than their local (Dunkeld) equivalents. By May, Anderson was expressing annoyance that Munich glass was to be installed in the new church windows. In an impassioned and somewhat repetitive letter he appealed to Duke to 'keep clear' of it, since its bright, dominant character detracted from the architecture rather than decorating it:

> The interior of a church should be so designed that everything of furniture and decoration should be so subordinated to the structure that the general effect is one harmonious whole & if any glass, sculpture or painting distorts this, it is instantly to be suppressed . . .
> Take warning from Glasgow Cathedral, or the Parliament House here, where the blazing impudence of the glass prevents you from seeing anything but itself.[9]

The words of this extract might easily have come from Pugin's own pen. They were not, however, sufficient to persuade Duke, although by this time a friend and admirer, to let the architect design the glass himself.

By July the matter was forgotten, with Anderson busy designing sediliae for the chancel, which necessitated higher walls than originally planned, arguing in defence of the extra cost that 'windows well elevated from the floor have always a good effect'. In the same letter, Anderson expressed his pleasure that the work was 'giving satisfaction' asking Duke to 'be sure and tell me what the Bishop of Brechin says [about it]. He is so awfully critical'. These remarks confirm his ignorance of Forbes' involvement in securing him the commission, as well as providing an interesting insight into the Bishop's personality. Within a few days, Anderson was in communication with Duke again:

> The Irvingites or as they now call themselves the Catholic Apostolic Church are about to build a new church here. They have called upon me regarding it, but of course they are considering other names as well as my own. Would you have the kindness to write me a note stating your own & the opinions generally of my designs for the restoration of St. Vigeans & the manner in which it is being carried out. You might also mention the name of any notabilities who have visited the work and have approved of what is being done. Your early attention to this will greatly oblige . . .[10]

A few days later Anderson was able to write back thanking Duke for the 'very flattering recommendatory letter' which he had so promptly despatched.

In September and October of 1871, Anderson's strength of character was displayed as he dealt with two new and difficult problems. The first of these related to his disagreement with the authorities at the church over the restoration of the tower, revealed in the extract letter which follows:

> I . . . return the photo of the English Church. I do not think it would be correct to finish the tower of St. Vigeans other than I have already showed on the drawing. It must be remembered . . . that we must go by Scotch and not English precedents.[11]

This was by no means the end of the matter. On 18 October the architect was summoned by the Building Committee, who, in the interim, had instructed him to complete the tower with a battlemented parapet. The minutes record that Anderson was 'unable to carry out their instructions satisfactorily' since he felt that to do so 'would not be a restoration'. His reasoning was straightforward: the base of the tower resembled those at Dunning and Muthill, and it was therefore appropriate to provide St Vigean's with a saddleback top, in accordance with these precedents. Swayed by his arguments and his tenacity the Committee finally accepted his recommendation. Within a week, however, the architect was again on the defensive. Accusations that Smith, his Clerk of Works, was in

Plate 21. St Vigean's Church, Arbroath (National Monuments Record of Scotland).

collusion with contractors had reached the ears of Duke, who wrote asking that he be removed. As was customary at the time, the Clerk of Works was paid by the client, and Anderson's hands were therefore tied. While writing to confirm that Smith was being removed, Anderson forcibly defended his integrity, principle and competence, concluding that he had no qualms about transferring him to a commission 'involving three times the outlay on St. Vigeans'.

After these setbacks, the restoration proceeded smoothly through the winter months. On 14 February 1872, a distraught Anderson wrote a tearstained note to Duke.

> I am sorry I have been able to do nothing for you since I was last at St. Vigeans. When I returned I found our child very ill and a day or two afterwards the doctor pronounced it to be an aggravated case of typhoid fever. Since then I have been able to do nothing & have only had my clothes off twice & that for a few hours only.
>
> The poor little darling has suffered terribly & several times we have been waiting for her last sigh. The doctors have given her up but still she clings to life. At this moment she seems better to my eye than when the doctor paid his farewell visit to her.
>
> 4.45 p.m.
>
> I grieve to say our only darling died at 1–15 today. I fear I shall be unable to do anything till next week.[12]

Plate 22. St Vigean's Church, Arbroath, interior (*Academy Architecture —
Edinburgh, 1893*).

The poignancy of these words needs no amplification. Annie Ross
Anderson, aged 8, was laid to rest in Warriston Cemetery, her grave
marked by a simple but beautiful stone decorated with a quatrefoil relief
depicting a child on Christ's knee.

   The St Vigean's commission was therefore completed in the shadow of
immense personal grief, the building, restored with consummate taste and
the utmost care, reopening on 9 May 1872 (Plates 21 and 22). The
architect's achievements were well appreciated at St Vigeans, particularly
by Duke, who had given a paper on the church's archaeology to the
Society of Antiquaries of Scotland the month before, stating that the very
fact of Anderson's involvement was 'a sufficient guarantee for the char-

acter of the work'. The clergyman went on to describe what this had involved. Anderson had removed the eighteenth century external stair to the tower, raised its level to make a belfry, replaced the parapet and installed a saddleback roof, building a new stair turret at the south-east corner. A new apse was added and the north aisle was replaced. Radical surgery was also needed inside. As well as rebuilding the south aisle arcade, a new roof and a new floor were also provided. If the changes made were at times drastic and occasionally speculative, the restored church was structurally, functionally and aesthetically vastly superior to the crumbling pastiche that had preceded it. Having done so much in circumstances that were frequently harrowing, Anderson was afterwards asked to reduce his account. This he refused to do, having made 'moderate charges for everything, omitted some things, and made a handsome deduction from the total'. No offence was taken at this justifiable refusal, and in due course he was asked to design the church's communion plate. The plate, superbly decorated with finely wrought Celtic ornament, is still highly prized by the congregation.

Shortly after his arrival at St Vigeans in 1871, Anderson became a member of the Society of Antiquaries of Scotland, and may even have been present when Duke delivered his paper in April 1872. This was an association which would put Anderson in touch with a highly influential group of men. Already in membership when he joined were John, the youthful Third Marquess of Bute, the Marquess of Lothian, the Earl of Northesk and the highly respected solicitor and historian, William Forbes Skene. The membership also included prominent architects such as Andrew Heiton of Perth, John James Stevenson of London and David MacGibbon of Edinburgh. In these days antiquarianism and architecture walked hand in hand: since architects still used the stylistic syntax of bygone ages in their designs for buildings, they were anxious to expand their knowledge of archaeological remains. At the same time, ancient artefacts were often unearthed in the course of building restoration, adding historical interest to an already absorbing task. On 13 January 1873, Anderson presented his first paper to the Antiquaries. In studying the crypt of Roslin Chapel, he had discovered ancient diagrams on the walls. With the help of illustrations (Plate 23) he pointed out relationships between the markings he had found and parts of the executed building, although none corresponded exactly with built work. This, he contended, explained their presence on the walls. In ancient practice, final details were worked out on the floor. The diagrams must therefore have been 'mere trials or tentative drawings to solve questions in construction'.[13]

Anderson's visit to Roslin and his detailed study there was an indication of his abiding interest in the sketching and measured drawing of historic buildings, an activity he had pursued ever since his student days at the

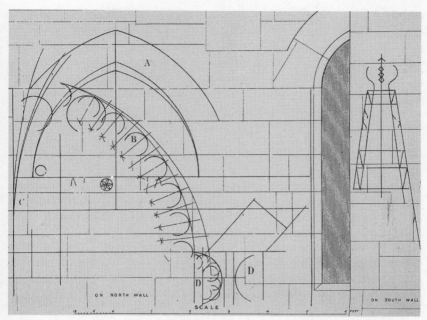

Plate 23. Working drawings in crypt, Roslin, illustrated by R. Anderson (*Proceedings of the Society of Antiquaries of Scotland, 1873*).

Trustees' School of Design. Whenever circumstances allowed, he would visit ancient buildings in the neighbourhood of commissions, either in search of ideas or simply to record what he saw. A pocket sketch book surviving from the 1870s contains a silhouette of the west front of Brechin Cathedral, perhaps sketched on his visits to St Vigeans in an attempt to establish local characteristics.[14] Details of wrought iron work from the gates were jotted down, as were sections of the beautiful and austere arch mouldings of the Maison Dieu Chapel, situated close by. A series of notes indicates that Anderson also visited and sketched at Balvaird Castle near Strathmiglo, Myers Castle near Auchtermuchty, Pitcarlie near Newburgh, and Pitairthie near Dunino, also in Fife. In the course of pursuing his ever growing practice, Anderson occasionally made trips to England, visiting the London craft firms Burlison and Grylls or Farmer and Brindley, suppliers to Scott, and now providing his former pupil with stained glass and ornamental carving respectively. On these occasions, the opportunity was taken to visit, study and sketch contemporary buildings, such as the church work of James Brooks at St Chad's, Neol Square, St Columba's, Haggerston, or St Saviour's, Hoxton, buildings in the severest form of 'vigorous' Gothic. J.L. Pearson's work at St Peter's, Vauxhall, very much in the same mould, also took his eye. As might be expected, Anderson, in the true Scott tradition, was not interested in reproduction for its own sake: the lessons of antiquity had to lead to thoroughly modern buildings, hence his study of like-minded architects.

Perhaps surprisingly for a man of such persuasions, Anderson in 1873 entered into partnership with David Bryce, then in his seventieth year, and with his nephew, John Bryce. Bryce was well aware of the achievements of his new partner, then in his thirty-ninth year. Drawings of Anderson commissions for this period bear the Bryce address, 131 George Street, suggesting that the offices may have combined as a result of the amalgamation.[15] The partnership was over within the year, however. The reasons for the dissolution are now beyond recall, but may well have been connected with fundamental differences of architectural approach. At around this time, on one of his London trips, Anderson had been making clear his theoretical stance in conversation with R.W. Billings, who some years earlier had returned to his native land. He had visited one of Billings' water works structures in London, observing that it had been designed to look like a castle, and had raised the matter on seeing the elderly architect. Anderson found that his efforts to convince his old acquaintance that he should never have dressed up his buildings in borrowed forms were in vain.[16] This was a conversation Anderson would never forget, and while working alongside Bryce, he must have recalled that the man whose approach he so strongly opposed had in fact collaborated with, and indeed inspired, his elderly partner.

During the brief partnership, Anderson was commissioned by the Marquess of Bute to report on the cloistral buildings at the west end of Paisley Abbey.[17] The young Marquess was becoming more and more deeply immersed in ecclesiastical history, and had discovered that some of his ancestors were buried at Paisley Abbey. The cloistral buildings were under threat of demolition by the town council, who wanted to widen the road. The council had taken the advice of a local antiquary, a Mr Semple, who had assured all concerned that none of these buildings were old enough to warrant preservation. Anderson's study reached an opposite conclusion, that the vaulting of the ground floor of the threatened building, as well as the walls, were original work dating from the time of the Abbey's construction under Abbot Thomas Tarvas. In spite of Anderson's report and a widespread outcry at the proposed demolition, it went ahead, bringing the road absurdly close to the Abbey's front door, and leaving the 'marks of attachment' on the main walls. It seems obvious from the remaining stonework that the architect was right, and that the Paisley authorities should have accepted the Marquess' offer of £10 000 for town improvements, an offer conditional upon the cloistral buildings remaining. While the project was frustrated, it enhanced Anderson's standing with Lord Bute and consolidated his reputation among his antiquarian associates.

Immediately after the dissolution of the partnership with Bryce, Anderson and his staff moved to 44 Northumberland Street, next door to the Royal Engineers' Office. One of the first tasks undertaken there was the preparation of the contract and working drawings for the new Catholic Apostolic Church, which was to be erected nearby, in East London Street. Anderson had won the limited competition, full details of which no longer survive. The client's brief was quite specific: the building had to be 'Norman in style', and the nave had to be free of obstructions so that the congregation could see the clergy at all times.[18] The reasons for these preferences are clear. The Church's origins date back to the 1830s, during which period it was influenced by the theology of Edward Irving, the brilliant but eccentric ex-Church of Scotland minister who was then based in London. Irving's millenarian eschatology and acceptance of charismatic manifestations were allied to an elaborate liturgy, introduced by the MP Henry Drummond and his circle, and which demanded elaborate buildings as well as elaborate church furnishings. The Church was governed by a 'college of Apostles', operating through a fourfold ministry of 'prophets, evangelists, pastors and teachers', supported in turn by a multitude of lesser orders, most of these officials being drawn from the laity. Catholic Apostolic services were frequent and must have been glorious to behold, with the various office bearers dressed in richly coloured cassocks, mozzettas, copes, albs, maniples, dalmatics, rochets or surplices, according to rank. The services were austere but beautiful and were based on liturgical writings still regarded today as models of their kind. Occasionally the services would be punctuated by utterances in 'tongues'. It was highly desirable that the congregation should have unimpeded views of such magnificent ceremony.

The Catholic Apostolics quite clearly borrowed some of their ideas from the writings of Pugin and the Ecclesiologists, and in many cases went beyond them. Lamps had to burn pure olive oil, in accordance with scriptural precedent, churches were provided with tabernacles for the reserved sacrament; thuribles, faldstools and thrones were also in use. Anderson's response to the client's demands could, therefore, be more or less satisfied with a church designed in broad conformity with the ecclesiological canons with which he was already so familiar. In consequence his design was for a church in austere, transitional Norman, consisting of an aisle-less nave in the proportions of a double cube, together with a long chancel terminating in a rounded apse. The aisles he provided in the chancel were to be used as a side chapel and to hold an organ. A grand organ was to be placed on the west internal wall and was to abut on to the intended west tower, of which little is known except that it was to be square in section. The pinnacles visible in Anderson's drawings appear to derive from sketches made in his notebook at Glastonbury Abbey. The design, as well as reflecting the architect's preference for understatement, also mirrors the reserve and gravity aimed at in Catholic Apostolic ritual, while making practical provision for it in a giant undercroft, which was honeycombed with changing rooms.

Although Catholic Apostolics practised tithing, and notwithstanding the middle and upper class composition of the Edinburgh congregation, the full realisation of the architect's initial scheme was to prove impossible, perhaps because of the congregation's small size. The church was consecrated on 22 April 1876, by which point some £17 000 had been spent. By 1884, revised plans for the west end, costing £5000, were prepared, involving a large porch and baptistery and a cheaper tower of the cylindrical, Brechin type. The tower was never built (Plate 24). Between 1893 and 1897 Phoebe Traquair covered the interior of the church with biblical murals, decorating Anderson's chancel arch with a glorious, apocalyptic depiction of apostles, prophets, evangelists and pastors (Plate 25). Also visible is Anderson's massive baldacchino in white marble, added in 1893.[19] The Catholic Apostolic Church in Edinburgh was Anderson's largest commission to date, and a landmark in Scottish neo-Norman design. A tremendous coup in its own right, the commission brought Anderson into contact with a thrusting young Catholic Apostolic advocate who was destined for greater things, and whose path he would often cross in the future: John Hay Atholl McDonald.

As early as 1873, Anderson had been preparing designs for the Episcopalians of Stonehaven, which had been Bishop Forbes' first charge, a connection which may explain Anderson's participation. One design involved a broach spire, a second a saddleback tower, both of which were rejected in favour of a less ambitious design in the Norman/Gothic transitional style already adopted for the Catholic Apostolic Church.[20] The laying of the foundation stone by Forbes in 1875 was his last public act. Within a few weeks of carrying out this happy duty, the bishop was struck down by an illness, from which he soon died.

In September 1874, Anderson had been working at Iona on the instructions of W.F. Skene, Bishop Forbes' full cousin, and his recent collaborator in producing a revised introduction to Adamnan's *Life of St. Columba*. Skene had commissioned Anderson, on behalf of the Duke of Argyll, Iona's owner, to effect the consolidation and partial restoration of the ecclesiastical ruins there. A letter from Anderson to Skene, written in an intimate but deferential tone, reveals that Anderson had sent to Edinburgh for masons and to Glasgow for scaffolding in order to start work on what amounted to the first serious restoration at Iona. This work involved a great deal of rubbish removal and some exciting discoveries, a necessary prelude to later restorations. At the Nunnery, Anderson had cleared away rubbish, built up gaps in the walls and restored the freestone corners. On the south side, under a pile of rubble, a cross wall and the

Plate 24. Frontage, Catholic Apostolic Church, Edinburgh (National Monuments Record of Scotland).

Plate 25. Interior, Catholic Apostolic Church, Edinburgh (National Monuments Record of Scotland).

base of an ancient stone altar had been uncovered, and this Anderson sketched in his letter. Accumulations of soil were also cleared away, revealing several ancient grave stones. At the Cathedral, an 'enormous amount of rubbish and fallen walls' were cleared away, enabling the cloister court and ambulatory to be seen. The transepts and nave were cleared out. A few artefacts were found, a key, a ring, some pottery, but nothing of great significance.[21]

Anderson's letter also gives an impression of his energy and zest for life: 'The bathing is splendid here and I have not missed a day', he wrote, going on to say to Skene (who was in Germany) that 'I am sure you have'nt better air, milk, eggs, butter and salt water. I could stay another month here with pleasure'. But this was impossible, for reasons which he outlined as follows:

> The Edinburgh University extension will be my next magnum opus. The Committee have decided to invite a few architects to submit preliminary sketches. Six have been applied to, Bryce, Cousins, Wardrop, Lessels, Peddie & Kinnear & self. I understand Bryce has declined. I do not know if any of the others have. As the plans are to be sent in by the 1st of November & they expect us to visit several buildings in England it will require very close application to this to get done in time.[22]

The Iona commission was not completed until the spring of 1876, by which point all possible consolidation work had been carried out, the time taken reflecting the weather and the need to import skilled workmen from the mainland. The Duke of Argyll was well pleased, having been informed by Anderson that the cathedral was ready for reroofing. By the time this stage was reached, Stonehaven Episcopal church was in the course of erection. In many ways it was a sister commission to the Iona restoration. Not only had Forbes a strong interest in both churches, Anderson's designs for Stonehaven owe much to his engagement with the buildings of Iona. The exterior of Stonehaven, although deriving from the Catholic Apostolic design, was given a stepped string course reminiscent of the east wall of the Iona Nunnery (Plate 26). Inside the church, the mouldings of the west gable replicate those at the Nunnery with complete fidelity, rising in a double step at each side.

In parallel with these commissions, Anderson had been busy on competition designs for the first new schools to be built in Edinburgh under the provisions of the Education (Scotland) Act of 1872. Prior to this Act, schooling had long been organised and provided by churches and charitable bodies, but the provision was not uniform in quality and the funding arrangements were often precarious. The Act provided for the incorporation of existing schools into the state-controlled system, where school governance would become the responsibility of school boards. The

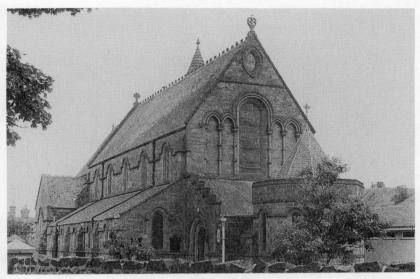

Plate 26. St James' Church, Stonehaven (Author).

boards, elected in each parish and burgh, could call on Parliamentary grants and local rates income for the provision and maintenance of schools, new or already established. The new Edinburgh School Board had approached Anderson, William Beattie, MacGibbon and Ross, Moffat and Aitken and Pilkington and Bell. In May 1874, Anderson's designs were awarded the first premium, and with it the commission to carry out West Fountainbridge, Causewayside and Stockbridge schools. Moffat was awarded second premium, together with the commission for Leith Walk and Bristo schools, while Beattie was given the third premium and the commission for North Canongate school.[23] The competition had called for designs for two sites, differing very significantly from each other. The first of these was Leith Walk, where the space available was regularly shaped and ample. At Fountainbridge, the site consisted of a gap between two sets of high buildings, and was much more difficult.

The schools took shape during the period 1874–6. Fountainbridge, on the most difficult site, was set back from the street behind its own little court. Its planning was in the form of an inverted T, the crossbar of which faced the street. Male and female staff rooms and the pupils' cloakrooms were located in this section. Behind the front block, on the stem of the T, were the co-educational infant and juvenile schools, together with separate classrooms for the older boys and girls.[24] Playgrounds were situated on either side. The Fountainbridge frontage was in the form of a giant Gothic order, stretching through the school's three floors and well into the gable

Plate 27. Fountainbridge School, Edinburgh. (National Monuments Record of Scotland).

(Plate 27). Anderson's drawings for Causewayside indicate that this school, too, had a narrow frontage. Again, Anderson opted for a T plan and chose the simple lines of early Geometric Gothic.[25] At Stockbridge, now the only surviving school, Anderson found more scope for his talents. The triangular site was difficult enough, but allowed a good frontage to Hamilton Place. Employing an L-shaped plan to optimise the space available, the architect, in true Puginan spirit, next allocated his interior spaces to meet the requirements of the users. On the Hamilton Place elevation, the infant classrooms were divided up by moveable partitions.

Plate 28. Stockbridge School, Edinburgh (Author).

At both extremities of this section, lofty stairs were cantilevered out on exposed iron beams, one set leading into the school's north wing, where a range of diversely sized rooms was provided for older pupils and staff. On the Hamilton Place elevation (Plate 28) the high quality of Anderson's early Gothic is again displayed, the whole composition based on asymmetricality, and owing much to the functionally dictated positioning of chimneys and the elegant roof ventilator. Other typical Anderson touches are the reinforcing arches, borrowed from early Gothic and castellated structures. In 1921, Sir John James Burnet indicated that Anderson's schools had been sought out and studied by several generations of architects. Even operating under severe spatial and cost constraints, he had set new standards. In contrast with this considerable achievement, Moffat and Aitken's mediocre school near Leith Walk exemplifies the poor command of Gothic that was still widespread.

In parallel with his Edinburgh schools, and arising from his involvement there, Anderson was asked to compete with Moffat, Pilkington and Bell, Little and Paxton of Kirkcaldy and John Milne of St Andrews for the design of new schools for the Kirkcaldy School Board. The Board intended to erect one school in the east and one in the west of their town. The Kirkcaldy architects refused to compete, and in May 1874 the competitive designs were put on public display in the Town Hall.[26] In May 1874, a Board motion to award both schools to Anderson was

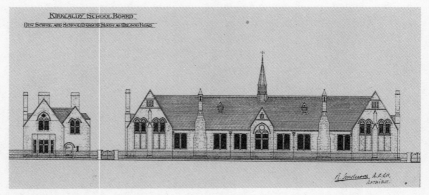

Plate 29. Kirkcaldy West School, design drawing (Anderson Office Drawings, Edinburgh University).

defeated by five votes to four, and the architect was awarded the west school, the east school going to Milne. The building of the west school began in 1875, on a spacious plot above old coal workings, necessitating arched foundations. The tenders submitted give the following details:

		£
Mason — Alexander Fraser, Pathhead		2,796 – 10 – 0
Joiner — Wm. Little & Sons, Kirkcaldy		1,488 – 8 – 6
Plasterer — Alex McPherson, St. Andrews		179 – 0 – 0
Plumber — Alex Torrance, Kirkcaldy		289 – 0 – 0
Slater — Wm. Muir, Kirkcaldy		295 – 9 – 8
		5,048 – 8 – 2

The two schools, built of local stone from Deu and Dubbie quarries, were completed in 1876. The west school's finish thence became the local standard for building specifications, so carefully was it carried out (Plate 29). Again, its appearance depends on the simple but elegant Gothic motifs preferred by the architect and their interrelationship with broad expanses of wall plane.

While working on the schools, Anderson had also produced his competition designs for the new Edinburgh University Medical School. As indicated in his letter to Skene, the submission timetable was tight, so tight that it was in fact extended from 1 November 1874 to 1 January 1875. The competition had arisen out of the massive accommodation problems being faced by the medical faculty, which was housed in the western side of Robert Adam's Old College. In 1871 five professors had brought this long-standing matter to a head by putting in a requisition for more space to fit in larger student numbers and to provide for the growing levels of practical and laboratory work being introduced into the curriculum. Negotiations for extra land in the immediate vicinity of both the Old College and William Adam's old Infirmary across Nicholson Street had been going on throughout the previous decade, but had been inconclusive. Late in 1871, the University Senate agreed to purchase Park Place, to the south of Teviot Row. The ground here was nearly level, Bryce's new Royal Infirmary stood nearby, and the Old College was also close at hand. After some tenements in Teviot Row were finally purchased, it was decided to proceed with the building project. The final list of architects to be approached for designs comprised Lessels, Cousin, Peddie and Kinnear, Wardrop and Reid and Anderson himself.[28] As indicated to Skene, Bryce had declined the invitation to compete, as was his practice.

The *Builder* of 23 January revealed that four schemes had been submitted and were under consideration. Cousin and Lessels, in their customary fashion, had decided to collaborate. It also revealed the thinking of the Building Committee, who, 'while desirous of seeing due attention to style, discouraged elaborate ornamentation'. Prominent in their thoughts were the facilities so urgently required, which were to include an anatomical museum, a lecture theatre, and a 'College hall' for academic gatherings. A 'preference for roof lights' was also expressed. Given the coincidence of the practical bias of the Building Committee with Anderson's own architectural philosophy, it is hardly surprising that he undertook a research programme of incredible intensity prior to submitting his entry. His researches are contained in a pocket book, where over seventy pages are crammed with details from a whirlwind British and continental trip.[29] This encompassed visits to Liverpool University, Owens College, Manchester, University College, London, Oxford University, South Kensington Museum, the Albert Hall, the Sorbonne, universities and like institutions at Utrecht, Amsterdam, Berlin, Leipzig, Bonn and Aachen.

In these places every remotely relevant detail caught his eye, and he scribbled in his book plans of anatomy rooms, 'bone rooms', measurements of desks, glass specifications, details of piping arrangements and lighting and gutter fixtures. At Liverpool he took the opportunity to record interior details at St George's Hall. At London University he noted that north light was best for microscope work. At Oxford he noted, significantly, that Wren's semicircular Sheldonian Theatre 'holds 4,000 when crowded' and that the stairs leading to its horseshoe galleries were positioned against the flat wall. At the Albert Hall all that seemed to interest him were seat details. On 19 October 1874 he scribbled down the plan of the circular anatomy theatre at St Bartholomew's Hospital, London, noting also the position of the lecturer's table. At the Sorbonne,

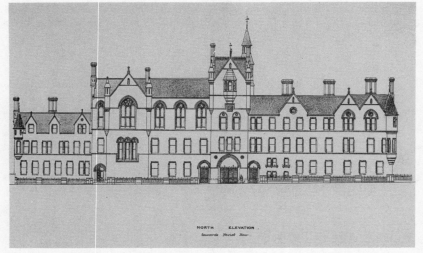

NORTH ELEVATION .

Plate 30. Wardrop and Reid's design for Edinburgh University Medical School (Anderson Office Drawings, Edinburgh University).

he drew a sketch plan of a semicircular lecture theatre, where a passage skirted round the perimeter. At the time, German technical and scientific education was in high repute, but not everything he observed in that country was to his liking. At one institution he noted 'Anatomy Class Room Badly Lighted'. At another he noted 'Dr. Ludwig's lecture room frightfully close and badly ventilated. Wants height'. At the Bonn Anatomy School, opened just two years earlier, he noted that 'classrooms are octagons with very large windows — much rattling during wind'. He did, however, approve of the laboratories at the Chemical Institute in Bonn, and learned there that glass was best for furniture where acids were in use. When he returned, he was armed with ideas on layouts, lighting, furniture and the latest equipment, information which would impress as well as prove useful.

The *Builder* of 23 January had also provided a brief description of each competition entry. Cousin and Lessels' design was in Venetian Gothic, with a large dome surmounting the hall. Peddie and Kinnear, hedging their bets, submitted both a classical and a Gothic design; presumably Peddie was responsible for the first and Kinnear the second. None of these designs are believed to survive. Wardrop and Reid's design does, however, exist. These architects had chosen the Gothic style, perhaps to harmonise with the Baronial style of the Royal Infirmary next door and George Heriot's Hospital in Jacobean diagonally opposite. The design was pedestrian — a fairly nondescript Geometric Gothic building, asymmetrically massed, with plate glass windows (Plate 30). The internal

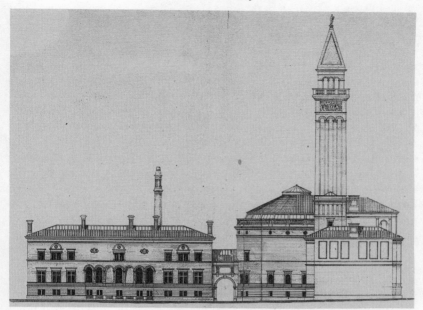

Plate 31. Elevation from Anderson's accepted scheme for Edinburgh
University Medical School (Anderson Office Drawings, Edinburgh University).

planning was, however, chaotic. The architects failed to provide an
interlinking circulation system, there were quite a number of changes to
floor levels, and arrangements within departments were irregular and
confusing. Perhaps surprisingly, therefore, two of the nine professors
involved in the decision voted for Wardrop and Reid's scheme, although
four voted for Anderson's. The remaining three were undecided, but no
support appears to have been forthcoming for the other two schemes. A
subcommittee appointed to look specifically at 'Circulation and Services'
then settled the matter by reporting that Anderson's plan met their
requirements best. The award was communicated to Anderson on 29
January 1875, and the other competitors each received a hundred guineas
for expenses.

Anderson's winning designs were for a complex of buildings which
hugged the boundary line of the irregular but almost square parcel of
ground between Teviot Row and Stable Lane. Along the Teviot Row
(north) axis he placed the main frontage of the complex, to house the
materia medica and medical jurisprudence departments. Behind this lay
an open court, much of which was to be taken up by a great semicircular
graduation hall. Parallel to the main frontage, the south block was to
contain an anatomical museum and the anatomy department, while on
the west, a block with irregular projections into Middle Meadow Walk

was to house physiology, midwifery and pathology. A small court
surrounded by other teaching blocks completed the complex on the south.
The buildings were to be symmetrical on the Teviot Row elevation and
asymmetrical elsewhere, and were in the Italian Renaissance style,
described in newspaper reports as 'Cinque Cento'. The great surprise of
the design was an extremely bold campanile of square section and
pyramidal top, completely unsolicited, and modelled on St Mark's,
Venice. Its graceful proportions and crisp but delicate detailing completed the complex of buildings, and would have made the Medical School
visible from many parts of Edinburgh. One of Anderson's drawings shows
it in its initial position (Plate 31).

It is impossible to say finally what prompted Anderson to choose the
Early Renaissance style for the new school, although it has been suggested
that the Royal Scottish Museum in Chambers Street might have inspired
it. It is also possible that Anderson may have been aware that the other
designs being submitted were predominantly Gothic, and wanted to catch
the assessors' eyes with something different, without compromising the
functional flexibility which the Gothic style would have allowed. Credibility is given to this suggestion by a report appearing in the *Scotsman* of
7 April 1877. In discussing the style of the new buildings, it described how

> it naturally commended itself to an architect so wisely heedful of the
> practical, on account of its plasticity and adaptability to varied
> internal arrangements.[30]

If not conclusive on the matter of style, the newspaper report made the
architect's basic design philosophy absolutely clear, continuing that

> In catering for the difficult task of providing for the varied require-
> ments of ten distinct professors, Mr. Anderson proceeded on the
> sound principle, too often disregarded by architects, of first securing
> the necessary accommodation in the most desirable shape, and then
> considering what sort of elevations would adapt themselves to the
> interior thus adjusted, so as to secure an artistic ensemble. The result
> is a building with a distinctly pronounced organic character. Every
> external feature expresses the nature of the internal arrangements,
> and shows how kindly the beautiful adjusts itself to the useful when
> the latter has been, in the first instance, conscientiously consulted.[31]

The internal arrangements just referred to were simple, direct and
clear. Each block of buildings was to be given single axial corridors, off
which the variously shaped rooms were to be located. Stairs were to be
placed at the ends of blocks, and departments could access each other
easily, as departmental corridors were connected to each other, or to
stairs, at both ends. The studies made in England and abroad were selectively incorporated. The college hall, like the Sheldonian Theatre, was for
functional reasons modelled on Roman amphitheatres. Microscopy was

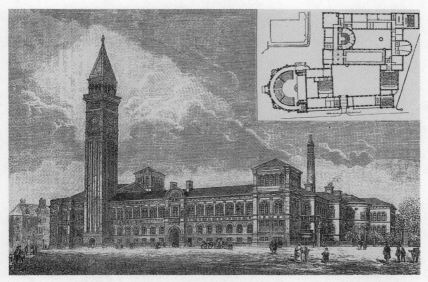

Plate 32. Edinburgh University Medical School (Grant's *Old and New Edinburgh*, Vol. II, 1883).

given north light (as in Wardrop and Reid's design) and lecture theatres, often steeply raked, were provided on semicircular lines. By mid-1877, nothing had been built. Negotiations for properties on the boundaries of the site had been continuing, as had discussions with the various professors in the Medical School, intent on bringing to the matter their 'mature deliberation and experience'.[32] When specifications were finally called for on 6 June 1877, the plans had changed. Property had been acquired at the east end of Teviot Row, thus enabling the graduation hall to be swung out from its position in the large courtyard. This in turn allowed some replanning of the departments adjoining. An extra floor was added to the west pavilion of the Teviot Row elevation, and the east pavilion was supplanted by the campanile (Plate 32). These modifications apart, the initial plans were basically unchanged. While the designs had been finalised, funds were not available to undertake the whole scheme, and when building started early in 1878 it was on the basis that the graduation hall and campanile were to be deferred. Tenders for the south block were scrutinised late in January that year, to be followed soon afterwards by tenders for the north block. Building was periodically stopped as professors argued the case for last minute alterations with the Building Committee, who eventually disallowed changes in 1883. The school was completed in 1886 (Plates 33 and 34).

In July 1880, Anderson was given a further opportunity to hammer home the design philosophy behind the school. A Mr Scott Moncrieff

Plate 33. West elevation, Edinburgh University Medical School (National Monuments Record of Scotland).

complained that the boiler house chimney had only been decorated, and not disguised. Through the *Scotsman*'s pages he observed that

This is no doubt frequently done, for example at the Calton Jail you have the chimney disguised as a mediaeval watch tower, at the Hydropathic Establishment at Craiglockhart and many other places the chimney takes the form of an Egyptian obelisk. At the Natural History Museum, South Kensington, thousands of pounds were spent dressing up the ventilation shafts as Italian campanili, and at a printing office in the High Street you may see a large chimney in the form of a Scotch Thistle.[33]

In the event, the chimney was erected according to plan, form following function as it had done throughout the commission. In line with the architect's practical orientation, the school was stoutly constructed with thick walls and heavy iron beams throughout. These structural members are boldly displayed on ceilings and staircases in many parts of the building. In an earlier cost-cutting exercise Anderson had put forward a number of suggestions which included slighter construction, but this was not implemented. In order to ensure that the highest standards of execution and commercial probity were achieved, Anderson entrusted the project's supervision from the very beginning to Allan Clark, a Hawick man who had spent a period of time working in London. Clark carried

Plate 34. Main quadrangle, Edinburgh University Medical School (National Monuments Record of Scotland).

out his duties as clerk of works with great distinction from the very beginning through to the completion of the great graduation hall, a period of twenty years. If the school and church competitions in Edinburgh had brought Anderson to the notice of many of its citizens, his achievement at the Medical School ensured that he was henceforth regarded as the city's first architect. Bryce, who had previously worn this mantle, had died just after the Medical School started building.

Prior to this point, Anderson in June 1876 visited London at the behest of the Caledonian Railway, which was in the process of rationalising its operations in central Glasgow. The railway's southern system terminated at Bridge Street Station, on the south side of the Clyde. Passengers wishing to travel further northwards or elsewhere in the central belt of Scotland had to traverse the city in order to catch connecting trains at the Railway's Buchanan Street Station, which also served as the starting point for journeys southwards. Clearly these arrangements were unsatisfactory. Moreover, the railway's staff worked in an overcrowded office in

Buchanan Street. A new station and terminus, on the north side of the
Clyde, was obviously required. New station buildings would also provide
an opportunity to rehouse the railway's staff.[34] It was anticipated that
Parliamentary approval for the changes, including permission to bridge
the Clyde, would be given and, as early as 1873, Blyth and Cunningham
of Edinburgh, the country's most experienced designers of bridges and
railway systems, had been consulted. Their plans for a new station at
Gordon Street were approved by the railway's board on 18 October 1876,
and shortly afterwards Parliamentary permission was granted.

How Anderson came to be involved is not entirely clear. There was no
competition, and it would appear that he was simply proposed by
Cunningham, who must have been aware of his recent achievements in
Edinburgh. On 1 May 1877, the railway board's minutes record that 'Mr.
Cunningham and Mr. Anderson attended, and submitted designs for the
new station buildings, one of which was approved of and initialled
accordingly'.[35] The same minutes give a picture of a board of directors
totally embroiled in the problems of running an expanding railway —
dealing with frequent accident investigations, checking passenger and
mileage statistics to verify their market share, and having to raise new
capital regularly from shareholders who looked for good returns. It is
highly probable that the directors were simply too busy to deal with the
administration of an architectural competition, hence the manner and
swiftness with which the decision to appoint Anderson was taken.

On 26 February 1878, invitations to tender for the new station buildings
were published in the national press. Later that year Watt and Wilson's
tender for £172 586.13.5 was accepted. By the time the builders were
permitted to start, a number of dwellings, offices and stores had been
cleared from the site, and the new station was well advanced. Anderson's
plans for the new buildings were stamped with the simplicity and clarity
which characterised the other great project in progress in Edinburgh at
the same time. Given that the site was bounded on the north and west
by Gordon Street and Hope Street, respectively, it was logical to locate
the main entrance at their intersection, and for the circulation to radiate
in both directions from this point. The ground floors of the buildings were
designed to accommodate booking offices, luggage depositories, waiting
and refreshment rooms, offices for the Stationmaster, superintendents and
other officials, with the whole general staff of the railway allocated to other
floors. All ranks, from clerks to the board, were to be located in a series
of variously sized rooms. These functions were to be accommodated along
central spinal corridors nine feet wide on each of nine storeys, including
basement and attics. Anderson had at his disposal 242 feet of frontage on
Gordon Street and 302 feet on Hope Street. At the junction of these two
axes he placed a large square tower, intended to hold the board room. A

Plate 35. Central Station Buildings (later Central Hotel), Glasgow (National Monuments Record of Scotland).

stone entrance stairway was set in the angle between the tower and the edge of the Gordon Street frontage.

The new buildings were stoutly constructed: the corridors were floored with concrete slabs laid on malleable iron joists, and in the 2 foot 6 inch gap beneath were three channels, the centre one bearing heating pipes and the other two for ventilation. The floors of the offices were laid on wooden joists again undergirded with malleable iron.[36] This immensely strong grid was encased in thick walls of Dunmore stone. The style of the buildings was described as 'an adaptation of the Renaissance order' and a 'modification of the Queen Anne style'. Its inspiration was clearly the architecture of the sixteenth and seventeenth centuries, at the point where the mullioned and transomed windows of late Gothic were intermixed with the semicircular arches and pediments of the Renaissance. The scale of the buildings and the pointed roof of Anderson's square tower strongly suggests Flemish town halls of that era. Anderson had two requirements of the windows, that they expressed the rooms behind them and that they admitted sufficient light. As well as achieving these objectives, they were used to give visual variety to the two major facades, which were otherwise left undecorated (Plate 35). In July 1879 the new line across the Clyde was completed, and the new station was opened for use. Above and around it, Anderson's noble edifice was beginning to rise.

A few months later, preparations were in hand for the accommodation of the workmen who were about to start on the third of Anderson's great concurrent projects of the 1870s and 1880s, the rebuilding of Mount Stuart, near Rothesay on the island of Bute, the residence of John, the Third Marquess of Bute. In December 1877 a fire had destroyed the central portion of the old Mount Stuart, a neo-Palladian building designed in the previous century by Alexander McGill and which had subsequently been worked on by the Adam office. Anderson, in good standing with Lord Bute as a result of the Paisley Abbey episode and their common membership of the Society of Antiquaries, was, in the spring of 1878, asked to survey the burnt out house and to produce designs for its rebuilding in sympathy with McGill's wings, which had both survived the fire. An alternative proposal, to build a completely new house at Torr Wood, a little inland from Mount Stuart, was never pursued.[37] Anderson's plans would have resulted in a rectangular block larger than the old corps de logis, nearly symmetrical, with two bay windows to the landward side of the house and a square two-storey entrance hall off the door between these bays. New kitchen offices were to have been formed in an oblong around a courtyard. The old house would have been transformed into a nineteenth century home where the rule of symmetry deferred to functional utility. Elevations, if ever drawn, do not survive.

The plans, however, bear evidence of a change of heart on Bute's part — a loose and sketchy hand, in all probability Anderson's, has superimposed on these designs a large cube containing a smaller cube inside.[38] The idea of Mount Stuart in its finally built form appears, therefore, to have been born in 1878, as a result of the discussion of Anderson's first scheme. On 2 October 1879, Bute was writing to his wife about the next set of designs.

> Anderson's plans are exceedingly nice. The house seems to bid fair to be a splendid palace. There were only a few things, partly in regard to the picturesque and partly the luxurious wh. I suggested alterations in to him. And these I shall see better in the model, when I am in Edinburgh.[39]

Mount Stuart in its final form had the most elementary of plans. It consisted of a huge cubical block placed between the two wings surviving from the old house, and at its heart lay a large and lofty hall, again cubical, round which the rooms were deployed. On the ground floor, on the seaward side of the house, a large library and drawing room were located, while opposite, on the landward side, an entrance hall and dining room were inserted. The great hall, rising through three storeys, gave way on one side to a grand staircase, and on the other to an outer hall. This magnificent space was to become the architectural centrepiece of the project, and in due course its arcades would be clad in the finest marble, alabaster and porphyry that money could buy. On the first floor, accessed from the grand staircase, bedrooms for Lord Bute, Lady Bute and their family were planned along the seaward side, with other bedrooms occupying the rest of the floor. The next two levels were for guest bedrooms and servants' quarters. Outside the main block, the plans for extended kitchen offices were retained in altered form, and a conservatory was to be built, offset at the opposite end of the house by plans for an apsidal chapel. The whole conception was as clear and logical as the retention of the original wings would allow.

The choice of style was Gothic. Bute's youthful conversion to Roman Catholicism had led to his immersion in the history, early liturgy and ritualism of his faith. Imbued with the spirit of Romanticism, he had developed a passion for all things medieval, and had at Cardiff Castle and Castle Coch collaborated with the arch-medievalist architect William Burges, in creating beautifully eccentric Gothic palaces, where lavishly expensive and elaborate interiors were progressively added, under his own guidance. Lord Bute would frequent these surroundings gorgeously clad in the robes of medieval saints. On the face of it, Anderson was a most unlikely successor to Burges in providing a Gothic palace for a man at once so saintly, sensuous and autocratic. The buildings and other artefacts designed by Burges had an innocent, almost naive, quality and a sculpturesque, rotund feel in contrast to the lean and spartan functional lines preferred by Anderson. Nevertheless Anderson, like Burges, was a Gothic specialist, the finest in Scotland, and it was Lord Bute's declared policy to employ a variety of architects at his many properties, in order to share their ideas. In any event, Anderson's designs pleased him greatly.

The house was built between 1880 and 1885. It was well advanced structurally by 1882, the delay in completion arising from a combination of factors, including the necessity to bring a great many of the building materials by sea, and the house's isolated location on Bute. It was intended from the outset that the new house should be lit by electricity, making it the first of its kind in Scotland. A London consultant, Wilson Phipson, was made responsible for the heating and ventilation system. Anderson as usual built robustly, reinforcing the structure with heavy metal beams. As the facades took shape, their inspiration became clear. The secular Gothic halls and houses of Cordes and Figeac, illustrated in Anderson's book of continental tour studies, were here realised on a

Plate 36. Mount Stuart, 1880s (A.H. Millar, *Castles and Mansions of Renfrewshire and Buteshire*).

remote Scottish site, in red Corsehill sandstone. Fascinated by the relationship between the sharp yet delicate details of windows and doors and the unbroken wall planes of these French palaces, Anderson had already emulated them in his school buildings, particularly at Kirkcaldy, and was at last able to utilise their example on a scale larger than the originals. At Cordes and Figeac the placing of doors and windows was asymmetrical, reflecting the requirements of usage; this, too, was the principle employed at Mount Stuart, where form expressed function, even in the positioning and design of chimneys and the outward expression of stairways. The end result was no picturesque contrivance. It arose from the architect's desire to express purpose and function in an honest manner, and while it would be wrong to say that aesthetic adjustments did not take place, there is no evidence that compromises were made. The crispness and discipline of Mount Stuart's imposing facades convey a sense of gravitas rather than exuberance and confirm the architect's intellectual approach (Plate 36). Over the next two decades Bute and Anderson would collaborate in extending the pile, with Bute himself, as ever, assuming responsibility for interior design.

While the 1870s were dominated by the three great projects just described, a number of smaller works were also carried out. Not surprisingly, these included several churches for Episcopalian congregations. At Dunimarle Castle, a mock Tudor building near Culross, Anderson provided a small but vigorous church, dedicated to St Serf, for Mrs Sharpe Erskine. This building was intended for the Episcopalians of Culross, and in due course would serve as the donor's mortuary chapel. The style adopted was late twelfth century, taken from the earliest parts

Plate 37. St Serf's Church, Dunimarle (Author).

of the nearby Culross Abbey.[40] The church was opened and consecrated on 1 July 1876, its austere wall planes suggesting the influence of James Brooks. The massive buttressing and the belfry of the west gable again derive from Anderson's studies of the Abbey Barn, Caen (Plate 37). Inside, the massively thick walls were decorated with stencilling, with elaborate encaustic tiling enriching the floor of the apsidal chancel. In September 1874, Anderson had been in correspondence with Sir H.J. Seton, advising him of difficulties in extending the existing Episcopalian church at Stirling. This resulted in plans for a new building, an elegant early Gothic design with five bays and an apsidal chancel, altered at the discussion stage to a square-ended one. Although the plans allowed for a fine broach spire with lucarnes, it was never a serious proposition given the financial position (Plate 38). The church, dedicated in 1875, has a splendidly proportioned interior, a little let down by the rough quality of the brickwork filling the spandrels of the nave arcades.

While he was engaged on the Iona restoration, Anderson had also undertaken some small-scale school work in the vicinity, including a tiny extension to Telford's original Iona school, a new school at Pennycross, on Mull (Plate 39) and extensions to the school at Balevulin, on Tiree.[41] While in the neighbourhood, he was also asked to report on the ecclesiastical ruins at Oronsay by a Captain Stuart of Colonsay. A further and more important restoration commission arose in late 1875, when Anderson was asked by the Marquess of Lothian, a fellow Antiquary, to make

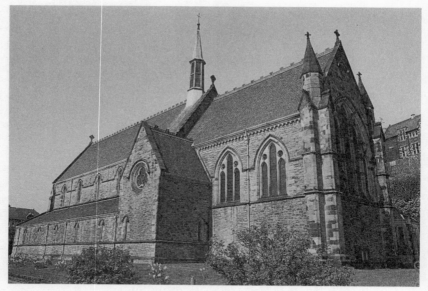

Plate 38. Holy Trinity Church, Stirling (Author).

Plate 39. Pennycross School, Mull (Author).

structural repairs to Jedburgh Abbey. The nave arcades were in danger of collapse and the south wall and one of its two ornately carved doors lay in ruins. Scott, who was in Edinburgh in connection with the new St Mary's Episcopal Cathedral, visited the site and agreed with Anderson's recommendation that light wooden tie beams be used to hold the arcades

Plate 40. Replacement door in south wall of nave, Jedburgh Abbey (Author).

in position.[42] The south wall was also rebuilt, and a replacement door, identical to its ancient sister, was provided (Plate 40). Old work and new were carefully differentiated. In 1879 Anderson's office, located at Wemyss Place since 1877, received a visit from Lord Dunpark, who commissioned restoration work at the ancient St Bride's Church, Douglas. The previous year some work on the outbuildings at Yester House was completed. At this point a 'Runic cross of red granite' was also erected in memory of Anderson's former supporter, the late Dean Ramsay, at St John's Church, Edinburgh.

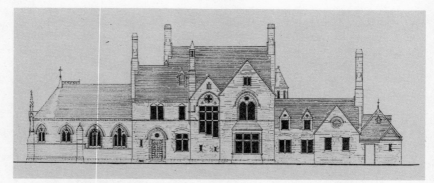

Plate 41. Design for Brechin Diocesan Residence (Anderson Office Drawings, Edinburgh University).

The range and volume of work undertaken during this period testifies to the tremendous regard in which the architect was now held. At the same time there were irritations as well as successes. Designs prepared in 1876 for a new diocesan residence for the successor to the late Bishop Forbes (Plate 41) came to nothing, as the project was scrapped. A mediocre competition design prepared for a new Free Church in Kirkcaldy was unsuccessful, the contract won by Matthews of Aberdeen, a fellow Scott pupil. A commission for a new Anglican church at Tynemouth, near Newcastle, was deferred because of resistance from the local bishop. Competitive designs for a new Episcopal church at Greenock were unsuccessful, as was a design submitted to the Episcopalians of Old St Paul's, Edinburgh. One of the most interesting of the frustrated projects was the commission to design a new Episcopal church for the congregation at Leven, in Fife. Contract drawings were completed in 1878. Anderson produced a design for 200 sittings, approximately 50 more than was wanted. The cost was £2000, considerably in excess of the figure the vestry had anticipated. Nevertheless, the work was put out to tender, resulting in a dispute between the selected builder and Anderson over the material to be used. After taking legal advice, the church abandoned Anderson's scheme. Matthews and Mackenzie of Aberdeen were given the commission and produced a cheaper building, much less distinguished than Anderson's design. Surviving drawings reveal a beautifully proportioned church with a Brechin round tower of the kind Anderson had sketched some years earlier (Plate 42). Towers of this type would reappear in future designs.

The setbacks were perhaps inevitable for a practice growing exponentially: it was impossible, with an increasing workload and increasing dependence on a growing staff, to do equal justice to each commission. Anderson's diary for 1879 preserves the hectic atmosphere of these

Plate 42. Unbuilt design for Leven Episcopal Church (Anderson Office Drawings, Edinburgh University).

years.[43] The architect was now embroiled in the lifestyle which had once characterised his late mentor Scott, rushing from one end of the country to the other in trains, visiting clients, sites, quarries and woodyards, while at the same time grappling with the affairs of the office. Like Scott, who had died in 1878, Anderson did not however neglect professional affairs. Although he was too busy to prepare further papers for the Society of Antiquaries, Anderson kept fully involved in the business of the Edinburgh Architectural Association. The Association, formed in late 1858, had initially been christened the 'Edinburgh Young Men's Architectural Association', and was set up to provide a forum for the younger practitioners, who felt they were not well enough catered for by the Architectural Institute. This latter body had, by the early 1870s, 'silently disappeared', an attempted merger with the Edinburgh Architectural

Association having failed in the interim. The Association was therefore the Institute's logical successor, as far as Edinburgh architects were concerned. Its activities included the preparation and criticism of essays, talks on design, and architectural outings. It grew from strength to strength and attracted the city's finest architects, in due course building up a library. Anderson, Hippolyte Blanc, David MacGibbon and Thomas Ross were prominent in its affairs. The latter architects had already begun to show the interest in old Scottish architecture that would lead to their masterwork, the *Castellated and Domestic Architecture of Scotland*. Thomas Ross in November 1869 had read a paper on sketching, and had suggested that an Association Sketch Book, contributed to by members, should be inaugurated.

This represented an interest near and dear to Anderson's heart, and in 1875 he proposed a motion:

> that the Edinburgh Architectural Association should undertake as part of their annual work the publication of a volume of Sketches and Measured Drawings of Old Scottish Architecture, and that a special Committee of the Association be appointed to superintend its production.[44]

This was agreed, and Anderson joined the Committee of Management, contributing drawings of the choir windows at Brechin and drawings of the chapter house windows at Glenluce Abbey to the first edition. While maintaining his allegiance to the Association, Anderson had also faithfully and regularly contributed drawings to the annual exhibitions of the Royal Scottish Academy, an organisation to which he was also immensely committed, and with which he was on good terms, having been involved in negotiations with the mercurial William Fettes Douglas, a future president, with whom he discussed painting, lighting and heating alterations at the National Gallery in late 1879.

From 1877 onwards, Anderson had become increasingly familiar with the relatively undiscovered Edinburgh suburbs of Currie and Colinton on the south-west side of the city. That year he had designed a double villa at Colinton, and shortly afterwards drew plans for Baberton Court, erected a little later in Currie. Now in his forty-fifth year, the architect made the decision to build himself a new house at Colinton. On 14 July 1879 he bought a piece of ground bordering on Woodhall Road from the Company of Merchants. It was a long narrow strip of over two acres, and ran from north to south, bounded on the west and east sides by two public roads, as yet unmade. Anderson divided the land into two long narrow plots, building a smallish house on the westernmost strip. The result was 'Allermuir', named after a summit in the Pentlands directly to the south. The house was designed on two axes, one running from west to east and facing the garden, and containing two superimposed public rooms of good

Plate 43. 'Allermuir', Colinton. (Royal Incorporation of Architects in Scotland).

proportion. A double bay window provided extra light on each floor and afforded fine views of Allermuir Hill (Plate 43). At right angles to this, on the other axis, the architect provided a range of bedrooms, with kitchen offices filling the angle between the two wings. At the house's west end, the main door gave entrance to a generous hall, from which a handsome oak staircase arose. At the north end of the house trees were planted, deliberately obscuring the elevation. The plan was clarity itself; all rooms radiated sensibly from the entrance hall, and the kitchen was logically and conveniently placed for service.

The house was designed in the Scots Jacobean style. During and beyond the Jacobean period, Scottish domestic architecture had become less defensive in character, and occasionally incorporated English motifs. At 'Allermuir' these were represented in the bays and oriel of the garden frontage, which were blended with sash windows in a manner both functional and historically authentic. The end result strongly resembled the east range at Pinkie House, Musselburgh, built in 1613. Inside, Anderson panelled the walls extensively in oak, breaking up the ceilings with simple Jacobean mouldings. He also panelled the entrance to each of the bay windows in a semicircle, adding variety to the rectangularity of the house, while emphasising the depth and solidity of the walls, a device that would turn up again and again in his work. The house was

the essence of Scottishness. Asymmetrical, crowstepped and unosten-
tatious, it was the culmination of the architect's preoccupation with old
Scottish buildings, and in particular the relationship between their form
and function. At the same time the house, in all its simplicity, emits a
sense of great refinement and completeness. 'Allermuir' would in due
course inspire Anderson to design a number of larger buildings in the
same vein. Its significance was, however, far wider. It signalled the death
knell of the Scots Baronial style, in all its excess and extravagance.
Drawings of the house were exhibited in the Royal Scottish Academy's
1880 exhibition. In due course its influence would be visible in the work
of many of the best architects of the next generation.

For Anderson and his wife, the house was more than an architectural
statement; it was home, a place of relaxation, hospitality, and happiness
that they would occupy for the rest of their lives. From this base Robert
and Mary would play a full part in the social life of the new suburb, much
of which stemmed from their involvement in the local Episcopal church,
which then met in temporary accommodation. Anderson, whose previous
Episcopal connections are something of a mystery, soon became a
vestryman, active and conscientious in his church's affairs.[45] The carving
above the house's main entrance speaks volumes: the words 'Adsit Deus'
(let God be present) convey something of the quiet faith which pervaded
his thinking and informed his work. Beneath, the monogram 'RRA 1879',
carved in typical Jacobean fashion, conveys a sense of arrival. It was at
once a gesture of affection and tribute to his long deceased mother, whose
maiden name, Rowand, he had recently adopted as his middle name. At
the same time the resultant double-barrelled title was far more sonorous
than plain 'Robert Anderson', and much more in keeping with his status
as Scotland's foremost architect.

5

Scotland's Premier Architect

By 1880, Anderson had attracted a galaxy of talented pupils and assistants to his office. From the mid-1870s onwards, in true Scott fashion, he had gradually delegated most of the drafting and the bulk of the detailed administration to these young men. Among their number was Archibald MacPherson who, from 1873 to 1876, honed his fine drafting skills and built up his experience on the major commissions of that period, prior to taking up a prospective partnership.[1] His successors also proved to be extremely competent. One of these was John Watson who, in the early 1880s, worked in the office as an assistant. He too was a superb draughtsman, deeply involved in Anderson's pet projects, spending up to three months a year sketching historic Scots architecture, and sitting on the Edinburgh Architectural Association's Sketch Book Committee when its first volume of drawings was published in 1875/6.[2] Another outstanding pupil, Arthur George Sydney Mitchell, was in the latter stages of his training by 1880. Mitchell was a graduate, and was the son of Sir Arthur Mitchell, the Queen's Commissioner for Lunacy in Scotland. Sir Arthur Mitchell was a very active member of the Society of Antiquaries and knew Anderson well.

At around this time, George Washington Browne took up a post as Anderson's chief assistant. He too had impeccable credentials, having started his career with Campbell Douglas and Sellars in Glasgow from 1873 to 1875, following this with two years' experience in the London office of Douglas' former partner, John James Stevenson.[3] Anderson and Stevenson had worked together with Scott in 1858. Browne had next spent some time under A.W. Blomfield, leaving in 1878 when he won the Pugin Scholarship, which enabled him to undertake a British study tour. In due course his studies from this tour would be published in book form. Before joining Anderson, Browne had also spent a short period in W.E. Nesfield's office in London. His arrival in Edinburgh said a great deal about Anderson's reputation south of the Tweed. These promising assistants found a

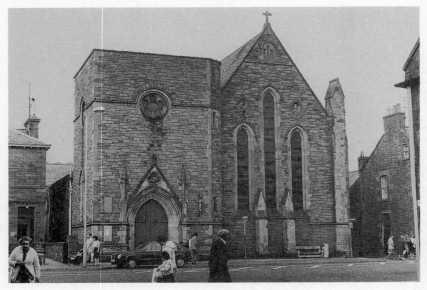

Plate 44. St John's Church, Forfar (Author).

wide portfolio of commissions in hand in 1880, and an immense amount of work.

As usual, church commissions were much in evidence. In 1878 the Episcopalians of Forfar had travelled out to Stonehaven to examine Anderson's work there, and, suitably impressed, had asked him to design their new church.[4] The foundation stone was laid in October 1879, and the new building, seated for 600, soon took shape, consisting of four bays and a long chancel with a north aisle. The main door, elaborately carved, was located in the base of its tower, on the left of the frontage (Plate 44). In keeping with Anderson's fondness for chronological transitions, the style changed from early Gothic to Geometric Gothic, moving from west to east. The influence of the 'vigorous' style of Brooks or Pearson can again be detected on the sides and rear of the building. Inside, an unusual roof incorporating tie beams, kingposts and supporting struts was provided. The chancel floor was paved in Godwin's encaustic tiles in black, red and yellow, its walls decorated with alternating bands of white alabaster and red terracotta titles. These tiles were also used as a cladding material for the entire south wall of the church. Anderson had a few years earlier refaced the interior of Kelton Church, near Castle Douglas, with similar tiles, producing a warm, dark effect, potentially good but marred by efflorescence. At Forfar, the terracotta tiles were of uneven flatness, which may explain their more sparing use in later commissions. Drawings

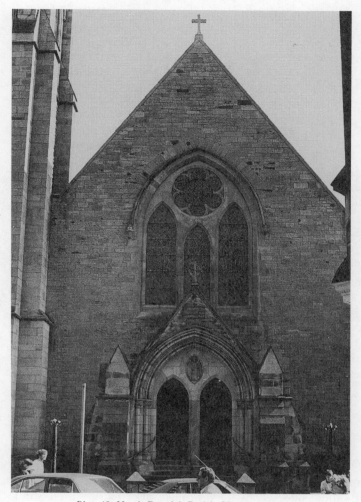

Plate 45. North Berwick Parish Church (Author).

showing the effect of the intended 150 foot tower still hang in the church, its completion thwarted by the lack of funds.

In 1879 and 1880, discussions with the Rev. G.W. Sprott of North Berwick Parish Church, a clergyman with a deep interest in ecclesiology, resulted in the preparation of three designs for a new church, one with a broach spire, one with a saddleback tower and the selected design, cruciform and towerless.[5] This was built, on a very restricted budget, for a congregation of 750, much of which had to be accommodated in galleries. Its finish (Plate 45) is reminiscent of Forfar, particularly in the

Plate 46. Nos 4 and 6 Nile Grove, Edinburgh (Author).

plate tracery of the chancel windows. A second church from this period was less successful. In August 1880, some designs were produced for St John's Church, to be built in Edinburgh's Canongate. A beautiful five-bay Gothic design was rejected in favour of a more or less rectangular Presbyterian preaching box, again in Gothic, with a U-shaped gallery and a pulpit on the back wall. On the frontage, stairs were contained in two Franco-Scottish tourelles. The result was visually unimposing and was heavily criticised in the *Builder*, whose reporter felt it lacked proportion and that it looked distinctly odd. Anderson defended the design on the grounds that funds were very restricted, and that an attempt had been made to make the most of 'simple constructive necessities'.[6] Quite clearly, this had not worked. While most of Anderson's church designs were inhibited by a lack of finance, it is scarcely a valid excuse for such an unprepossessing building, and all the more regrettable in view of the initial design.

Interesting developments were also taking place on the domestic front. After the completion of 'Allermuir', a second house belonging to Anderson was erected in the neighbouring plot. This house, 'Torduff', was also named after a summit in the Pentlands, and was let out by Anderson until the 1890s, when it was sold. A vigorous, somewhat daunting Gothic house on the exterior, it was nevertheless very well planned. At the same time,

Plate 47. Fettes College Sanatorium (now Malcolm House) (Author).

Anderson was busy in Edinburgh, at Morningside, on the Braid Estate, where town and country met. It was here that a whole scheme of speculative building, spanning thirty years, was begun. Anderson's involvement as feuing architect and designer may have come about through his connections with W.F. Skene. Although Skene had retired and was devoting all his time to his historical works, his firm, Skene Edwards and Garson, were solicitors to Lady Cathcart, who owned the land. Together with James Slater the builder, Anderson began to develop the first of the streets, Nile Grove. Numbers 4 and 6 were among the earliest houses to be built, and breathe the spirit of 'Allermuir' (Plate 46). These, again, were owned by Anderson, and let out as an investment. Number 8 followed soon afterwards, a large and undistinguished villa with a balcony at attic level in the 'Torduff' manner.

At about the same time, the little Gothic sanatorium at Fettes College was in the course of construction. This well massed building (Plate 47) was as usual simply planned, its rooms entered from corridors running along the two floors of the main axis. On the top storey the passage was given a pointed barrel roof, again featured in the largest room there. Anderson's thoughtful and familiar touches can be found everywhere: heating pipes are exposed at key points, the window ironmongery has been specially made, red cresting tiles adorn the roof ridge and inside, encaustic tiles have again been used. Nearby is its sister building, the north lodge cottage. If the opportunities given to Anderson at Fettes were slight compared with those given to David Bryce, the quality of his work is at least comparable.

In the autumn of 1880, Anderson received information which must have given him mixed feelings. At a time when his practice was, to put it mildly, hard pressed, the Directors of the Caledonian Railway decided that the nearly complete railway offices at the new Glasgow Central Station should, if possible, be converted to a luxury hotel. The *Glasgow Herald* of 5 October that year, announcing the change of plan for the 'handsome buildings', stated that the structures had been examined by 'professional men' whose opinion it was that 'their conversion under revised plans may easily be accomplished'. At a board meeting the next month, Anderson, with the aid of drawings, explained how the alterations could be made, stating, somewhat buoyantly, that before finally deciding on the internal arrangements, he should visit 'other great hotels, and also have the advantage of advice from a competent Railway Hotel Manager'.[7] Once his researches were completed, reconstruction began. Contrary to the sanguine reports submitted, this turned out to be a task of horrendous proportions. The grand staircase at the corner of Gordon Street and Hope Street had to be pulled down, together with the east staircase in Gordon Street. The tower was no longer to be used for board rooms and offices, and instead would contain a great staircase, gently climbing to all floors. At the bottom end of Hope Street, a two-storey dining room, 76 feet by 30, had to be created. This involved cutting away a complete section of the second floor, and demolishing a hundred feet of walls 2 feet 6 inches thick, which divided up a number of rooms.[8]

This left the conversion of the offices, which averaged 37 feet by 18 feet, into hotel rooms. The large doors into the corridors had to be walled up and the offices divided into rooms of either two or three apartments, calling for many more partition walls. The hotel bedrooms were to average 18 feet by 11 feet in size, and were each to have a fireplace, receiving daylight from the large double casement windows originally intended for the stricken offices. The bedrooms were to be provided with three doors, one to the corridor and one to each of the rooms on either side. This soul destroying work gave the builders 'no small difficulty', compounded at the rear of the building, where many new windows had to be opened up and many of the original ones filled. At roof level, attics were added to increase the accommodation to 400 rooms, now contained in seven floors. If the reconstruction of the station buildings produced frustration and difficulty, it must have pleased all concerned that the revised structure could be furnished and decorated with a sumptuousness befitting its new status. This involved wainscotting all the rooms in oak, walnut or mahogany, with classical columns in the corridors, and a handsome main staircase with a fine ironwork baluster. In the dining room and main hall, plaster cornicing and ceiling mouldings would in due course complement wood panelling a floor high.[9]

The task eventually took until mid-1883 to complete, the final cost of the new Central Hotel amounting to £363 806–19–11, of which £229 918–0–7 went to Watt and Wilson, the main contractor, with £78 135–17–6 spent on fittings and furniture, most of the balance accounted for by land purchase costs.[10] A newspaper report of a speech made at Watt and Wilson's topping out party, on 28 June 1883, reveals the lengths to which those involved had been put.[11] It confirmed that the job of conversion had been 'dreich' and 'troublesome', a 'source of worry to everybody concerned — the directors, committee, architect and ourselves'. Some appreciation of the immensity of the task can still be obtained in the eastern stairwell of the Gordon Street block. There the stumps of massive iron beams and patches of brickwork tell the story with unusual eloquence.

Late in 1880, Washington Browne's draughtsmanship was in evidence when Anderson submitted his design for the completion of Bryce's Free St George's church in Shandwick Place, Edinburgh.[12] The church had been erected without its tower in 1869, in a baroque style. Bryce's un-executed design for the tower had involved two elaborate, superimposed clusters of Corinthian columns. Browne prepared a card-mounted pencil sketch of Anderson's design, which, as well as illustrating his intention, also displayed Browne's sketching technique to advantage. He drew in a very competent if fussy style, with a penchant for impressionistic flecks of pencil in the manner of Pugin himself. The design caused controversy from the moment it appeared. Anderson had chosen to complete the church in a Venetian style, with a tall square campanile modelled on another, more famous church also dedicated to St George, San Giorgio Maggiore in Venice. In early 1882, as the tower began to rise, the *Builder* enthused that it was the 'most important' of 'all the recent additions to the ecclesiastical edifices in the city'.[13]

On 22 March, Professor Blackie of Edinburgh University wrote a witty letter to the *Scotsman* stating that the tower was 'in defiance of the rudimentary axioms of aesthetical science', being 'neither congruous with the building from which it rises nor with the parts of which itself is composed'. The next day two letters were published, one agreeing with Blackie, although regretting the church had not been designed in the Gothic style. Another wrote that 'there is nothing in the proportions or position of Free St. George's inconsistent with the addition of its tower'. On 24 March, George Reid of the Royal Scottish Academy came to Anderson's defence:

> Professor Blackie cannot be speaking seriously when he advocates the propriety of making the nose ugly, because the rest of the face happens to be so. Let us have at least one redeeming feature.

> I am not concerned with Mr. Bryce's intentions; let his part of the
> work speak for itself, or let those who admire it do so. If Mr.
> Anderson has succeeded in adding a beautiful feature to it, he
> deserves our thanks.[14]

Blackie replied firmly that, 'judged by the acknowledged principles of
aesthetic science, the church of Free St. George's is weighed in the balance
and found wanting'. This good natured but serious dispute is hard to
understand in the light of the visual evidence (Plate 48). Anderson was
too professional an architect to produce a tower at marked variance with
an existing building; it seems probable, though, that his intention was to
tone down the church's baroque exuberance. If the controversy proved
anything, it was simply that Bryce's architecture had fallen from favour.
Many of the other correspondents, as well as a senior Academician, had
expressed a strong disliking for the church, and none had anything
positive to say about it.

In 1881, the office moved to 24 Hill Street, another New Town address.
By this point it was clear that Anderson needed to share the executive
strains of his huge practice, especially in the light of developments at Glasgow Central Station. That year, at the age of twenty-seven, Washington
Browne was made a partner.[15] Browne had already expressed his
aspirations by submitting an entry for the new Glasgow Municipal
Buildings competition. His design was of the highest quality: it was for a
long, low, boldly rusticated classical edifice, with pedimented windows
spaced far apart, its composition completed by a tall campanile topped
with a lantern, rising from the Cochrane Street elevation.[16] This elegant,
understated design may well have owed something to Anderson's guidance. In any case, it was unsuccessful. Several years were to elapse before
Browne's personal touch was discernible in designs emanating from the
partnership; even then, this would be restricted to fairly minor works,
since the office's main task was to complete a whole range of buildings
started prior to his arrival. While this cloaked Browne in virtual anon-
ymity, it represented an unparalleled opportunity to a young architect
ready for responsibility and in need of experience. Browne's dignified
bearing made him an ideal substitute for Anderson in all but the most
important meetings with clients. At least once, he was entrusted with a
visit to Mount Stuart to 'take instructions', and was also involved at the
University.

One of the most important buildings coming to fruition in the days of
'Anderson and Browne' was the new clubhouse for the Scottish Conservative Club, Edinburgh. An entry in Anderson's diary records that, in 1879,
he had met the club's committee and gone over the plans, the outcome
being that the internal arrangements were 'approved of', but that the
elevation was 'to be revised'. The club had been founded in the late 1870s,

Plate 48. St George's West Church, Shandwick Place, Edinburgh
(Author).

and was inundated with applications for admission from its earliest days.
By the early 1880s, its membership had to be restricted to 2000, and there
was a substantial waiting list. Notwithstanding the fact that the club's
fees were modest, it was financially very successful, and was therefore in
a position to proceed with the new building it quite obviously needed. A
prime site in Princes Street was acquired in March 1880, and the revised
elevations were agreed in sufficient time to let Anderson exhibit them at
the Royal Scottish Academy in 1881. From 1882 to 1884 the building,
based on a free interpretation of early Italian Renaissance palazzi, gradually took shape. The style was a natural choice for two reasons: Barry

had made it fashionable for club architecture over the previous three or four decades, and Princes Street already boasted major classical works by Adam and Playfair, as well as a palazzo in Venetian Renaissance, the Life Association Building, on which Barry himself had collaborated with the local architect, David Rhind.

Prior to the Club's opening on 1 February 1884, a newspaper reporter, attuned to the architect's thinking, noted that it

> shows in all its arrangements an adaptation of means to secure the ends for which such a building exists, which bespeaks the most thoughtful care, extending to the smallest details, on the part of the architect.[17]

Inside, on the ground floor, Anderson had provided a magnificent hall and staircase, accessed from an outer vestibule. To the left, an L-shaped reading room afforded views of Princes Street through a canted bay window, a feature continued through the next two floors. A corridor on the ground floor, lit by stained glass windows, led to the remaining apartments, a library, some parlours, a lavatory, and several billiards rooms. The building stretched back 140 feet, compared with a frontage of just over 67 feet. On the first floor, a dining room occupied the whole front portion of the building, including the next stage of the bay window. Immediately behind, a corridor led to a private dining room, the secretary's and steward's rooms, and some lavatories. On the next floor was the members' smoking room, which again occupied the front portion of the building and gave fine views of Princes Street. A lesser smoking room, card room, lavatories, members' bedrooms and a room for waiters took up the rest of the floor.

The top storey was given over to the more practical functions. Nineteen members' bedrooms, divided into five sets, were each provided with bathrooms. Alongside was a bedroom for boot attendants, a footman's room, and a brushing room, all connected to the bedrooms by electric bells, which Anderson had also installed at 'Allermuir'. In conformity with the existing rules of propriety, and in recognition of the lifestyle of the membership, service quarters, kitchen offices and stores were pushed to the building's extremities. Menservants' apartments, wine cellars, stores and boiler rooms were located in the basement. Tucked behind the dormer windows of the roof were rooms for female servants, and at the back, kitchens, pantries and larders. Above this, and beneath a flat roof to the rear, were a laundry and drying space.

One of the journalists surveying the club praised the unique device of placing the kitchen arrangements at the top of the house, since it prevented cooking smells from permeating the other apartments. He was equally complimentary about the ingenious system of discreet service stairs, food and wine lifts, and the pneumatic tube apparatus for despatching orders to the kitchen. The same journalist also noted the

Plate 49. Main stair, Conservative Club, Edinburgh (National Monuments Record of Scotland).

sumptuousness of the materials used for decoration, and the superb quality of the workmanship.[18] Oak, walnut and sequoia panelling was used for the walls, and many of the corridors were paved in mosaic and lit through stained glass. Entrance hall and grand staircase were particularly imposing. The hall was warmed by an oak and marble fireplace, and floored in mosaic. The stair, of Arbroath stone, was 8 feet 6 inches wide, and treated 'in the Italian manner', with a carved oak balustrade and handrail. The staircase was mounted on arcades, affording fine perspectival views, and was lit by a large three light window of stained glass, by Ballantyne, featuring Britannia and emblems of literature and politics (Plate 49). This august and punctiliously planned building eventually cost £32 000, the site and furnishings amounting to £38 000. The work was carried out by Arthur Colville.[19]

At the beginning of 1883, Anderson submitted to the Royal Scottish
Academy's Annual Exhibition drawings of the Normand Memorial Hall,
a classical building erected in Dysart, Fife, together with drawings of the
Lady Flora Hastings Homes, Colinton. In prior years, the Academy had
been reminded of his pre-eminence in Scotland when he submitted
drawings of his more prestigious works, such as the Central Hotel or the
Conservative Club. On 10 February, a week prior to the opening of the
annual exhibition, the members of the Academy met together to vote on
a vacancy in their ranks caused by the death of Sir Daniel MacNee the
painter. In keeping with the rules of the Academy's Charter, only those
in full membership were entitled to vote. The new Academician would be
chosen from Associates of the Academy, a status conferred on Anderson
in 1876. Not surprisingly, perhaps, the ballot resulted in the replacement
of one painter with another: W.D. McKay was raised to full membership.
In the wake of these events, Anderson resigned. At the point at which he
took this action, there was only one living representative of the architectural profession in full membership, John Dick Peddie, who over the
1860s and 1870s had built up a large practice in partnership with the
Baronial and Gothic specialist, Charles Kinnear. Peddie had resigned as
secretary in 1876, ostensibly on health grounds, but immediately pre-
ceding his election as MP for Kilmarnock Burghs.[20]

While Anderson was undoubtedly hurt that an institution which had
previously elected David Bryce and the largely uninspired Peddie should
reject him, his protest stemmed from a deeper complaint; that an
Academy pledged by its Royal Charter to the support of architecture
virtually ignored it in most spheres of its activity. In common with Scott
and Pugin, it seemed to Anderson that architecture was the mistress art.
The function of a painting was to adorn a building; paintings were for
buildings and not the reverse. The Academy's attitude, in his eyes,
betrayed an ignorance of the history of art — it was only in recent centuries that the framed picture had evolved as an object separate from the
building it was intended to adorn. That it should usurp architecture was
an absurd aberration. Anderson was determined that the Academy's dis-
torted view of the importance of architecture should not go unchallenged.
Subsequent events would prove that his resignation was only the first step
in his protest. That year, recognition came from a different but equally
prestigious quarter: the Royal Society of Edinburgh elected him a Fellow.

The year 1883 also witnessed the death of Charles Reid of Wardrop
and Reid. His partner, James Maitland Wardrop, had died the previous
June leaving Hew Montgomerie Wardrop, aged 27, in charge of a huge
practice, with several major commissions outstanding.[21] The firm had
started in 1849, when James Maitland Wardrop had gone into practice
with Thomas Brown, introducing a style much influenced by Bryce.

Brown retired in 1873, at which point Charles Reid, chief draughtsman, was taken into partnership, the business continuing in a strong Baronial vein. Brown had enjoyed good connections with the farming community and Wardrop with the landed gentry, explaining two strands of the practice's work, which also included prison, courthouse, bank and church commissions.[22] It was a huge practice, one of the country's largest, and had to its credit the remodelling of Callendar House, Falkirk (1869–77) where its showier proclivities can be seen. Other commissions included the addition of a wing to Culzean Castle (1875–8) and alterations at Haddo House, where a good quality (if discernibly Victorian) refurbishment had been carried out. Integration with the Anderson practice was typical of the closely knit Edinburgh architectural fraternity, but as with the Bryce merger, involved potentially conflicting ideologies.

Shortly after the amalgamation, the practice moved to the Wardrop and Reid address, 19 St Andrew Square. Thereafter, the partners' involvements in the various commissions seem to have been along predictable lines. Wardrop (no doubt under Anderson's guidance) handled the work emanating from his father's practice, while Anderson handled all other new work, with the exception of a few commissions dealt with by Browne. This reflected the sources of the commissions rather than any discrimination against Browne. The completion of Beaufort Castle, Beauly, for Lord Lovat had been inherited by Wardrop from his father. Designs had been prepared as early as 1880, and work had begun when Wardrop, and then Reid, died. The building was gutted by fire in the 1930s, but photographs taken earlier still enable the extent and character of the work to be seen.[23] The building had been extensively and showily 'Baronalised' in typical Wardrop and Reid manner. It did, however, incorporate a good chapel with Geometric tracery and an open timber roof. Anderson's involvement in this commission, direct or indirect, remains a mystery. Wardrop was also busy at this time producing plans for the reconstruction of the Hirsel, Coldstream, which were never carried out.

Among the many commissions keeping Anderson (and no doubt Browne) fully stretched at this time were the rebuilding of St Mary's Parish Church, Hawick, which had previously been gutted by fire, and an addition to the nave of the ancient Kirkliston Parish Church. In 1884, Browne was involved in designs for Nile Grove in the Braid Estate, where on the north side two of his terraces were coming to completion, numbers 9–23 and 29–39. The houses at Braid were intended for the 'middle classes' who wanted to escape from the flatted accommodation at the centre of the town. Provision was made for servants in each house, and careful attention had been given to the sanitary and drainage arrangements.[24] A comparison between Browne's houses and those designed by

New Church Tynemouth
Detail of West Gable Nº 16.

Half Exterior Elevation.   Half Interior Elevation.

Scale Plan

Plate 50. St Augustine's Church, North Shields, contract drawing. (Anderson Office Drawings, Edinburgh University).

Anderson reveals a softer approach, using shallower roof pitches and smoother masonry finishes, although both sets of buildings have much in common, the most notable points being the external expression of internal layout and the sparing use of classical motifs. In Browne's houses more than in Anderson's, a faint echo of Norman Shaw's Queen Anne-style terraces at Bedford Park, London can be detected. At around this time Browne also designed a house for Professor Ewart the zoologist, at Bog Road in Penicuik.[25] The house (now a hotel) was of two floors and an attic, asymmetrically and functionally planned. This time, in the absence of any inhibitions, the exterior was tackled with Queen Anne freedom, featuring half timbering, pargetting and corbels carved as snakes and crocodiles.

Meanwhile, in North Shields, after a number of false starts, St Augustine's church was coming to completion. The bishop objecting to its erection had since died, and a site had been donated by a Captain Linskill, at the junction of Washington Terrace and Jackson Street. The captain also gave £1000 to which the Duke of Northumberland added £500 and a £60 per annum endowment.[26] The design of the church eventually erected differed considerably from those Anderson had first submitted: it was cruciform, towerless and the nave had a north and south aisle. Inside, a barrel roof with projecting tie beams complemented walls lined with fine red brick, a device producing a velvety ambience and which was to turn up increasingly in Anderson's church work. The general design of the church was loosely based on St Andrew's, St Andrews, photographs of which survive at North Shields. The style was early Gothic, possibly owing something to Arbroath or Pluscarden Abbeys, the clerk of works was David Lindsay of Edinburgh, and the contractor was G.F. Shotton, of Tynemouth (Plate 50). As this commission at last drew to a close, another was beginning at Glencorse, near Penicuik. Here a clergyman of the Established Church with ecclesiological leanings insisted on his new church being correctly oriented, forcing Anderson to rotate his plans through 180 degrees. The result was a church in a vigorous Butterfieldian mould (Plate 51) incorporating the saddleback tower Anderson had so many times offered clients in vain.[27] Inside the walls were clad in dark red brick, the communion table sat in the chancel, and a gallery ran along the back of the west wall.

Another Anderson commission in progress in 1884 was the conversion of a section of Biel House, East Lothian into a private chapel for Miss Constance Nisbet Hamilton. Biel House was a building in monastic and battlemented Gothic, largely the responsibility of William Atkinson. The alterations involved a new roof of open timber, collar braced, and the creation of a raised chancel and seating. A wheel window was inserted into the west wall, and the windows to the south converted to Perpendicular tracery.[28] In late November Miss Hamilton invited Anderson to call and visit the chapel in its completed state and to enjoy a few days of relaxation. Pressure of work would not allow the latter, but Anderson arranged an overnight stay to see the chapel both by gaslight and daylight. Miss Hamilton was evidently satisfied with the work, com-

Plate 51. Glencorse Parish Church (Author).

missioning a porch with an ogee arch in 1886 and some structural alterations to the main house in 1887, which included the provision of a sacristy for the chapel. A half-timbered estate cottage was commissioned in 1886. The year 1884 had also witnessed Edinburgh University's tercentenary celebrations. The University took the opportunity to recognise Anderson's work at the medical school, conferring on him the Honorary Degree of Doctor of Laws.

Anderson's church work to date had been impressive, but would pale into insignificance compared with the design coming to fruition at Govan. In 1875, the Rev. John McLeod was brought there by the congregation of Govan Old Parish Church. A son of the manse from Fuinary in Morven, Macleod had captivated his previous congregation at Duns with the conviction of his preaching and his commanding presence. On his arrival, Macleod immediately began a programme of church extension, at which he worked unceasingly until his death. This would eventually result in the remarkable total of thirty-three *quoad sacra* or daughter churches. The old church was inadequate for the numbers flocking in. This enabled him to initiate one of his great visionary projects, the creation of a church in Govan where the industrial ugliness of the shipyards could be transcended and worship heightened through the introduction of liturgy, and where daily services could be held, ideas novel to the Established Church.[29] Anderson had been consulted in 1876, initially in connection with the extension of the existing church. Further meetings took place in 1879, and by 1882 the idea of a new church had crystallised and extra ground was being acquired.

In July that year, Anderson twice met Macleod in London, firstly to go over plans, and secondly to discuss how galleries could be incorporated.[30] The latter question was crucial for Macleod, who 'wanted to "grip" his people, and see every face in the congregation', but at the same time did not wish galleries to mar the associational effects of an archaeologically accurate Gothic building. Probably at Anderson's instigation, they visited St Peter's Church, Eaton Square, a classical Commissioner's church built earlier in the century to the designs of Henry Hakewill, and subsequently altered internally by A.W. Blomfield.[31] The placing of galleries in this church provided the solution to the problem at Govan, and Anderson made measured sketches to work into the design. Macleod had visited Italy, and had noted that the great Franciscan basilicas were laid out so that the arcades did not interfere with the view of the preacher, and, as a result, the arcades at Govan were intended for access only. By October 1882 the design was completed. In December 1883 the drawings for the roof were sent to Macleod, together with an alternative scheme for a tower. In January 1884, Anderson was in Glasgow arranging for the Building Committee to place contracts. The last service was held in the old church on 18 March that year, after which it was moved stone by stone to Golspie Street and rededicated as Elderpark Parish Church. Between this time and 1888 the new church took shape, more or less to the original designs.

The end result had much in common with Anderson's earlier churches: it consisted of a lofty nave in the Early Gothic style, heavily buttressed, with shallow side aisles leading to a chancel, originally short through lack of funds but lengthened in 1908. On its north side the foundation for a heavily buttressed tower with pinnacles and octagonal spire was laid. A side chapel for daily services stood at the north-east corner, the complex surrounded by the blackened sheds of Scotland's most famous shipyards. Inside, Anderson employed a number of familiar devices. At the base of the chancel arch, on each side, pointed doorways were formed. This the architect had already done in the Romanesque style at the Catholic

Plate 52. Interior, Govan Old Parish Church (Scottish Civic Trust).

Apostolic Church in Edinburgh, another church without side aisles. Its derivation is unclear. Among the possible precedents is Gerona Cathedral, where the doorways lead to an ambulatory round the apse. More probably, Anderson would know it from the work of James Gillespie Graham at the chapel of Murthly Castle, where Alexander Christie had been employed, or at St Mary's Roman Catholic Cathedral in Edinburgh. The great glory of the interior was and is, however, the view towards the giant oculus and triple lancets of the chancel, modelled on Pluscarden Priory (Plate 52). The walls were lined in dark red brick, offset by the cream stone of arcades and dressings, and giving the warm and dark effect Anderson so much liked. Galleries were provided on the west wall and in the north transept, where they were not intrusive. Above, the architect provided one of his most unusual roofs, a trefoil barrel, planked over, the centre portion of which was plastered and ribbed. The nave was lit by stained glass, mainly by Kempe, who, this once, was persuaded to design for a non-Anglican congregation.

The interior had been much debated; the Building Committee had voiced reservations about the red brick linings, but were eventually persuaded by Anderson that the material was both cost effective and aesthetically acceptable.[32] The architect was less successful in arguing the case for his alternative tower design (Plate 53). This was to be a scaled-up version of the design for Leven Episcopal Church, a round tower of the Brechin type. A tower of this kind would have been cheaper than the octagonal spire preferred by the others. These arguments proved to be academic: the lack of funds prevented the building of a tower of any kind.

Plate 53. Govan Old Parish Church, design with round tower (Anderson Office Drawings, Edinburgh University).

On a happier note, Anderson designed the organ case, pulpit, communion tables and choir stalls, which were made by Whytock and Reid. He also designed the gas fittings, made by Starkie Gardiner of London. The cost of the church rose to £27 000, a tribute to Macleod's strenuous fund raising efforts. The great shipbuilding families gave generously. Sir William and Lady Pearce gave over £7000. The Misses Steven of Bellahouston provided the funds for the Steven Chapel, as well as substantial funds for the main building. Mrs John Elder gave £2000. The partnership between Anderson and Macleod had worked well. Both were intense and serious men, dispositions that had helped them reach the heights of their chosen professions, manifested in their recently conferred honorary doctorates. Contemporary photographs disclose strong facial resemblances, down to the heavy walrus moustache favoured by each man. If Macleod raised Scoto-Catholicism to prominence at Govan, Anderson housed it in a building that would set standards for Scottish ecclesiology for years to come.

The year 1885 saw Hew Wardrop with two important commissions in hand, major additions to the Place of Tilliefoure, near Ballater, for F. Gregson, and the remodelling of Ballochmyle House, near Mauchline, for Claude Alexander. Both commissions were managed entirely by Wardrop, although it is most likely that Anderson advised on the designs. Tilliefoure involved extensions to a turreted, crowstepped and harled seventeenth century house. The extensions made the house's horizontal emphasis even more pronounced. Robert Lorimer, training in the practice at this point, was closely involved in the project. Late in 1885, Wardrop began to work at Ballochmyle. Claude Alexander, descended from a family of successful merchants and entrepreneurs, had himself been an eminent soldier, and had lately served as MP for South Ayrshire. Alexander would shortly be knighted. The original house dated from 1760 and was by John Adam, appearing in *Vitruvius Scoticus*. It was a symmetrical classical house with two wings linked to the main block by quadrantal arms. On several occasions the house had been extended, destroying its symmetry but maintaining its classical character. No doubt connected with the changing circumstances of its owner, the remit on this occasion was for greatly increased accommodation and, therefore, more drastic treatment. Designs were completed in February 1886, and by April that year Wardrop was writing to Lady Alexander about estimates.[33] The alterations involved new public rooms, hall, stairway and entrance as well as kitchen extensions. More bedrooms for guests and servants were added at the top of the house, calling for a steeper roof punctuated by dormers. Outside, the Adam wings were removed, and the additional accommodation was expressed in an asymmetrical series of bays and dormers, the provision of an ogival cupola suggesting a stylistic transition from English Jacobean to early classical. The hand of Anderson was unmistakeable.

Late in 1885, Washington Browne resigned. By this point his book, *Pugin Studentship Drawings*, was in publication, and he was ready for the course he had perhaps always intended. In some ways, there was little incentive for him to stay, since the partnership was still deeply engaged in large long-term projects which had not called for his personal design skills. His later works point to a preference for more flamboyant styles than he had been permitted to exercise in the Anderson office, adumbrated to some extent in his 'busy' pencil sketching technique. Earlier in 1885, Browne had deputised for Anderson at Mount Stuart, where the joiner work was in its closing stages. Matters were not proceeding to the satisfaction of Lord Bute, who confided to his secretary and friend, G.E. Sneyd that 'Anderson has been very careless, and the work's very ill done', an observation at variance with the growing reputation the architect was acquiring for his attention to every aspect of craftsmanship.[34] The complaint may have arisen out of the infrequency of the visits made from Edinburgh, but was perhaps also related to an incident that had occurred the previous October, when Anderson had visited Athens with Lord Bute.

Bute had been planning since at least 1882 to erect a Byzantine-style chapel for the Roman Catholics of Troon. In a letter to his wife he had

Plate 54. S. Sophia's Church, Galston (Author).

revealed his passion for the lore of the Eastern church, and had crudely
sketched out a cruciform and domed Byzantine chapel as a rough guide
to his spouse, whom he had empowered to engage an architect. Her choice
may have been governed by Lord Bute's suggestions that Anderson 'or
anyone else' would do, that Pullan, a Byzantine expert 'seems rather a
brute' and that 'Englishmen are a-sea with Scotch tradesmen'.[35] Not
surprisingly, Anderson had been selected, and the trip to Athens, among
other things, would have enabled Anderson to see the small Byzantine
cathedral there. The architect had, however, displeased Bute, making a
'a very bad effect . . . by refusing to pay the whole cost of sending his
plans' (presumably for the new church).[36] The rift was short lived and
the church, erected at Galston rather than Troon, took shape in 1885–6,
almost exactly to Lord Bute's requirements, with one important exception. Instead of culminating in a dome, the building was given a conical
spirelet in the Georgian or Armenian manner, Lord Bute indicating in a
letter to his wife that 'the spire (?) is very pretty and much better adapted
to our climate'.[37] Anderson's functional leanings had again carried the
day. The church, dedicated to S. Sophia, was completed in smooth red
brick and painted white inside, the first in the Byzantine style to be
erected in Scotland. It cost in excess of £5000, proving to be much dearer
than a Gothic building of similar capacity because of its complicated
construction (Plate 54).

During these years a number of opportunities were given to strengthen relations with Lord Bute, arising from the erection of the National Portrait Gallery and Museum of Antiquities. This had started in 1885, but the project had been alive since 1882, the year that John Ritchie Findlay became a member of the Board of Manufactures. Findlay was senior partner in the firm which owned the *Scotsman* newspaper, and was then fifty-eight years old. He was a shy man with a warm personality, liberal both in his thinking and his charitable activities. His liberality with his personal wealth assumed a new order of magnitude in 1882 when he anonymously offered to endow to the nation, through the Board of Manufactures, £10 000 towards a National Portrait Gallery, provided an equal amount could be provided from public resources. His endowment was matched, and the project began.[38] At the same time the Society of Antiquaries, meeting in the Royal Institution at the Mound, was having accommodation problems with its publicly owned antiquarian collection, a fact well known to Findlay, a member since 1873, and now its secretary. The Treasury had been approached about a new home for the Antiquaries' collection, but merely suggested a reshuffle of the activities taking place in the Royal Institution, with the Government Art School, under the Board of Manufactures, spilling over into the Museum of Science and Art in Chambers Street. This was considered unacceptable.[39]

Findlay anonymously solved the problem with a further endowment of £20 000, intended to provide a home for the Portrait Gallery and the Antiquaries' collection in the same building. Anderson, architect to the Board, had previously been involved in minor additions and alterations at the Mound. By late 1884 a rectangle of ground occupying 260 feet of the frontage of Queen Street, and with a depth of 70 feet, had been purchased for £7500 and Anderson's plans had been prepared, submitted and approved. It was felt that the site, basically north facing, would be ideal for a gallery, since it would admit plenty of light and keep the building separate and thus less at risk from fire. The donor had stipulated that the building should be isolated, probably for reasons of identity as much as from fire considerations. Anderson's designs were typical of his architectural philosophy. In accordance with late-Victorian thinking, galleries and museums called for broad areas of exhibition space, plenty of light, and generous access facilities. All these criteria could be met in a long rectangular building of three floors, with a central main entrance. The building's east side was to be dedicated to the antiquarian collection, and the west side to the portrait gallery. Light was to be provided at ground floor level by eight large Gothic windows, four on either side of the entrance, and, on the floor above, by a continuous band of paired Gothic openings. On the upper storey, a large apartment coincided with the arcaded central court of the entrance hall. The top floor walls were to consist of blank masonry, light being admitted to the upper galleries through the roof.

As usual, Anderson outlined this straightforward rationale in his releases to the press, explaining that the Gothic style had been adopted for 'considerations of utility as well as beauty', since it allowed the flexible fenestral arrangements that were needed.[40] The choice of style might also have been influenced by the Board's intention that the frontage of the building should incorporate statues of historical Scottish figures. The concept, inextricably linked with the idea of the gallery itself, carried strong late-romantic overtones of nationalism and heroism. The design of the gallery's exterior again derives from Cordes and Figeac, thus explaining its frequently noted resemblance to Mount Stuart. The original contract drawings show the Queen Street frontage of the building terminating in two Franco-Scottish tourelles. These would have underscored the building's predominantly French inspiration, and, indeed, had already appeared on a smaller scale at St John's Church, Canongate. The elaborate pointed doorway had also been executed in embryo at Forfar Episcopal Church and the two-storey arcaded ambulatory in the building's centre had already been seen on a grander scale at Mount Stuart. Anderson was never ashamed to repeat a motif he considered to be successful.

When construction began, the finances were not sufficient to carry out the building's east and west terminations, although in 1887 Findlay would anonymously provide the money to complete them. He did not, however, approve of the two tourelles, partly because they excluded light but also because he was dissatisfied with their appearance.[41] Niched octagonal turrets, a vast improvement on the tourelles, were eventually substituted. An alternative plan to leave the building's ends unadorned was also considered, but was scrapped. Anderson's selection of materials brought no surprises. As at Mount Stuart, red Corsehill sandstone was used, in due course proving too brittle for the ornate carving to survive Edinburgh's atmosphere. Also present in the entrance hall was a quantity of smooth red brick, which complemented the colouring of the arcades. The building committee set up to monitor the gallery's progress included Sir William Fettes Douglas, President of the Royal Scottish Academy, a man whose intellectual inflexibility was only exceeded by his lack of discretion. It was during Douglas' presidency that Anderson had resigned his associateship. The minutes of the meetings between architect and committee, in all their brevity, still convey a frosty atmosphere and a tendency to indelicacy.[42]

There was, however, ample opportunity to engage in more rewarding pursuits, as over the years the elaborate scheme of decoration for the gallery was debated with Lord Bute, among others, and progressively carried out. In due course the murals of the entrance hall were executed

Plate 55. National Portrait Gallery and Museum of Antiquities, Edinburgh
(National Monuments Record of Scotland).

by William Hole, and the statues were one by one added to the exterior.
The gallery was officially opened on 15 July 1889, while the decoration
was not completed until many years later. When designing the gallery,
Anderson must have been conscious that, as the natural heir to Playfair
and Bryce, he was in a position to make an architectural statement for
posterity. This may partly explain the insertion of a bold red Gothic
palace in the bland expanse of Edinburgh's New Town (Plate 55).

While Wardrop was busy at Tillifoure, Ballochmyle and Udny Castle
(a Baronial house built by his father near Aberdeen), Anderson toiled not
only at the Portrait Gallery, but on a range of new and important
commissions. These included the erection of a dome to complete Robert
Adam's Old College at Edinburgh University. Adam had planned a
graceful tapering dome, to be built of timber and lead and rising to about
twice the width of its base. Anderson, in contrast, decided on a larger
structure incorporating more masonry in order to provide accommodation
for the Professor of Fine Arts and to house the bust of Robert Cox, a
Writer to the Signet who had left a legacy for the dome's completion. The
lower stages were erected by the spring of 1887, and it soon became clear

Plate 56. Dome, Old College, Edinburgh University (National Monuments Record of Scotland).

that Anderson was neither adhering closely to Adam's plan nor to classical precedent. A rounded stair turret, particularly prominent when viewed from inside the quadrangle, had been grafted on to the exterior of drum and dome. This asymmetrical excrescence expressed the presence of a stair in an almost Baronial manner.[43] When the structure was in due course completed, its lantern was topped with a sculpture of a youth bearing the torch of knowledge, executed by John Hutchison, RSA (Plate 56).

Just round the corner, in Parliament Square, the memorial to the Duke of Buccleuch was also in the course of construction at the same time. This monument showed signs of Anderson's growing fascination with the complexities of the late phase of Gothic.[44] It was hexagonal in section and

Plate 57. Buccleuch Memorial, Parliament Square, Edinburgh (Author).

consisted of four stages, each elaborately furnished with bronze work, the whole pile surmounted by a statue of the late Duke (Plate 57). Also at an advanced stage at the same time was the Ardgowan Estate Office in Greenock, for Sir Michael Shaw Stewart, Lord Lieutenant of Renfrewshire. An old baronial mansion with an eighteenth century extension, the former home of Shaw Stewart's ancestors, had previously served as the estate office, but was in decay and in the path of a new stretch of the Caledonian Railway. Anderson's design, in a classical style of c. 1700, was asymmetrically massed, cleverly paying homage to the earlier building with beautifully detailed vestigial Jacobean touches on the upper storeys and rear of the new structure. Inside, surveyors', legal and cash depart-

Plate 58. Ardgowan Estate Office, Greenock (Author).

ments were housed in a series of logically planned offices which allowed ready access to the rooms provided for the factor and Sir Michael himself (Plate 58). Nearer home, at Currie, work was also beginning on a large house for Bruce, the paper manufacturer. Here Anderson provided an expanded 'Allermuir' in red sandstone, the planning following the familiar pattern with sensible circulation and straight corridors.[45]

In 1885 and 1886, two enquiries that could have led to even more absorbing commissions were received. An information leak from the War Office revealed that extensions to Edinburgh Castle were planned. Lord Balfour of Burleigh objected to the lack of public consultation which he felt the Castle's historical and architectural importance warranted. Articles in the Edinburgh press indicated that Balfour had 'rightly interpreted the mind of the citizens of Edinburgh and of Scotsmen generally'. Although it was disclosed that a mere £1200 was involved, the press, reflecting changing tastes, were adamant that 'gimcrack illustrations of the old Scottish baronial style' would not be tolerated.[46] At this stage Constance Nisbet Hamilton of Biel entered into the controversy, making private representations that Rowand Anderson should be consulted, and shortly afterwards a newspaper article appeared, suggesting this would happen. Anderson's thank you note to Biel expressed the hope that 'Edinburgh Castle may at last get justice done to it'.[47] In spite of the outcry, a drawbridge and gatehouse, designed by R. Lawson Scott of the Royal Engineers, were erected in 1887–8, coinciding with the restoration of the Portcullis Gate by Hippolyte Blanc, for which funds had been provided by Nelson the publisher.

The second of these false alarms concerned the restoration of Holyrood

Abbey Church, which the Marquess of Lothian was considering as a gesture to mark Queen Victoria's Jubilee. A confidant, Andrew Ross, was asked to present him with an objective summary of the general arguments for and against restoration, in view of the possibility of voluble objections from the John Ruskin-inspired Society for the Protection of Ancient Buildings, whose non-restorationist views were commanding an ever growing following.[48] The Society believed that the concept of restoration was inherently flawed, since it was impossible to recreate buildings that had disappeared, and that to tamper with the ruins was practically sacrilegious. It did, however, approve of small-scale repairs necessary to consolidate remains to prevent them from disintegration, but only in the rarest of circumstances. Lothian was unimpressed by the Society's position, and shortly afterwards Anderson was asked to report on the feasibility and cost of the Abbey's restoration. In his response he pointed out that the walls of the ruin were strong, that decay was only superficial, and that there was a large body of evidence on which to base a faithful restoration. An estimate of £25 000–30 000, covering the restoration of the nave only, was provided as a rough guide.[49]

Anderson also observed that the foundations of the choir and transepts still existed and that if funds could be collected for their restoration, Holyrood could become the 'Westminster Abbey of Scotland'. His report next took a remarkable turn, revealing his widening vision:

> The greatest drawback we have to progress in the Arts in Scotland is the absence of buildings capable of absorbing all the best art works that can be procured in stone, metal, wood, glass &c &c.
>
> At the present time for such works we have to go to England or abroad. If we had the shell of such a building as Holyrood Abbey it would be a school for art workmen for many years to come and on this ground a strong appeal could be made to the working classes of Scotland, because it would raise the standards of workmanship, and the money they give now would all come back to them tenfold in employment.[50]

He acknowledged that such a scheme might take £70 000, but that it could be spread over three years. He suggested that subscriptions could be collected nationwide and that he would 'go as low as shillings and six-pences from working people and pennies from children'. The restoration was never carried out, but this would not be sufficient to dampen Anderson's growing enthusiasm for improving the training of 'artwork-men'. This would find its full expression in later years.

Since 1887 was the year of Queen Victoria's Golden Jubilee, Tennyson, as Poet Laureate, had suggested in some celebratory lines that the nation should:

Raise a stately memorial
Some Imperial Institute
Rich in symbol and ornament
Which may speak to the centuries.[51]

The injunction had fallen on receptive ears, and a rectangular site in 'Albertopolis', midway between the Albert Hall and Waterhouse's new Natural History Museum to the south, was chosen. The architects invited to compete were T.N. Deane, Aston Webb, T.E. Collcutt, T.G. Jackson and A.W. Blomfield, as well as Anderson. The panel of judges included Alfred Waterhouse. The location assigned to the proposed building virtually dictated its symmetrical treatment. It was to stand parallel to Waterhouse's Natural History Museum, and a line drawn southwards from the Albert Hall bisected the site. The choice of style raised several possibilities. Nearby, both the Albert Hall and the original quadrangle of the Victoria and Albert Museum were in classical styles, still regarded in many quarters as the most appropriate style for civic architecture. In this instance, too, associational arguments were particularly valid. It would have been appropriate to let the architecture of other great empires evoke the glory of Victoria's realm. However, the proximity of Waterhouse's building and Norman Shaw's Albert Hall Mansions both raised the possibility of a bolder, more eclectic and more fashionable treatment.

In the event, Anderson opted for a version of the classical style which he stated was from 'the middle of the last century', but which in fact bore all the hallmarks of 'Wrenaissance', a style possessing the added advantage of specifically British and Metropolitan connotations.[52] As was his wont, Anderson studied the building's function most carefully, a matter to which Waterhouse was sure to pay particular attention. A large exhibition court was positioned in the centre of his plan, flanked by two generous museum spaces divided up by colonnades. Straight corridors on all sides of the building's perimeter provided clear-cut circulation, radiating from an entrance hall in the centre of the frontage. Off these corridors reading rooms, libraries, laboratories, restaurants and even lecture theatres were to be provided. The basement was to house stores, workshops and cellars. Anderson's elevations disclosed a long, low facade, to be built in red brick with cream stone dressings, and rising from a rusticated base. An attic storey rose from the centre of the facade, pierced with Wren-like circular windows and adorned with a sculpture-filled pediment culminating in a statue of Britannia. The office, hard pressed as ever, had struggled to meet the deadlines, in spite of extra drafting labour having been hired. A rather poor perspective drawing was hurriedly produced by W.F. Bidlake, one of several talented English assistants gaining experience in the practice at the time.

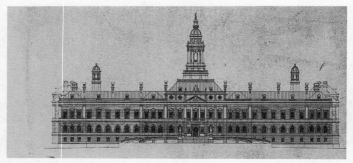

Plate 59. Design for Imperial Institute Competition (Anderson Office Drawings, Edinburgh University).

A.H. Mackmurdo, on a trip north, had been shown the design by an enthusiastic Hew Wardrop, and wrote a letter of fulsome praise to Anderson on 15 June that year:

> I have never seen so pure and vigorous a piece of architecture as that you have given the world the chance of realising. Its monumental character, strong silence, homogeneity and purity are sublime. The mosaic you will enhance it with by the arts of painting and sculpture will make it appeal to and satisfy every fine sentiment and mood in man.[53]

Mackmurdo was particularly well placed to comment on the 'vigorous' character of the design, having himself come from the office of one of the most prominent exponents of that style, James Brooks, whose work Anderson admired. Mackmurdo's enthusiasm for his fellow Scot's competition entry was also fired by his love of Wren, testified to by his 1884 book, *Wren's City Churches*, in which his famous Art Nouveau graphic style had first appeared. The assessors, however, were not so favourably impressed. On 15 June Waterhouse wrote to Anderson that, while his designs had been 'greatly admired, especially by H.R.H.', Collcutt's design had been selected.[54]

The winning entry was in a richly ornamented version of the fashionable Queen Anne style, with a campanile, and was well planned. Deane's entry, in the words of a contemporary commentator was for 'a really stately . . . classic group of buildings', but had sacrificed the planning for architectural effect. Jackson's design was described by the same commentator as 'a jumble of late Gothic and Flemish' with a tower built on 'the principle . . . of the Tower of Babel'.[55] Aston Webb's design was an unsatisfactory composition with an advanced tower which would have detracted from the facade, while Blomfield's entry had a disproportionately large dome which dominated the building's centre.

Anderson's design quite obviously lacked the picturesque qualities the

Plate 60. Queen's Hall, Charlestown (Author).

assessors were looking for. It was too early for its time; within a few decades, however, the picturesque appeal of Queen Anne would abate in favour of a quieter, more classical approach.

The architect had been let down, too, by the standard of draughtsmanship displayed in his submission. While the other designs were superbly executed, the publication of Bidlake's poor perspective gave those who never saw the full set of plans a misleading impression of the quality of his proposal. To correct this misunderstanding, Anderson arranged for the delicately detailed geometric version of his design drawings to be published in the *Architect* of 12 August (Plate 59). Notwithstanding the honour associated with Holyrood and with the Imperial Institute, the fact remains that Anderson was frustrated in his attempts to celebrate Queen Victoria's Jubilee on a grand architectural scale. He did, however, find a lesser outlet — a commission to build a small public hall at Charlestown, Fife, not far from Culross on the north shore of the Forth. The Queen's Hall (Plate 60) was again carried out in the Scots Jacobean style, with crow steps and tall pediments highlighted in dressed stone against harled walls and red slate roof.

The year 1887 ended tragically with the untimely death of Hew Wardrop at Udny Castle on 4 November. That same year Washington Browne won the competition for the design of Edinburgh Central Library on George IV Bridge, events punctuating the end of an era. Many years were to elapse before Anderson was again to assume a partner. His affection for Wardrop and his grief at his parting can nevertheless be gauged from his continued use of Wardrop's name in the firm's title until the turn of the century. It is clear, however, that Wardrop's own design philosophy was very much influenced by Anderson's thinking. None of the commissions with which he was associated looked remotely like the work of the Wardrop and Reid partnership which he had inherited, and all bore the familiar Anderson stamp. Matters were different with Browne, who, released from the confines of other men's designs, displayed his liking for rich detail, visible in the Francois Premier styling of his new library. Nevertheless, even in independent practice Browne would occasionally produce buildings closely resembling Anderson designs, such as Langlees House near Lanark, which is very obviously based on 'Allermuir'. The two men, notwithstanding their different preferences, both designed buildings characterised by careful planning and a sense of dignity and refinement, quite at odds with the picturesque-influenced structures erected in mid-century. If Browne had developed his sophisticated taste elsewhere, it was enhanced and sharpened during his days with Anderson.

6

Rebuilder of Cathedrals

Dunblane Cathedral had stood in ruins since the time of the Reformation. In the 1550s and 1560s, its woodwork had been stripped off by the Reformers, causing the nave roof to collapse. In 1818 and 1860, repairs had been made to the choir, which had remained in use as a place of Protestant worship.[1] These involved the replacement of the original roof which had become unsafe, and the insertion of new window tracery. As a ruin, the Cathedral was much loved and admired. It had been drawn by Slezer and Billings, and Ruskin had praised it in his Edinburgh lectures in 1853. Sir George Gilbert Scott had examined it in 1872, and Anderson himself had at one time made a special study of it.[2] The impetus for its restoration came from the Rev. Alexander Ritchie, who was inducted as parish minister in July 1886. On 25 November that year, Ritchie called a meeting of his Kirk Session, at which point a decision was made to approach the heritors about the seating accommodation, which was considered inadequate for 810 communicants and adherents.[3] Prior to this the heritors themselves, aware that Ritchie had been involved in restoration work at Whithorn, his previous charge, had been moving in the same direction, and had commissioned a report from Anderson. His findings were positive:

> I am of opinion that the walls are strong enough to carry new roofs, and that the decay though considerable, is only superficial . . . as the decay . . . seen all about the walls has been caused chiefly by the water soaking into them from the uncovered wall heads and window cills, the first step to arrest this is to get the building covered in.[4]

One of the leading elders, James Webster Barty, a Dunblane solicitor, had also been discussing the feasibility of restoration with Mrs Wallace of Glassingall, whose generosity would eventually make it possible.

In August 1887, while the matter was under consideration, Anderson, much admired in Glasgow, met a party from the Glasgow Institute of Architects, explaining to them how he intended to undertake the restoration. This resulted in a letter from their president, David Thomson, expressing their 'great satisfaction' at the 'conservative manner' in which the task was to be carried out. The Glasgow architects were pleased that 'as the existing work is not to be touched except where necessary for its preservation, the historical and architectural interest will not be impaired'.[5] By the summer of 1888, although nothing had been done, fund raising was in progress. At that point the Archaeological Institute of Great Britain met Anderson at Dunblane, and when he outlined his plans they again met with general approval.

In July 1888, the Society for the Protection of Ancient Buildings advised in its annual report that

> The fate of this most important building still hangs in the balance. A very large amount of the Committee's time has been expended upon opposing the scheme for bringing the nave into use, and it has been shown conclusively in letters to the public press and to the different Government offices concerned that the proposed scheme must necessarily be of a destructive character. It is hoped that by next year we may be able to state that the scheme has been abandoned.[6]

On 14 December that year, an executive committee of the principal heritors and the minister, formed to effect the restoration, met for the first time. A letter from the Board of Manufactures was read out. The Cathedral, which was Crown property, had recently been conveyed to the Board, who now insisted that plans and estimates be submitted to them first for approval. With three parties directly interested in the restoration, the architect, the Restoration Committee and the Board of Manufactures, the likelihood of tension and disagreement was greatly increased. On 10 January 1889 the Board met with the Restoration Committee, and it was decided that the opinion of practical builders be sought regarding the suitability of the walls to hold a new roof. The three builders consulted all agreed that a roof of the type proposed by Anderson could be erected with perfect safety once his recommendations to repair the walls had been implemented.

However, the opposition to the restoration continued. On 9 May 1889 Thackeray Turner, Secretary of the 'Antiscrape', wrote to the Chief Commissioner of Works alleging that 'the restoration of the nave as a church will involve the addition of much new work and the destruction of much of the existing original work'.[7] This the Commissioner annotated with red query marks. Turner's letter continued with the allegation that it was not feasible to restore the nave walls because it was 'impossible to say what they once were'. This too was queried in red. The observations of the SPAB, although ultimately dismissed, were taken seriously enough.

At around this time, Ruskin himself had entered the fray with a letter stating that:

> Restorations are either architects' jobs or ministers' vanities, and they are the worst sort of swindling and boasting. That of Dunblane Abbey, the loveliest ruins in Scotland (and, in its way the loveliest in the world), would be the most vulgar brutality Scotland has committed since the Reformation.
>
> I had rather she had run a railroad through it and thrown the stones of it into the brook.[8]

But there was another danger — for hundreds of years the nave floor had been used as a burial ground. A local property owner threatened an interdict if the restoration was commenced. The Board of Manufactures took senior legal advice on this question, resulting in the conclusion that the legality of interments was extremely doubtful, since the nave was Crown property. In addition to this, it was not intended to disturb or desecrate graves, and so it was likely that opposition would be overcome. In spite of this tangle of forces restoration began on 16 September 1889, and satisfactory progress had been made by the following spring.

As intended from the outset, Anderson had the whole of the nave and aisles scaffolded in order to repair the wall heads. Where the old work was sound, although chipped and superficially decayed, it was left alone. Immediately afterwards, a pointed barrel roof of oak was put on. In order to make it fit some parts of the walls had to be rebuilt because they had been penetrated by vegetation and displaced. Anderson on a later occasion produced a box of roots taken out at the time as an object lesson in their destructive power. The minor repairs were then put in hand. In Anderson's words,

> these consisted chiefly of cutting out parts that could no longer hold together, and repairing them with sound new stone . . . making good the rybats of the windows where they were so decayed that they could not be glazed, and repairing the walls where there appeared any sign of weakness.[9]

Once the glazing had been completed and the nave had been made safe from the elements, the choir was next repaired. The wall sealing up the chancel arch was removed. The wall heads were made good and a new roof was put on. The cathedral floor was then tackled. The surface soil and vegetation in the nave were removed to a depth of eight inches, once a map of the various graves had been made. A six-inch layer of concrete was spread on top, then asphalted, after which the floor was tiled in patterned freestone of red, yellow and black colour. As far as possible, the existing tombstones were displayed. Where this could not be done, inscriptions were cut on the new surface.

While building operations were in progress, a series of wrangles on archaeological matters was taking place.[10] Anderson was of the opinion that, on certain areas of the walls, ashlar had at one time been removed and substituted with rubble. After the initial disapproval of the Board, he was allowed to replace patches of rubble in many areas of the church with ashlar. The arguments also extended to window tracery. The choir windows, in the Perpendicular style, had been supplied earlier in the century. Anderson held that they should be allowed to remain, as part of the church's architectural history. Instead, Anderson was ordered to provide new windows with Geometric tracery, to harmonise with the windows on the west gable. At the north-west angle of the nave, two aisle windows had flat, late Gothic arches, and were out of character with those alongside. Anderson maintained that, as these had originally resembled the other windows, they should be altered. He was again overruled. Matters became heated on the question of furniture. Anderson's designs for pulpit, choir screen and table were rejected by the Board. These were in a later style than the early Gothic of most of the church. Anderson had originally designed them in an earlier style but had changed his mind, to the incumbent's regret. Nevertheless, the Restoration Committee as a whole accepted the revisions. Their decision was overturned by the Board, who, in spite of couching their resolution in carefully framed language so as to 'hurt the architect's feelings as little as possible', failed to avoid giving offence. Anderson's response was to write a long letter stating that their views were 'entirely unsupported by the history of art'. It made no difference. The Board was a resolute body which had among its membership Sir Noel Paton, John H.A. McDonald, by this time the Lord Justice Clerk, and Sir George Reid, who by then had succeeded Fettes Douglas as President of the Royal Scottish Academy.

It is recorded that 'Dr. Anderson seems not to have received the decision of the Board with good grace', later informing the Restoration Committee that 'he had not prepared new designs and was much too occupied to do so'. In due course he relented, eventually supplying revised drawings for the pulpit, screen, font and organ case. Most of the controversies hinged on one basic point. Should a church in the course of restoration be restored to the style of a single period of time? The Board's opinion was that all should harmonise. Sir John Stirling Maxwell was almost certainly right when in later years he attributed the disagreement to Anderson's firm belief that buildings in which everything conformed to the same style were apt to be cold and lifeless.[11] On a later occasion, Ritchie recalled that 'Dr. Anderson was of a very determined nature, and it was difficult to get him to alter his views to conform to the wishes of others'. While these developments say a great deal about Anderson's vulnerability and personal pride, they also speak volumes about the deep sincerity of his views, which had been carefully arrived at after great reflection. The architect eventually became philosophical about the disputes. Speaking of the alterations to the choir tracery he later observed that 'those who had the final word here decided that it must be removed'.[12]

Over against this controversy the restored church took shape, its interior decoration presenting some interesting choices and dilemmas. The Marquess of Bute, by then a member of the Board of Manufactures, became deeply interested in the holes discovered beneath the two large windows over the chancel arch. Since it was likely that these holes had once held a rood loft, Bute was anxious that a new one should be supplied, but this was not done. The Marquess, who was specially interested in heraldry, was, however, consulted about the decoration of the bosses of the nave roof, and on this occasion his suggestion was accepted. The arms of the seven Earls of Strathearn were chosen for the seven bosses on the north side, while six on the south side were to be decorated with the arms of the Earls of Strathearn from Maurice to Walter, the seventh of these bearing the arms of King James II, the first Royal Superior. Anderson had also at one stage suggested the colouring of the nave roof, but this was held over and eventually abandoned for financial reasons.

In 1893 Anderson presented a paper on the restoration to the Edinburgh Architectural Association. At its close, he summarised his views:

> The lesson I want to enforce . . . is that, Dunblane Cathedral might at any time, but for this restoration, have collapsed into a heap of ruins, and neither the architectural nor the pictorial aspect would have remained to delight us . . . I do not say that the work I have done is above criticism as all the work of human hands is faulty, and were it otherwise, there would be no progress; but I feel confident that all who see it will feel that the old Dunblane Cathedral is still there . . . and that the promoters of this work did well to resist all the pressure that was brought to bear on them to leave the building to the elements and to false and impossible methods of so-called preservation, with the certainty of its total ruin in the near future.[13]

The Clerk of Works was George Kermack, and Robert Lorimer was chief draughtsman. James Slater, the builder, was paid about £10 500, James L. Arnott was paid £1675 for plumbing and gasfitting, and A.D. McKay £612–16–8 for slaterwork. Glazing amounted to £337–3–2, and some £5000 of additional work was carried out under Kermack's supervision. Anderson's fee was £1500, implying a total cost of some £30 000. Mrs Wallace of Glassingall, together with friends and relations, gave £19 000. The heritors contributed £3000, the balance coming from public subscriptions. If the restoration had not run smoothly, its outcome was, by general agreement, the finest Scottish work of its kind to date, setting the highest possible standards for others to emulate (Plates 61 and 62).

Plate 61. Dunblane Cathedral, as restored (National Monuments Record of Scotland).

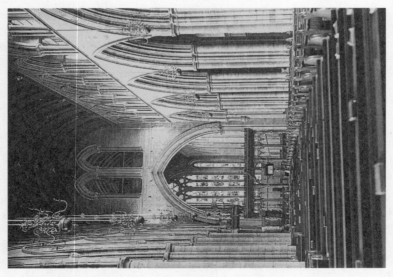

Plate 62. Interior, Dunblane Cathedral, as restored (National Monuments Record of Scotland).

Just prior to the commencement of the Dunblane restoration, preparations for the Edinburgh Congress of the National Association for the Advancement of Art and its Application to Industry were at an advanced stage. The Association seems to have existed for the arrangement of congresses and the publication of transactions in an effort both to popularise art and to promote its application to manufactures. Its list of office bearers for 1889, as well as containing a large number of baronets and peers of the realm, reads like a 'Who's Who' of late Victorian art and design. Among its vice-presidents were Sir J.E. Millais and Sir Frederick Leighton, the President of the Royal Academy. A.H. Mackmurdo was one of its two honorary secretaries, and Walter Crane, Professor Herkomer and E.J. Poynter were members of its central council. Each congress necessitated the formation of a local committee, and the Edinburgh committee was heavily populated with Anderson's social and professional contacts. The Lord Provost of Edinburgh was chairman. John Hay Atholl McDonald, the Lord Justice Clerk, was a vice-chairman, as was Sir William Muir, Principal of Edinburgh University. J.R. Findlay, as well as being a vice-chairman of the Edinburgh committee, was also a member of the central council. Findlay had just been revealed as the donor of the new National Portrait Gallery and Museum of Antiquities, and it was here that the congress was held.

In his keynote speech the Association's President, the Marquis of Lorne, alluded to two matters of current concern. One was the existence of sixty art industry associations in Germany, which, with about 40 000 members, posed both a challenge and a threat to British design. The second was the architectural disfigurement of cities, exemplified locally by the grim range of barracks at the west end of the Castle Rock, or the factory chimney spoiling the 'fine valley' beyond the North Bridge. The President of the Section of Applied Art was no less a figure than William Morris. Naturally enough, his presidential speech dealt with the first question, while Rowand Anderson, as President of the Section of Architecture, dealt in his official speech with matters loosely related to the second. Although topics of high import such as these were very prominent on the Congress's agenda, papers on 'French Impressionism and its Influence on English Art' or 'The Picturesque in Sculpture' relieved the undoubtedly didactic tenor of much that was said. Anderson's contribution was not confined to his presidential speech. The Transactions of the Edinburgh Congress disclose that he was active in the discussions which succeeded the various papers. Throughout, his architectural philosophy is revealed in depth.

The theme of his presidential address was *The Place of Architecture in the Domain of Art*. As far as Anderson was concerned, this was grossly misunderstood as a result of

the artificial distinction of fine art as opposed to useful or mechanical
art . . . the foundation of Academies of art, in which architecture has
been relegated to a very secondary position — the use of the word
artist to distinguish those who paint pictures from those who make
them — the almost entire exclusion of architecture from literature
dealing with art, or where it is admitted, its treatment from the
pictorial point of view, and the artificial and modern distinction
between architecture and building – all this, I say, has had the effect
of warping the public understanding of art.

Furthermore,

architecture . . . has come to be, in the minds of many, the art of
applying decoration or ornament to buildings which could serve their
purpose equally well without them. In support of this . . . I recall to
your notice, what Mr. Ruskin has said. In his 'Lectures on Architecture' we are told that no person can be an architect who is not a
great sculptor or painter, otherwise he is only a builder. In his 'Seven
Lamps of Architecture', he says Architecture is the art which so
disposes and adorns the edifices raised by man that the sight of them
contributes to their mental health, power and pleasure.[14]

To refute these mistakes, Anderson asserted that

such doctrines as these are contradicted by everything we see in
nature, and all we can learn from Grecian and mediaeval art. Art is
not applied to any object in nature; the beauty we see there, or what
seems by contrast the ugliness in the lower animals and plants, is
inseparable from their environment and the purposes for which they
have been created. In the great art epochs of Greece and the Middle
Ages there was no division of art into fine and mechanical — there
was only one art, whether seen in a painting, a piece of sculpture, a
building, or the commonest object of everyday use, and the degree
of beauty we see in, and the satisfaction we derive from them, is their
fitness and expression more or less successfully worked out of the idea
that called them into existence.[15]

While painting and sculpture could directly imitate nature,

architecture on the other hand, in order to express its ideas, has to
create its own forms; but in doing so it must follow closely the laws
and methods of nature, particularly that all structure should be
functional, adapted to its purpose, and modelled to express or
emphasize that; but in dealing with the decoration of surfaces, and
those points of the structure that seem to call for such, then it may
imitate the forms of nature in plant and animal life, but under certain
restrictions included under the head of conventionalism. The success
with which all this is done is the measure of its fitness and its
resultant beauty.

In organising matter, the architect therefore calls into play more of the creative force than either the painter or the sculptor . . .

Architecture and the constructive arts . . . provide us with the comfortable home and the luxurious mansion; with buildings where our youth are educated, and suffering humanity receives all the care that skill and liberality can do to alleviate bodily affliction; with all those edifices for carrying on the functions of local and imperial business arising out of our national life; with the solemn temples where man offers his homage to his creator . . . Therefore I hold that architecture is entitled at least to an equality of position, consideration and respect.[15]

Anderson next proceeded to amplify, exemplify and work out the consequences of his position; beginning with a potted history of architecture, in which he singled out Greek, Romanesque and Gothic as examples of styles in which aesthetic expression had grown naturally from the realisation of function. In particular he attributed the transition from Roman into Gothic to functional and rational factors such as the limitation of the rounded arch and vault in relation to increased building sizes. Since Renaissance times, he felt, art 'has always followed literature', an example of this being the ousting of Palladian architecture by neo-classicism in the wake of the publications of the Dilettante Society and the various new discoveries in the field of Greek archaeology. This in turn was superseded when the Romantic writers and the antiquarian studies of Carter, Rickman and Pugin made an impact, epitomised in the new Houses of Parliament.[16] All this had led to architecture from the Renaissance up to his own day being more concerned with the 'features, details and proportions of ancient buildings' than with the production of buildings adapted to and deriving their expression from their purposes. Not only had the public misunderstood the nature of architecture; so too had a vast number of its practitioners.

Anderson at once proceeded to the remedy for the state of affairs thus diagnosed:

It is impossible that we can ever have a new style of architecture . . . as all the possible methods of construction are known to us; but although we cannot have that, we can give to our buildings a new and truer expression than they have had since the decline of mediaeval art. We have all the experience of the past at our service, as well as the ever increasing and expanding science of the present day, and in addition a command of wealth, material and appliances infinitely beyond what was at the service of those who reared the buildings from which we have been drawing all our architectural knowledge.

It is in this direction, I hold, that we must look for progress in architecture.[17]

As well as spelling out his manifesto for the future regeneration of architecture, Anderson was of course justifying his own design practice, working from plan to facade, using the whole palette of historical styles as a source, always subject to the proviso that style should never compromise, mask or falsify function.

His speech next focussed on local examples. The Calton Jail was 'a toy castle . . . devoid of expression and utterly meaningless', made totally ridiculous because a castle is a place to 'keep people out' and a jail 'to keep people in'. The writings and sayings of Pugin, Scott, Alexander Christie and even Patrick Allan Fraser had clearly not passed him by. In due course the analysis was applied to the Baronial style, made popular as a result of Sir Walter Scott's writings and the publications of Billings.

> Now if you examine the plans of an old Scottish Mansion you can read them like a book, from the foundations to the chimney tops. You can distinguish the original tower that the family once lived in and held their own against all comers. The walls are from six to fourteen feet thick, and everything is planned for the purpose of keeping out intruders. You will then notice an addition when the family became richer and times were not so warlike: the walls are much thinner, but there are still sundry provisions for resisting a sudden attack. As time rolled on, and it was no longer necessary to provide for defence, you find a still larger addition; but now everything is done for comfort and a peaceful country life, the whole group becoming a wonderfully picturesque and readable chapter in the history of architecture: but it was never built to look picturesque or interesting — such was never thought of by the builders.[18]

In contrast, the modern imitation could not be read from outside to inside. The walls were of one thickness, the building evidently modern. The battlements and towers contradicted the large drawingroom windows, the gables and roofs were stuck on at random for appearance's sake, at the expense of sound construction. Thus, the Baronial revival was roundly dismissed.

Anderson's paper was not only remarkable for the clarity of its main thrust; it also turned prophetically towards the aesthetic of the machine.

> Who has looked down into the engine room of one of the great ocean going steamers, and not felt the impression of an irresistible power that rests not day nor night. Look at a shearing or punching machine that opens or closes its jaw and cuts or punches just as easily as cutting paper; the steam hammer, planing machine, and pumping machines all have the same clear expression of their purpose . . . The designing of machinery, whether for peace or war, has now reached such a high standard of excellence in function, form and expression that one is justified in saying that these things are entitled to rank as works of art as much as a painting, a piece of sculpture, or a building.[19]

Revolutionary though it may have seemed, such a statement was the logical outcome of Anderson's position. Did it, however, mean that fitness and adaptation for purpose were alone sufficient to guarantee beauty? 'I hold that beauty, if not entirely, is almost entirely composed of these two qualities' he continued, a statement expressing his belief that these conditions were necessary for beauty, but not quite sufficient. He knew from his own experience that aesthetic adjustments were often required even where fitness for purpose had been achieved.

Anderson's paper must have enhanced his standing in the eyes of most who heard it. His views were carefully thought out and forthrightly expressed. The same candour characterised his observations after G.S. Aitken had spoken on *The Architectural Education of the Public*. H.H. Statham had indicated earlier in the debate that he regarded Ruskin as

> an utterly false teacher of anything related to architecture. He was a mass of contradictions, and knew nothing about plans or construction. He was a perfectly unsafe teacher, and the public should know it.[20]

Anderson was

> very much pleased that Mr. Statham had had the courage to speak as he had done regarding Mr. Ruskin. After all Ruskin's eloquence and poetry, and not forgetting the enthusiasm he had created for art in this country, he had been a blind guide in regard to architecture. All his reasoning and all his poetry and sentiment had been based on Italian Gothic architecture, which was one of the most deficient, incomplete, and undeveloped styles of architecture they knew. It was pictorial and full of colour, and that had apparently been the great attraction for him, but it had none of the real essentials of constructive art.[21]

His fearless criticism was not just reserved for those absent and distant. Amplifying his earlier remarks on Academies, Anderson in his presidential speech had also taken the opportunity to broadside the Royal Scottish Academy:

> Although we have had in our midst for the last half century an Academy of Painting, Sculpture and Architecture, enjoying the prestige and privileges of a Royal Incorporation, generous support from the public, and substantial aid from the Government, whatever they may have done for painting and sculpture, it is certain they have done nothing for architecture.[22]

At the time of the Congress, Anderson's protest against the Academy was gaining momentum. From the mid-1880s onwards, there had been a movement within that institution pressing for a supplementary charter, and early in 1889 a draft charter had been submitted to the Privy Council for approval.[23] The draft made provision for 'fuller membership participation in Academy affairs'. It allowed for the removal of the restriction on the number of associates, and gave associates the right to vote in elections to associateship, to teach, to serve on the Hanging Committee, and to receive the annual accounts. The Academy also sought in its charter 'additional powers to enable it to institute lectureships, to purchase premises for schools, and in other ways to provide for art education'. Anderson, supported by a hundred and fifty-seven enquirers, at this point had engaged a solicitor to apply for a copy of the final draft application. A query from the Academy elicited the source of the enquiry, and the request was refused. An invitation welcoming suggestions was, however, given to the architects. This they did not take up. The Privy Council itself invited objections, to be submitted by 30 August. At the end of October a petition from Rowand Anderson and other architects was received, claiming that the Academy 'slighted and ignored architecture', and had misappropriated its funds.[24] The petitioners came from all over Scotland, from as far afield as Tain and the Orkneys, as well as from the main towns and cities. It was presented in full to the Privy Council, together with a 'memorial' four pages long. During the Congress, these objections were still under consideration.

In the months immediately succeeding the Congress, whilst engaged on some of his largest and most prestigious works, Anderson continued to press his case against the Academy. Early in 1890, a petition was lodged with it by Edinburgh Town Council. The Council had become increasingly concerned at the controversy and at the allegations of mismanagement of the Academy's affairs and funds. The Academy, on pressing the Council, discovered that a party of four architects, Rowand Anderson, David MacGibbon, Hippolyte Blanc and John McLachlan, had met with the Council and persuaded it to intervene.[25] The controversy raged in the press throughout the following spring, McLachlan clarifying in a published letter that the alleged misappropriation of funds related to the Academy's payment of pensions, not just to the needy, but to all members over a certain age. W.W. Robertson, another architect, in a later letter to the press expressed his scepticism about the new powers the Academy had requested. If it abused its present powers, what reason was there to believe the new powers would be any more productive?

The response of the Academicians and their supporters in the press was feeble. J.B. Gillies, a town councillor, queried the credentials of six signatories to Anderson's petition, who had described themselves as architects practising in Airdrie. Gillies doubted that the town could support six architects.[26] In other letters to the press, some writers had confused the issues raised by the architects with other matters, in particular the unsatisfactory system of art education introduced nationally by the government in 1858. Also mentioned was the ill feeling that had arisen between the Board of Manufactures and the Academy over requests for increased accommodation, appalling in a situation where its President also sat on the Board. Although many issues had been confused, it was plain that dissatisfaction with the various institutions and their roles was at a high pitch. In the event, the Town Council reversed its petition for an enquiry into the Academy's affairs, and in 1892, the supplementary charter was granted. Within a few months, four architects, Washington Browne, Hippolyte Blanc, John Honeyman and William Leiper were elected associates.[27] Credit for this belonged to one man.

As well as pursuing these controversies and attending to his committee work during the late 1880s, Anderson was also embroiled in the Dunblane restoration, the decoration of the Portrait Gallery, and the critical stages of the building of Edinburgh University's new graduation hall. In 1886, William McEwan, MP, head of the brewing business of that name and a member of the Edinburgh University Extension Committee, had offered £40 000 for the erection of the academic hall which had always been intended to sit alongside the Medical School. Parliament voted £8000, which enabled extra ground to be purchased. A hall of moderate size could have been built with these resources, but it occurred to McEwan that such a building would have been out of scale with the Medical School, so early in 1888 he advised that he would bear the cost of a larger scheme.[28] The enlarged hall could then be used by the whole university instead of the Medical School alone, permitting the original scheme for the complex to be taken a complete stage further. The Senate in March 1888 recorded their gratitude for this gift with the words that it 'forbids all terms of ordinary acknowledgement' and that it had 'no parallel in the whole history of the University'.[29] For this reason, the 'hall for all time coming should bear the name of its generous donor'. McEwan had accomplished at a stroke what years of fund raising had failed to do.

The hall was to seat at least 3000, and to cost in the region of £60 000–70 000. Early in 1888 drafting had started in the Anderson office, shortly after approval of his designs. The hall's location had been settled as far back as 1877, and on this occasion, the architect's research had largely been done in advance, at the time of the Medical School competition. A press statement subsequently explained the new building's underlying rationale:

> In designing the McEwan Hall the architect of course kept in view the special purposes to which it would be put in the life of the University. The requirements therefore were an ample floor space, a large platform, and abundant gallery accommodation for students and spectators. The design of the hall, semicircular in shape, is based on the form of the ancient Greek Theatre, which it is believed, is best adapted for the largest number of spectators both seeing and hearing well.[30]

In effect this meant that the flat end of the hall, abutting on to the Medical School, should incorporate the platform, and that seating and galleries should be deployed in semicircular fashion around the building's perimeter. An external corridor was to be built concentric with the outer walls, the two galleries sitting above it. The main entrance was to be situated at the half-way point of the semicircle and there were to be three staircases to the galleries, one on either side of the door, with the main one at the building's southern extremity.

The facade designs had evolved in three stages. In the first plans, when the hall was in the main courtyard, its lower storey harmonised with the buildings there, its upper levels walled in blank masonry. The semicircular pitched roof was to have been flat in section. By 1883, when illustrations of the hall's altered position were published, the roof of the first design had been retained, but the walls had acquired heavy full-length exterior buttresses in order to tie them in with the Medical School's facades. The elevations of the final design reveal subtle changes. The buttresses and cornice lines were retained, but the blind arcades of the upper storey were shallower and softer than the arcading of the School's frontage. The most striking changes were at roof level, where, beyond the balustrade, the interior walls and gallery arcades were expressed externally by buttresses. Above this, the roof was curved in section and ribbed to show its structure. Anderson had been influenced by Wren's Sheldonian Theatre; it is equally clear that while at Oxford he had also taken the trouble to study Radcliffe's Camera, by James Gibbs. Inside the hall, thirteen arcades two storeys high clasped the twin galleries, and above this a beautiful Renaissance frieze gave way to a coved clerestory of circular lights. The semidome of the ceiling culminated in an oculus.

Hundreds of drawings were required for this great project, making it necessary to employ part-time staff. Although the draughtsmen found the perspective views particularly difficult, they nevertheless managed to produce watercoloured drawings of stunning quality.[31] At operational level, supervision of the hall's construction was again entrusted to Allan Clark, whose talents had become apparent at the Medical School. The materials chosen for the hall mirrored Anderson's usual predilections. The columns of the giant arcades were to be of red Corsehill stone, mounted on grey freestone bases, and would be topped by gilded Corinthian capitals. All the stalls and pews were to be of oak, while the walls of the ground floor corridor were to be faced in smooth red brick, its floors in mosaic. On the hall's exterior, the blind upper storey was to be arcaded in red polished granite. Most of the contracts were won by Edinburgh firms. The main building work was to be carried out by W. & J. Kirkwood, the joinerwork by Shillinglaws, the plumbing by Barton & Son and the glazing by Coutts and Cameron.

The lighting arrangements, in typical Anderson fashion, were the outcome of 'painstaking care and unwearied experiment'.[32] Electric light had been decided on as the 'one and only light for such a hall', in a city with a public electric lighting department of high reputation. In due course, the solution was revealed. A giant electrolier carrying thirty-nine lamps of 200 candle power each would hang from the centre of the dome. Two hundred and sixty-four lamps along the cornice, obscured from view, would radiate light from the dome's sides. The gallery lights were installed carefully so as to avoid dazzling those on the platform. King & Co. of Leith were entrusted with the execution of this important work. A proper system of heating and ventilation was also essential for the McEwan Hall, and Wilson Phipson, the consultant employed at the Medical School and Mount Stuart, was again given the work. The ventilating system was designed to operate after crowds had assembled. At this point fresh air would be introduced through tubes, the used air escaping through ventilating shafts in the roof of the upper gallery. In 1894 McEwan would sanction a lantern to crown the roof of the hall.[33] This was not entirely decorative, as the used air from the shafts in the gallery would pass through it and into the atmosphere.

While attending to these practicalities, Anderson also designed an organ case in oak for the new organ, built by the Electric Organ Company of Birkenhead to the designs of Robert Hope Jones. This was to be situated behind the platform, and was to be 'elaborately carved and richly decorated in gold and colour'. A scheme of elaborate mural decoration was in 1894 entrusted to William Palin of London, recommended to the Building Committee by the Science and Art Department, South Kensington. Palin was to execute a huge allegorical scheme on the theme of *The Temple of Fame* above the proscenium opening and upper parts of the hall. In due course it would become apparent that this glorious ceremonial space had no peer in Scotland: that it was one of Anderson's greatest works (Plates 63 and 64). By the time it was completed, the University complex would cost in the region of a million pounds.

In train with the large commissions of these years, church and domestic work, as ever, took up a fair proportion of the practice's time. On the Braid estate, still spreading southwards, the new rows of terraced housing tended to be designed by assistants, who would present alternative drawings to Anderson for his selection and criticism. By this point much of Braid Avenue and Braid Road had been built up. In 1890, the 'Allermuir' style was in evidence at Luscar House, Carnock, near Dunfermline, both inside and out. Anderson here greatly extended an earlier house in the Manorial style (Plate 65). On the ecclesiastical front, a shift to late Gothic, reflecting the influence of Bodley, can be detected as early as 1886 at St James' Episcopal church, Inverleith, Edinburgh.

Plate 63. McEwan Hall, Edinburgh University (National Monuments Record of Scotland).

Inside, the arcades strongly resemble those at the Portrait Gallery, and a mural on the chancel wall, by William Hole, confirms the connection. In this mural, a figure of Christ is depicted holding a miniature of the church, complete with spire, in his hand. The intention was not matched by the act, however, and the church remained spireless.

At Colinton, where Anderson's own congregation had been worshipping in an 'Iron Hall', a movement for the erection of a new church was afoot in 1886. By 1887, a meeting to discuss designs had been held in Anderson's office. On 20 October, Mary Anderson cut the first sod of turf at a little inaugural ceremony marking the start of building.[34] The church, also in late Gothic, was sturdily built of local rubble with red Dumfriesshire dressings, and took shape in just over five months, under the supervision of two clerks of works, John Gibson and J. Liddle. The tower was originally intended to have a broach spire, but in due course received a leaded top of the seventeenth century type which had formerly graced the Tron Church in Edinburgh's High Street, which Anderson had refurnished in 1888 (Plate 66). Inside, a late Gothic pulpit and profuse wall and roof decoration, executed by Powell of Lincoln, testify to the architect's shifting tastes (Plate 67). From time to time he still visited English churches, photographing interiors, many of which were late

Plate 64. Interior, McEwan Hall, Edinburgh University (National Monuments Record of Scotland).

Gothic in style. Much of the money for the Colinton church was provided by Anderson and Oliver Riddell.

Another outlet for Anderson's late Gothic styling was provided in 1890, at Dunfermline Abbey Church, where Anderson was asked to design a new oak pulpit over the grave of Robert the Bruce. The carving, by Thomas Beattie, featured symbols of the four evangelists. The work was attacked as a manifestation of Popery by a local minister, the Rev. Jacob Primmer. These minority views did not prevent Anderson's return to Dunfermline within a few years to provide new steps and gates for the Abbey, and to redecorate the Abbey Church with stencil work. Three churches from the same period are also worthy of notice. At St Paul's Church, Greenock, a splendid west window partly compensates for the non-completion of the towers (Plate 68). South Morningside Free Church must be regarded as a sister church to Greenock; its tower is almost identical to that planned

Plate 65. Luscar House, Carnock (Author).

Plate 66. St Cuthbert's Church, Colinton (*Colinton Old and New*, 1926).

Plate 67. Interior, St Cuthbert's Church, Colinton (Author).

there (Plate 69). At Holy Trinity Episcopal Church, Dunfermline (Plate 70) a good west window illuminates ecclesiological arrangements and a deep chancel. The irregular placing of the north nave windows breaks up the interior wall space rather awkwardly. That apart, the church makes a good composition on a sloping site.

At the 1889 Art Congress held in the Portrait Gallery, one of the papers had dwelt 'on the Failure in the Results of the Government Art Schools and a Possible Remedy Therefor'. At the same congress, Professor Patrick Geddes had spoken 'On National and Municipal Encouragement of Art upon the Continent'. These papers manifested the great dissatisfaction that for many years had resulted from the Government's national scheme for art education, introduced by Henry Cole in the late 1850s and administered from South Kensington. In Edinburgh, a Treasury Minute of 1858 had curtailed the activities of the Trustees' School of Design, which was no longer permitted to educate beyond 'the antique' stage. Life classes were to be reserved strictly for intended painters and arranged by the Royal Scottish Academy. The situation worsened over the years as the national system was formalised and extended. In due course a range of charts for copying was introduced nationwide, and flair and freedom in drawing were discouraged. A system of national medals and diplomas was also instituted. The Trustees' School of Design had been reduced to the teaching of elementary, utilitarian drawing. To make matters worse, a system of partial 'payments by results' had been operating in all government schools since 1862. This related the salaries of drawing masters to the achievements of their pupils in the national competitions. The system was later extended to full 'payment by results', putting

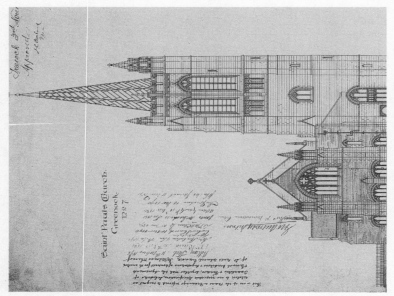

Plate 68. St Paul's Church, Greenock, contract drawings showing unexecuted tower (Anderson Office Drawings, Edinburgh University).

Plate 69. South Morningside Free Church, Edinburgh (Author).

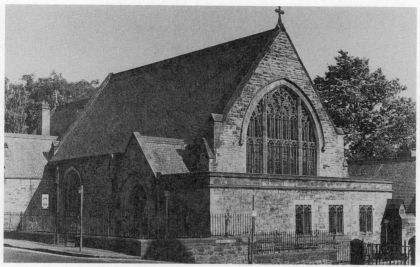

Plate 70. Holy Trinity Church, Dunfermline (Author).

tremendous pressure on teachers to make their students conform to South Kensington's somewhat circumscribed definitions of excellence. Drawing and painting thus became an end in itself, rather than serving design.[35]

The achievements of the Trustees' Academy over a century had been all but wiped out, and the contribution of Alexander Christie and Scott Lauder had been nullified at a stroke. A good education for craftsmen, designers and architects in Edinburgh had long since been impossible. This was a situation the Trustees' School of Design's most distinguished student was no longer prepared to tolerate. The feelings he had expressed to Lord Lothian a few years earlier had strengthened even further, and action was required. Injustice certainly figured in his thinking, but he was also motivated by his own experience of the craft and design workers he encountered daily in connection with his practice. Many of these men displayed a lack of education and design knowledge in his dealings with them. From 1890 onwards Anderson, together with sympathetic supporters, had been involved in discussions with the Board of Manufactures about the possibility of a new art school specifically intended to provide advanced education for craftsmen, architects and designers. The Board was the logical body to approach, since any new institution would, in effect, begin where the Trustees' School of Design had left off in 1858. Unable to reinstate the pre-1858 curriculum in their own school, the Board were sympathetic, and agreed to provide free accommodation in the Royal Institution and to help with administration.

The City Council was also approached, since it had been given a £4000

Exchequer grant for 'technical education', whereupon it voted £1000 to
the new school. Anderson and his supporters also gave generously, and
arrangements were made for the classes to start on 17 October 1892. An
advertisement was put in the newspapers announcing the new 'School of
Applied Art' and inviting applications from potential students. Class
hours would be from 8 to 10 a.m. on weekdays and 7 to 9 p.m. in the
evenings. Bursaries were available, and students had to show drafting
proficiency by submitting drawings or appropriate certificates. A number
of enquirers had to be turned away due to the constraints of space.[36]
Initially 68 students were enrolled, with 42 intending to stay for four
years, the period initially established for the full course. The school
eventually opened on 21 October, by which time only part of the equipment had arrived. These minor setbacks failed to dampen Anderson's
enthusiasm as he made the opening address in the presence of the Lord
Justice Clerk, representing the Board of Manufactures.

Anderson began with an explanation of the School's raison d'etre,
distinguishing the new institution from the Royal Academy's Life Class
and the nationally controlled Trustees' School of Design. In discussing
the reduced status of the latter, he was at pains to stress the good
intentions of the South Kensington system prior to its decline, and also
to emphasise that its 'great museum', the Victoria and Albert, was 'a
treasure house of art, and an inexhaustible source of information for
workers'. The new school was not a drawing school. In applied art,
drawing was a means to an end. In the new school, the teaching was to
be carried out by 'those engaged in the work they profess to teach'. Frank
Simon and George Watson, the two teachers of architecture, were 'two of
the best draughtsmen in Edinburgh'. The modelling teacher was Robert
Innes, 'well known as the best man we could get'. A colour teacher had
yet to be appointed, and Anderson himself had 'undertaken for a time the
general superintendence' of the school. The basis of the teaching was to
be 'an education in common in Classic, Renaissance and Mediaeval Arts'.
Anxious to dispel the notion that this was the province of architects alone,
he emphasised that 'all who contribute to a building must understand one
another. They must all be able to speak the same language'. Anderson's
architecture-led philosophy of the arts was fully revealed in his further
statement that the object of applied art was to 'realise the complete
conception of the architect', and that all must work 'as the men of old'.

The amount of 'architectural' study would vary with the occupation of
each student, who, when he 'has acquired enough for his particular art,
he will follow his own special work as far as it can be carried on in the
School'. The course of instruction was to be 'thoroughly practical and
varied to suit the student's interest'. Guest speakers in the various arts
were to be invited to 'tell us all they know'. In the colour classes the

students would learn how to 'mix up plain tints', to sketch and colour items from the school's collection, and to select and execute background tints. From this they would proceed to the arrangement and colouring of complex groups. Metal workers were to have good examples to work from, and a comprehensive collection was planned. 'Put workmen in contact with good work and you will quickly increase their intelligence and power'. Concluding his lecture, Anderson warned that 'Germany is covered with Industrial Art Schools' and that vast sums were spent in art education in Paris. This implied that 'if we don't waken up we shall be left behind', but it was to be remembered that the 'workmen of Edinburgh were not inferior to the French, Germans or Italians, in power and possibilities, but they must train for the race'.[37]

In preparation for the opening, Anderson had been busy selecting books and objects for the school. He had visited London and Paris and had spent £400 on a collection. This included casts of medieval work from English buildings, although it was also intended to amass examples from Scottish sources. A selection of photographs of French medieval work had also been purchased in Paris. Some 'good casts of classic work' were acquired from the Ecole des Beaux Arts and the British Museum, and the latter had also been asked to supply casts of classic gems, Italian medals and medieval seals, 'every one of which is a delight to look on'. It was hoped that the Board of Manufactures would allow access to the Tassie gems, 'one the finest collections extant', and a collection of casts and illustrations of heraldic work had been begun. A selection of casts from inscriptions on buildings and monuments had also been initiated, for the benefit of students of typography. Shortly afterwards, gifts began to arrive. Mrs Anderson donated a bundle of coloured materials, a number of Scottish seals, and a case of Indian moths and butterflies. G.S. Carfrae supplied drawings and tracings of 'decorative figure subjects' at the same time. In due course Copland and Lye of Glasgow presented coloured remnants and Thomas Bonnar presented a cast of an Italian gate panel. J.R. Findlay donated casts from the tomb of the Duke of Burgundy at Dijon, and Farmer and Brindley gifted Renaissance casts. Anderson's personal gifts followed: two Donatello casts, tapestries, oriental rugs, and an eclectic selection of books on historical architecture. As well as providing evidence of the wide attention the school was receiving, the gifts point to the unmistakeable resemblance between its aims and equipment and those of the pre-1858 Trustees' School of Design.

Anderson was convenor of the school's working committee, which also consisted of Hippolyte Blanc, W.W. Robertson, David MacGibbon, Thomas Bonnar, W. Scott Morton, Birnie Rhind, Robert K. Inches, George Waterston Jr and T.L. Gibson. Alexander Inglis was secretary, and, at a slightly later date, Washington Browne and John Kinross would also be involved. Outdoor classes were introduced, as at the pre-1858 Trustees' School of Design. J.J. Joass was a leader on these sketching outings, which visited such places as Corstorphine Church, Linlithgow Palace and Falkland Palace. Guest lectures and competitions were introduced, as promised. From the first, the students were enthusiastic about the new institution, which quickly grew from strength to strength. In due course, the school advertised its willingness to involve students in the preparation of designs for outside customers, and in October 1893 it was decided that three fellowships should be created for two years each, to study and draw old Scottish architecture and design, a development that marked the inception of the National Art Survey of Scotland.[38]

In 1891, the office had moved to 16 Rutland Square, Edinburgh, its final home, and the house next door (number 15) was bought as a town residence, no doubt reflecting the tremendous demands being made on the architect's time. That year a commission arising out of his deepening friendship with the Marquess of Bute began, at the University of St Andrews. Student facilities were inadequate, and in particular a dining hall was required. The matter was brought to the attention of Bute, who had been a Commissioner under the Universities (Scotland) Act since 1889 and had earlier endowed Glasgow University's Bute Hall (1878–84). Bute provided £1000, and Anderson drew up plans for a complex which also included a debating hall, a reading room, and other rooms. The total cost was estimated at £2800, with the Students' Union providing £650, leaving a balance of £1150 to be subscribed. The commission involved the conversion of 75 North Street, an ancient building associated with the Admirable Crichton, and adjoining property in Butts Wynd. The work involved the creation of a large hall with a crisp Jacobean ceiling and a series of small rooms. The exterior of the complex was repaired, harled, and finished in the Scots Jacobean style in keeping with the period in which it was built.[39]

During these years, when circumstances permitted, Anderson would occasionally take a holiday in Tangier, a city he had visited and fallen in love with at some point in the 1880s. Described by contemporaries as 'the seat of a rather extensive and gay European colony', Tangier offered an excellent climate and also gave access to Arab and African culture. Socially, it provided opportunities to rub shoulders with wealthy Americans, such as Ion Pericardis, who together with his wife kept a villa which was 'the show house of Tangiers'.[40] Anderson struck up a friendship with Pericardis, who shared his conservative political viewpoint, noting in a letter to Anderson that he had read of William McEwan giving a 'great blow to the Gladstonians' in the Commons.[41] One of the great attractions of Tangier was its horse riding. Race meetings took place at 'the Bubana', a racecourse two miles away. These were always spectacular occasions,

Plate 71. Eastern Telegraph Office, Tangier (Author).

producing a display of first class horse flesh and great flamboyance among the visitors as they mingled with the colourfully dressed Moors, Berbers or Riffs. Another more grisly occupation available to those with a sense of adventure was 'pig sticking', spearing wild boar in the 'Diplomatic Forest', slightly to the south of Tangier. Anderson himself was fond of riding, and some years later was present to see the Earl of Dumfries off on a horseback expedition, lending him his 'smoked goggles'.

In the early 1890s Anderson made the acquaintance of James Thompson, a young Scot who had moved to Tangier in order to set up in business as an architect's contractor, asking him to take charge of the erection of his holiday residence. This led to the execution of a deed of partnership, which appears to have covered the operation of a building business.[42] The first and only product of the collaboration was an office erected for the Eastern Telegraph Company c. 1892, and now in use as a school. This building has a number of characteristics pointing to Anderson's involvement in its design (Plate 71) and faintly resembles the Conservative Club in Edinburgh. The two men, however, 'found themselves to be incompatible'. In 1894 Anderson interested an Australian, Ernest Waller, in looking after property he had purchased in Tangier. Waller, who was a member of the Royal Caledonian Horticultural Society, came out for this purpose, but eventually set up nurseries on his own account, at Souani, in the suburbs.[43]

Anderson's own house, now demolished, remains a mystery. At one point he had designed a building called 'Emsallah House', its name suggesting that it would have been built on the Emsallah, slightly southwards of central Tangier.[44] It is, however, known that Anderson's house was eventually erected on the cliffs of the Marshan, overlooking the Mediterranean and behind the Sultan's palace. The space it once occupied is not large, and all that can now be said with certainty is that it was built of cement, and possibly not unlike the designs for Emsallah House.[45] Wherever and whatever his abode, Anderson clearly enjoyed Tangier on a number of levels: he relished the climate and the social and recreational opportunities that came with it, but perhaps more importantly, he took a delight in its people and their exotic culture. In later years, when failing health kept him away, he still interested himself in its political affairs, clipping out relevant newspaper articles and strongly advocating Moroccan independence. He also kept a translation of the Koran among his books. It is clear that during the century's final decade, years of prolific activity, Tangier was a place of stimulus and rest to a man of remarkable forcefulness and energy.

At this point the Bute connection yielded further work. On 16 November 1894 the corner stone of St Margaret's Memorial Roman Catholic Church was laid in Dunfermline, just across the road from the new Holy Trinity Episcopal Church. The Catholics of Dunfermline had been worshipping in temporary accommodation and Bute had intervened with a substantial gift and in the selection of Anderson as architect.[46] The full scheme envisaged again involved a Brechin-style tower, Anderson's final (and again unsuccessful) attempt to have a tower of this type erected (Plate 72). Funds ran out after £6000–7000 had been spent, enabling the building of the nave alone to be carried out. Meanwhile, at Mount Stuart the great architectural saga continued. Lord Bute was proceeding with the chapel, and Anderson was despatched to the old Cathedral of

Plate 72. St Margaret's Roman Catholic Church, Dunfermline (A.H. Millar, *Fife, Pictorial and Historical*, Vol. II, 1895).

Saragossa to obtain details of its octagonal lantern. The chapel was to be apsidal, with the east end in lofty French Gothic, while the walls were to be lined with white Carrara marble. In due course this glorious sanctuary took shape, the octagon framed in steel and supported on squinch arches, with a clerestory of ruby red glass, admired by Lord Bute in the Byzantine churches of Russia[47] (Plate 73). Bute, Rector of St Andrews University since 1892, chose Saragossa because of its associations with Pope Pedro de Luna, who, while regarded as an antipope elsewhere in Europe, had authorised the founding of the University. While on a research trip for this project, Anderson, accompanied by two monumental casters and his secretary Miss Hepburn, had sought out de Luna's remains at Savignan. A cast was made of his embalmed head and this was mounted on a Gothic plinth and gifted to the University, to Lord Bute's delight (Plate 74).

Plate 73. Mount Stuart Chapel, Bute (Valentine Ltd, Dundee).

Over against these fascinating developments, the frustrations of an architectural competition again intervened. In 1895 the Directors of the North British Railways had invited Anderson, William Leiper, John James Burnet, now an ARSA, Dunn and Findlay and W. Hamilton Beattie to submit designs for the new hotel and offices to be erected at Edinburgh's Waverley Station. Just prior to this, Hamilton Beattie had designed Jenner's in Princes Street for Charles Jenner, a Director of the North British Railway. The competitors had been given detailed instructions at the end of the previous October. Plans were submitted on 11 February, and on 14 February it was announced that W. Hamilton Beattie's design had won the competition. A furious Anderson wrote to the Secretary of the North British Railway on 16 February asking if the

Plate 74. Cast of Head of Pedro de Luna (St Andrews University). .

Directors 'had the plans, sections, reports and estimates examined by experts before coming to a decision'. The Railway in reply merely emphasised that it had exercised its prerogative. Anderson retorted that, in view of the time span between the submission of the designs and the final decision, it was clear that the entries had not been carefully examined, an insult to those involved, and confirmation of the rumour that the result was a foregone conclusion. His protests, he continued, should not be construed as arising from disappointment. He was anxious that the public should be acquainted with the unjust way in which the matter had been handled, finally making his point by having his letter printed and widely circulated. In the event, almost any of the entries would have improved on the much loved but rather dumpy building eventually erected.[48]

Plate 75. Glencoe House, Invercoe (Author).

Coinciding with the onward march of the School of Applied Art and its National Art Survey, Anderson had become increasingly concerned with the development of a national style in architecture. Four buildings from the 1890s exemplify the approach which he was attempting to foster in his architectural students. The first of these was the small library erected in memory of Alexander Crum of Thornliebank, who had died in 1893. Two much more substantial works in the same vein soon followed, at Glencoe House and Pollokshaws Burgh Buildings, both carried out on the same principles. Glencoe House was the new residence of Sir Donald Alexander Smith, Queen Victoria's 'favourite colonial'. Smith, aged 75 in 1895 when the house was started, had emigrated early in his life to Canada where he had risen through the ranks in the Hudson Bay Company, eventually becoming its Governor, which he still was. He had been actively involved in politics in Canada, and was a director of the Canadian Pacific Railway. Ten years earlier, it was Smith who had struck in the last spike of the rail link between the Atlantic and Pacific Oceans. Before his new house was completed, Smith would become Baron Strathcona and Mount Royal, and at around the same time would become Canadian High Commissioner in London.[49] Built on rising ground, the house was sensibly planned on two axes, presenting several floors of public rooms and bedrooms to Loch Leven, and on the landward side, gave magnificent views of the Pap of Glencoe. Unusually, Anderson built the house of local grey granite, offset with red sandstone dressings, and,

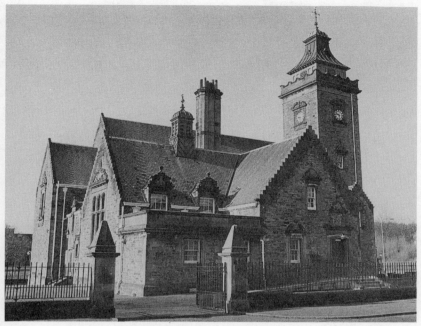

Plate 76. Pollokshaws Burgh Buildings (Author).

ignoring the local slate quarries, with a roof of red clay tiles in his Colinton manner (Plate 75).

Pollokshaws Burgh Buildings resulted from the blossoming friendship between Anderson and the youthful Sir John Stirling Maxwell, an acquaintance of the Marquess of Bute and a member of Anderson's social circle. Stirling Maxwell had in 1890 commissioned Rowand Anderson to add an entrance hall to his home, Pollok House. The new buildings, situated close by, were a gift from Stirling Maxwell to his local authority. When securing Anderson's services, he learned from the architect that he intended to reproduce as many features as possible of Glasgow's Old College in the new structure.[50] The Old College had been demolished to make way for a goods yard when the University was reconstructed at Gilmorehill. The new buildings, completed in 1897, were laid out in an L-shaped plan, to accommodate a large and small hall and subsidiary rooms. Anderson's tribute to the Old College came in the form of a tall steeple topped with a lead-covered structure of the Edinburgh Tron Church type, which had been the College's most prominent feature. The end result pleased Stirling Maxwell both from the point of view of usefulness and beauty (Plate 76). The final building in a series that had basically emanated from 'Allermuir' was designed in the 1890s but not

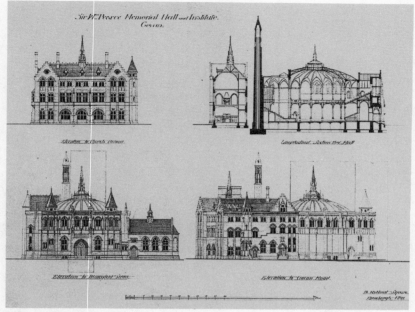

Plate 77. Designs for Pearce Institute, Govan (Anderson Office Drawings, Edinburgh University).

started until 1900: the Pearce Institute in Govan. Sir William Pearce, the proprietor of Fairfield's shipyard, had died in 1888, leaving a personal fortune of £1¼ million. Pearce, originally from Kent, had been a flamboyant entrepreneur, but also had the gift of 'sweet reasonableness', which endeared him to his workforce.[51] The Pearce family and friends decided to erect an institute to his memory in Govan, designed to provide social and recreational facilities for the people of that district. The new institute was to be administered by Govan Parish Church, and no doubt related to this, Anderson was commissioned. In 1891, a stunning Gothic design incorporating many Anderson hallmarks (Plate 77) was abandoned, and a Scots Jacobean design was later substituted. As usual, every minute detail of the client's brief was carefully considered and incorporated, and the plans were strikingly simple and utilitarian, the structure laid out in an irregular U shape to suit the site. The great hall (named after Dr Macleod, who died in 1898) is in a more elaborate Renaissance style, perhaps suggesting a chronological transition (Plate 78).

On 10 February 1897, Anderson received a telegram at 'Allermuir' from George Hay, Secretary of the Royal Scottish Academy, advising him that he had been elected an Honorary Member, one of the Academy's

Plate 78. Pearce Institute, Govan (National Monuments Record of Scotland).

rarest and highest honours. A telegram conveying the personal con-gratulations of Sir George Reid arrived simultaneously. Reid, President of the Academy, had been one of his greatest supporters in public controversies and must have been one of the leading advocates of this conciliatory measure. The rift was at last healed. That same day John Honeyman, one of the first batch of architects to be elected associates after Anderson's campaign, also sent a congratulatory note. Both these communications Anderson cherished. If the year had started well, it finished on a sourer note. In December 1897 the McEwan Hall was at last ready for its formal opening, its mural decorations complete. Anderson, William McEwan and a host of civic and academic dignitaries attended the opening ceremony. Amazingly, in all the solemn speeches, no reference whatsoever was made to the contribution of the architect, a gigantic gaffe by any standards. At a dinner a few days later in honour of Allan Clark, this loyal man deplored the omission of any reference to the one 'whose brain . . . created that beautiful design'. A draft letter to Aeneas Mackay, a senior judge, survives to show the torture this had inflicted on Anderson. The letter does not appear to have been sent, but when the Senate had been advised of the omission it was quick to place its gratitude on record by releasing an apologetic statement to the press.[52]

On balance, however, these lapses into self pity were few in number, were quickly regretted by Anderson, and may have been related to his advancing years and increasingly indifferent health. The closing years of the century were, on the whole, years of great fulfilment, the evidence suggesting that in spite of his many involvements, his mastery of

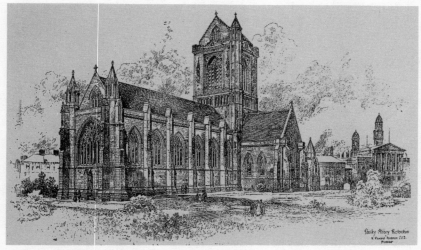

Plate 79. Anderson's designs for the restoration of Paisley Abbey (A.R. Howell *Paisley Abbey, its History, Architecture and Art*).

delegation enabled him to enter fully into the affairs of the Edinburgh Architectural Association and even to deliver architectural lectures and addresses to bodies such as the Franco-Scottish Society or the Literary Institute. In the century's last year, his personal attention was required in the west of Scotland, where his unique skills as a restorer were again in demand. At Bothwell Parish Church, at the instigation of the Rev. Dr Pagan, he restored the late fourteenth century choir, the only surviving remnant of the medieval church. Earth was removed from around the walls, the floor was lowered to its original level, and the Geometric window mullions and carving round the doorway were repaired, together with various monuments.[53] But there was a greater prize: Anderson had at last been allowed to undertake a commission he and the Marquess of Bute had hoped would come to pass for many years, the restoration of Paisley Abbey.

Paisley's nave had been restored by James Salmon in 1859, but the choir, transepts and tower had remained unbuilt since the collapse of the latter in 1540. The Rev. Thomas Gentles, the minister, raised £20 880 for the restoration, which Anderson estimated would cost £28 000, a figure which allowed for a new choir with open timber roof and a new nave roof to harmonise with the choir.[54] A saddleback roof was to be provided for the crossing tower, and the choir floor was to be of stone and encaustic tiles. Drawings of the church in its proposed state (Plate 79) show a single louvred opening on each side of the tower. The Building Committee, formed in 1898, had among its membership Sir John Stirling Maxwell and Sir Michael Shaw Stewart, and hence the choice of architect was never in any doubt. By the end of the century, however, it had become apparent that the hopes of the Committee for a complete restoration were ill-founded. Excavations at the base of the tower 'showed clearly that it was not the foundations that were at fault' when it fell. These were discovered to be sound, but the lower portions of the crossing piers were 'loose and bad, and the base quite inadequate'. One pier was particularly faulty, and it was concluded from this and the discovery of twisting on the other three that it had caused the collapse.[55] Disappointment was inevitable, but the unforeseen repairs nevertheless had to be made.

The year 1899 had also seen the commencement of a good sized church at Inchinnan for Lord Blythswood, a neighbour and friend of Stirling Maxwell. The time had come to replace the existing church, built in 1828 in Perpendicular Gothic, with something larger and more distinguished. With these important works in hand for the opening of the new century and an illustrious output behind him, Anderson must have had just cause for satisfaction. The School of Applied Art, in spite of more or less permanent financial insecurity, had produced a crop of graduates who were being snapped up, even by London offices. The National Art Survey was well established, its bursars producing remarkable records of historic Scottish architecture, furnishings and decoration. Long-term problems were making themselves apparent in several projects, but these were not significant enough to daunt the man who by example and argument had done more for Scottish architecture than any other.

7

Elder Statesman

Anderson, now in his sixty-sixth year, entered the new century with no intention of retiring. As if to prove the point, he had assumed two new partners in 1899, Frank Worthington Simon and A. Hunter Crawford. Simon had taught architectural drawing at the School of Applied Art until 1897, when increasing business forced him to resign. Beforehand, he had trained at the Ecole des Beaux Arts and had been in practice on his own account and with Charles E. Tweedie.[1] A. Hunter Crawford was from the biscuit-making family of that name, and was active in the Edinburgh Architectural Association. In due course the design skills of the new partners would be discernible at 32 Inverleith Place, Edinburgh (1900), and at Claremont Congregational Church, Blackpool (1901), the latter work quite obviously by Simon himself.[2]

In 1899 St Andrews University had, after a long delay, sanctioned the refurbishment of its senate room.[3] This room, in common with the library next door to it, was walled with bookcases, with a gallery running above, set on fluted wooden columns. In the centre of the ceiling a very rudimentary gasolier composed of crudely bent pipes provided a rather ugly focal point for the tables and chairs below. The room was poorly heated and ventilated, and toilet facilities were inadequate. Refurbishment was started late in 1899 with the removal of the bookcases, galleries and ceiling, the resurfacing of the walls with plaster and lath, and the installation of new windows. Early in the new century the walls were panelled in oak and a 'handsome and suitable mantelpiece and hearth' was supplied. Fans, radiators, boiler and toilet were fitted. The room was then completed in accordance with Anderson's personal aesthetic preferences. The fireplace was in purple veined alabaster, a material he had used over many years in church commissions. The pedimented oak overmantel was similar to examples at Glencoe or Pollokshaws. The room's crowning glory was, however, the new ceiling. A deep symmetrical moulding, decorated with leaves and sprays of flowers, no doubt inspired

Plate 80. Design for extensions to Pollok House (Anderson Office Drawings, Edinburgh University).

by the ceilings at Holyrood, stood out from its surface. In keeping with the mid-seventeenth century styling of the rest, Anderson installed a new gasolier, complete with brass balls and scrolls. The work was carried out by local tradesmen for £821–14–2.[4] Anderson must have been deeply satisfied that he had made his mark at the heart of the University. Immediately next door, in the library, the glass case containing the plaster cast of de Luna's head sat proudly on the Gothic plinth he had provided for it, while at the same time, the architect was designing a new pulpit and producing a scheme of redecoration for St Salvator's church.

In the first two years of the new century, with the exception of a new drill hall and offices designed for the 5th Volunteer Brigade, Royal Scots, at Leith, the practice's interests lay largely in the west. Here, the Pearce Institute was rising up, and nearby, the new parish church at Inchinnan was taking shape. Close by, work was about to start at Pollok House, Stirling Maxwell's home. After coming of age in 1888, Stirling Maxwell had chosen Pollok as his residence in preference to Keir House, near Dunblane, which was then taken by his brother, Archibald Stirling. Pollok House was a severe classical box built in the middle of the eighteenth century and attributed, somewhat speculatively, to William Adam.[5] Its most pressing requirements were new kitchen and bathroom facilities, up-to-date lighting, and more space for the library and art collection which Stirling Maxwell had inherited from his father. In 1890

Plate 81. Pollok House (Author).

Anderson had added an entrance hall to the house, complete with elegantly rising staircase and period plasterwork. His first plan for the latest phase of alterations was simply to extend the house at both sides, retaining the same number of storeys as the original block. This would scarcely have relieved the building's severity. A further scheme demonstrated much greater sensitivity: here the extensions were lifted forward and attached to the central block by neo-Palladian quadrantal arms (Plate 80).

Another scheme was accepted and in progress in 1901. In this final solution, a pair of short corridors led from the existing house into two single storey wings, one to house a library, the other a billiard room. Each wing was given a Venetian window, echoing that of the central entrance, these and the provision of swags compensating for the main block's blandness. In revising the plans for the garden, Anderson retained two ideas from the previous scheme, the introduction of quadrantal curves, finally incorporated in the terrace walls, and cupola-topped pavilions. Within the house, little of the original block was touched, except at basement level where the kitchens were converted into a generous and airy work space, with cast iron ranges by Cormack of Glasgow furnishing the room's perimeter. The alterations were completely successful, transforming a rather barren house into a modern home which, externally, presented a pleasing and harmonious appearance (Plate 81). The work was not completed until 1908.

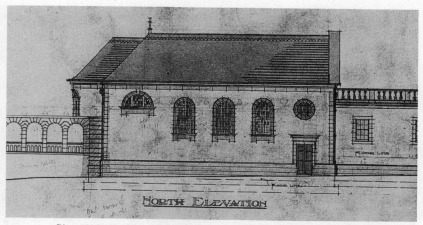

Plate 82. Keir House Chapel (Anderson Office Drawings, Edinburgh University).

While engaged at Pollok, Anderson was also working at Keir. The house had been designed at some point in the eighteenth century, but had subsequently undergone numerous extensions and alterations. A drawing-room wing had been added by David Hamilton, who was also responsible for providing Doric lodges and gates in 1820. Between 1845 and 1851 Alfred Jenoure, of whom little is known, was responsible for replacing the pedimented front of the house with a four-storey bow window which at one time had a glass roof. At some point during these years, Keir had also acquired walled gardens, bridges, tunnels, a water garden, a topiary yew house, cascades, an ice house, water house, garden house and stud house, inter alia.[6] Archibald Stirling seems to have been content to continue in this piecemeal tradition. In 1899–1900 Anderson installed new stairs and a lift, which was followed in 1902–3 by commissions for garden terrace walls and other exterior work, including a gardener's bothy. In due course a tempietto was requested. This was furnished with eight Corinthian columns and framed in steel. Finally, in 1910 Anderson produced sketch plans for a chapel, at the north-east corner of the house.[7] This was carried out in a plain classical style, and richly decorated in mosaics and marble (Plate 82). While Anderson must have had reservations about the disunity at Keir, the assignments were at least varied, and not subject to financial constraints.

The year 1900 had ended with the death of Lord Bute, who had suffered several strokes, thus bringing to a sad end a unique collaboration that had spanned three decades. In January 1901 Anderson was writing to Lady Bute about the cimborio at Mount Stuart Chapel, which Bute had not lived to see in its finished state. In due course this was completed under the Fourth Marquess, with whom Anderson had already struck up

Plate 83. Design for central feature, Queen Victoria Memorial (*Academy Architecture — Edinburgh, 1903*).

a friendship, and who later employed him to make alterations and to build a nursery wing. The house's final cost was rumoured to have been in the region of a million pounds. The sense of closure signalled by the ending of the century and the death of Bute was confirmed in 1901 by the death of Queen Victoria and the installation of Edward VII.

Anderson must, however, have been uplifted by the opportunity this gave him to prepare a competition design for the Queen Victoria Memorial. As well as Anderson, T.G. Jackson, Aston Webb, Ernest George and Sir Thomas Drew were invited to compete by Lord Esher, the chairman of the memorial committee. The memorial was to consist of a central feature in front of Buckingham Palace, together with a memorial arch at the east end of the Mall. The architects were to collaborate with Thomas Brock, the chosen sculptor, in the preparation of their schemes. The designs were prepared against a background of public controversy about the appropriateness of the memorial and the limited nature of the competition.[8]

Anderson's entry consisted of a *rond point*, fenced with a balustrade, culminating in a statue of the late queen (Plate 83). His design also provided for a semicircular parterre opposite Buckingham Gate in the Mall, which was again to be enclosed with a curving balustrade and filled with statuary. The centrepiece was to consist of an equestrian statue of Queen Elizabeth, set on a richly carved rectangular plinth, and surrounded by 'the leading men of her day', which included Drake, Raleigh, Shakespeare and Howard of Effingham. The third element in the design was a monumental archway into the Mall from Trafalgar Square.[9] Here Anderson intended to erect a Roman triumphal arch, heavily buttressed, and above, an aedicule containing an equestrian figure. His inspiration for this feature may have been the monument to Foulis of Ravelston, by William Ayton, which stood in Greyfriars churchyard, Edinburgh, and dated from 1636. On this occasion, in spite of the general recognition that Anderson's designs were 'handsome and scholarly', Aston Webb's rather grandiose scheme was preferred. In 1908–9, after several reductions in scale, Webb's scheme was executed, his entrance arch compromised by the need to incorporate in its structure office space for the Admiralty. As late as 1943, Stirling Maxwell still had grounds for entertaining the hope that Anderson's arch, which he felt was 'immeasurably finer' than Webb's, might still be carried out.[10]

Late in 1901, an honour of a different type came to Anderson: he was asked to write a preface to a new edition of Billings' *The Baronial and Ecclesiastical Antiquities of Scotland*, for Oliver and Boyd. His preface, entitled 'An Appreciation', set Billings' production in its historical context, clarifying the numerous points at which it surpassed Slezer's *Theatrum Scotiae*, Pennant's *Tour of Scotland*, and Grose's *The Antiquities of Scotland*; it was better drawn, contained a better selection of examples, and 'had disclosed a wealth of native Art hitherto practically unknown'. From this point onwards Anderson was uncompromising, regretting that those architects who had consulted Billings' works in the latter half of the nineteenth century had not done so 'from a sounder standpoint', assuming, with Billings, that the original designers of Baronial architecture had grouped their buildings to suit their natural situations. This had produced 'the many sham castles we see everywhere'. Anderson had no doubt that

> the builders of our Scottish houses and castles worked on no such principles. They never troubled themselves about picturesqueness or the composition of designs to suit sites. They did what suited their purposes and wants . . . and the result was . . . buildings that show an adaptation of means to an end, functional truth, with resulting intelligence, expression and picturesqueness.[11]

Anderson's 'Appreciation' was heavily qualified indeed. He was, however, pleased to note that better principles were prevailing, and that 'buildings are no longer made to look like what they are not, but their character is impressed on them by the various purposes that call them into existence'. Anderson next exhorted architects to follow in the footsteps of the ancient builders whose works Billings had illustrated, and to see their structures as essays in the provision of facilities and problem solving. Only by so doing, he felt, could modern architects produce 'buildings as thoroughly national in character, and representative of the social and political state of the time, as any building illustrated in this valuable work'. Thus, Anderson again crystallised the essential difference between mid-nineteenth century Baronial and his own approach to a national architecture. In so doing he had let one point slip. He had stated that Billings' work, when first published, had immediately gone into 'the front rank of architectural publications, and from this position it has not yet been displaced'. Even from as early as the 1870s it had been Anderson's intention to vie with Billings. At that point, Axel Hermann Haig had started to sketch ancient Scottish architecture in preparation for a book which he was to illustrate for Anderson, abandoned for reasons of cost. At the back of Anderson's mind as he wrote was the possibility that, one day, the National Art Survey, then in its seventh year, would be published, surpassing Billings and all others in quality and quantity, and providing an important source for the development of a national architecture worthy of the name. The words 'not yet' were charged with significance.

Since the death of Prince Albert in 1861, Queen Victoria had spent most of her widowhood at Osborne or Balmoral, where she had kept the Prince Consort's rooms as he had left them, as shrines to his memory. The new King, prior to his coronation in 1902, had decided to make changes. Together with the Comptroller of the Lord Chamberlain's Department, Sir Arthur Ellis, the Master of the Household, Lord Farquar, the Secretary of the Office of Works, Lord Esher, and Lionel Cust, the Surveyor of the King's Pictures, the King inspected each of his residences. Some were found to be badly heated, lacking in amenities, and not up to twentieth century standards. The changes were to be made on the direct instructions of the King, and under his personal supervision. When it was decided to tackle Balmoral, Anderson was selected as executant architect. A contemporary report on the outcome, preserved by Anderson, records that

> Mr. Anderson exactly grasped the King's own idea, which was to give greater comfort, roominess and convenience without destroying the air of simplicity, almost of homeliness, which has always been the distinguishing feature of Royalty's Highland dwelling place. Balmoral is scarcely a 'Castle', much less a 'Palace'. But it is now, thanks to his Majesty's own plans and Mr. Anderson's skill in carrying them out, a very handsome and commodious house, where a guest — be he an emperor or just a neighbour from Deeside – can find himself 'at home and in clover'.[12]

The additions and alterations at Balmoral included extensions to the kitchen wing, the installation of a new central heating system, the provision of a luggage lift, and alterations to the Balmoral Lodge Cottage, Bhaile-na-Coile. King Edward was 'greatly pleased' with Anderson's work, and, at some time in the autumn of 1902, summoned him to Balmoral to inform him that he was to be knighted at the coronation on 9 November that year.

The year 1902 also witnessed the end of the new partnership, Simon and Crawford leaving to form a separate partnership at a time when Anderson's personal prestige was never higher, and their own relatively lowly status never more apparent. For some unknown reason, a lawsuit was instigated.[13] Simon, who seems to have lacked the ability to settle, in due course left for Canada.

Meanwhile, the School of Applied Art was deep in financial crisis. After the first few years, Edinburgh City Council's support had been cut in half as a result of reduced government funding, causing the school to rely more and more on private subscriptions.[14] In 1899 John Stewart, a student, had won the RIBA's Owen Jones prize, with J. Hervey Rutherford and Ramsay Traquair jointly winning the Pugin Studentship Prize, achievements testifying to the high quality of the school's education. Mergers with the Government School of Design had been suggested by the Scotch Education Department in the closing years of the century, but hopes were dashed in 1901 when the Board of Manufactures' own finances were the subject of government review. In 1902 an approach was made to Heriot-Watt College, suggesting a merger on the condition that 'the system of education which has produced such good results should be continued and developed'.[15] Heriot-Watt responded by asking the Scotch Education Department for extra funding on the basis that it might merge with the School of Applied Art, as well as the Government School of Design, which, in the light of the impending curtailment of the Board of Manufactures' finances, had also made an approach.[16] By 1902 the School of Applied Art had exhausted its reserve funds, and while the Scotch Education Department prevaricated, it was forced to appeal to the City Council, citing thirty-one examples of municipal support for art schools throughout the country. In mid-1902, R. Anning Bell conducted an apparently routine inspection of the school on behalf of the Scotch Education Department, reporting on it in glowing terms. The drawings produced by its students were 'really wonderful', and their designs were 'remarkable for their reticence and dignity of treatment'. The students acquired 'a sense of beauty and proportion' from the study of ancient examples, and Bell was also impressed with the cast collection.

In September 1902 the Secretary of State eventually appointed a committee to examine all aspects of art education in Edinburgh. It reached the conclusion that the Board of Manufactures had been guilty

of 'dereliction of duty' since 1858, a surprising interpretation given the
constraints that had been imposed from that time onwards.[17] Interviews
with Anderson, Sir George Reid, William Hole and others then followed.
Reid concluded that a revision of Edinburgh's art education provision was
long overdue, but that Heriot-Watt might be an obstacle. While its design
courses concentrated more on technical aspects, its vastly superior student
numbers and financial strength gave it the balance of power in any
discussions of what might be taught in a merged institution. Anderson,
with customary forcefulness, began by explaining the rationale for the
School of Applied Art and then reminded the committee of its outstanding
achievements. This he followed with a statistically based condemnation
of Heriot-Watt's record:

> they have at the start one hundred pupils, but they melt away and
> they never see them again . . . For example . . . there are one hundred
> and ninety seven pupils in what is called Building 'Construction' and
> Architecture. The course of the class is for three years; they start with
> one hundred and ninety seven and finish with twenty six; then for
> Ornament and Design, the course lasts two years; they start with fifty
> five and finish with one.[18]

He, too, concluded that a new institution was required, and when asked
what role Heriot-Watt might play in it, he felt that it could contribute
nothing since it was 'not organised on such a footing'.

On hearing these statements, the Governors of Heriot-Watt were
justifiably incensed. They had not been consulted, and thus had been
denied the opportunity to make a case for their institution. They disputed
the implications of Anderson's statistics, and noted that the condemnation
had come from the director of a school which only a few years earlier had
requested a merger with Heriot-Watt. As a result of its investigations,
however flawed, the committee concluded that a new, single art institution was required in Edinburgh, and that the School of Applied Art
should be carried on until such a school was set up. When the new college
was established, the school should be transferred there, remaining under
the control of Sir Rowand Anderson 'for as long a time as he will continue
to exercise it'. It would take a few more years for the merger to come
about, but Anderson was at last able to relax knowing that his own school
would not be extinguished. During 1903 the School of Applied Art and
the Trustees' School of Design were combined as a short-term expedient.

In 1904 Anderson took a new partner, Arthur Forman Balfour Paul,
son of Sir James Balfour Paul, Lord Lyon King of Arms, who was an
active member of the Edinburgh Architectural Association. Paul had
trained in the Anderson office, entering practice in the closing years of
the old century. His largest work to date, the Sir William Fraser homes
at Colinton, showed clearly his espousal of Anderson's ideas to the point

Plate 84. Interior, Inchinnan Parish Church (National Monuments Record of Scotland).

where the complex's Scots Jacobean styling might easily be mistaken for Anderson's own work. By this time All Hallows Church, Inchinnan, for Lord Blythswood, was coming to completion. Unfortunately, the full scheme envisaged in the design drawings was not to be realised. By the time of the church's dedication on 6 June the planned western tower had been abandoned, and the spire had only been taken to parapet level. Lord Blythswood was alarmed at the church's mounting cost, and from this point onwards referred to the architect as 'Ruin' Anderson, spreading the message that he was expensive to employ.[19] Anderson, perhaps miscalculating the extent of Blythswood's generosity, had selected North-umbrian stone, Hampshire brick and black and while marble squares for the interior. The end result, if costly, was superb (Plate 84). If the donor had reservations about the cost, the incumbent at least was delighted. In later years Stirling Maxwell defended Anderson, explaining that he simply wanted the best for his clients.

Several miles to the south, at Paisley Abbey, similar sentiments to those expressed by Blythswood had already begun to form in the mind of the Rev. Dr Gentles. For five years he had watched the rebuilding of the crossing piers, stone by stone, noting how this was consuming the restoration funds. By 1904 the crossing had been rebuilt, St Mirin's Chapel and the transepts had been rejoined to the nave, and the tower had been taken above roof level. Relations had, however, gone sour in the process. Gentles, unable to accept the unforeseeable nature of the crossing repairs, blamed Anderson for failing to complete the restoration at the forecast cost, and a W.S. McKechnie, who had written to Anderson about the placing of a memorial plaque on the Abbey walls, had been forcibly rebuffed when the architect replied that 'I consider a brass on the wall an absurdity from every point of view'.[20] In spite of assurances from McKechnie that his authority and expertise were not being called in question, Anderson had despatched several fiery communications on the subject. By March 1904, however, an agreement was reached that Anderson should 'act if required' on the next stage of the restoration, as and when funds became available.

On a happier note, operations were about to begin at Culross Abbey Church, where a restoration had been planned since 1902. Initially the heritors there, led by Lord Elgin, had asked for the minimum to be done to keep costs low.[21] Anderson's first estimate of £2100 allowed for the replacement of the roof and the removal of galleries and other interior woodwork, all of which was in poor condition. Alternative estimates for a partial and then a complete restoration were obtained in 1903, and in 1905 a full restoration began. This involved the provision of a wheel window in the south transept, the opening of the north window in the chancel, new tracery for the east window, a new window in the south wall of the nave, the restoration of the north chancel aisle and the aisle on the east side of the south transept.[22] The work began in earnest with the removal of two giant sycamore trees at the entrance, much loved by the locals. Anderson had learned to distrust roots at Dunblane.[23] In 1906 an ancient side chapel had been opened up and a Norman window restored, and by the end of that year the work was more or less complete. The restoration was superbly done. Anderson opted for the simple grandeur of a wagon roof with surface ribs, relieved by a single exposed tie beam and kingpost near the chancel. Old and new masonry were clearly

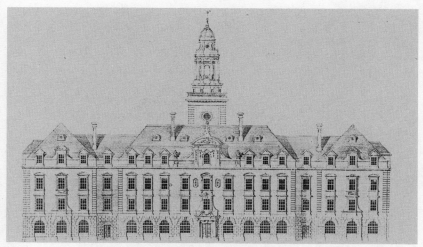

Plate 85. Designs for Dundee University (Dr D. Walker).

differentiated at every turn, and in the north transept a small-scale trefoil barrel roof was fitted, as at Govan. The heritors' pleasure was evident when in July 1908 they were finalising the finances. The architects had 'expressed their willingness to restrict their account to a percentage of 5%'. Lord Elgin voiced his gratitude for the fact that they had 'spared no pains and gone far beyond their ordinary professional duty'.[24]

The Edwardian period was also characterised by university work. In 1905 a commission came in for the conversion of Alexander Laing's late seventeenth century Old High School into a new engineering department for Edinburgh University. This involved the subdivision of the interior into laboratories and workshops linked by sliding doors, and the addition of a lecture theatre. A tower at the rear was heightened and given an ogival cupola. At the same time the partners were asked to convert Bryce's adjacent Old Surgical Hospital into physics laboratories.[25] Once again, the challenge was almost entirely functional. However, a greater opportunity was to emerge at Dundee. At some time prior to 1906 Anderson had been invited to submit designs for a completely new building at University College, then controlled by St Andrews University (Plate 85). This had fallen through as a result of funding difficulties, and less radical expansion was therefore planned in the shape of new physics and engineering laboratories. At the end of 1906 a letter was sent to Anderson calling him to a meeting at Dundee, at which he was to be advised that a local architect would design the buildings, and that he was to act as consultant.[26] At the meeting, Anderson managed successfully to persuade the college council that even at the age of seventy-two he should be entrusted with the whole commission.

Plate 86. Physics and Engineering Laboratories, Dundee University (Author).

The physics laboratories were designed in 1907 and complete by 1909. The conditions under which Anderson worked were favourable: the site, at the rear of the complex, was a good one, £12 500 was supplied by the Carnegie Fund, and to assist with the planning, Professor Keunen, the Dutch Professor of Physics, was on hand to advise. The planning of the engineering laboratories followed in 1909–10 with the assistance of Professor Gibson. The complex, enclosing what is now referred to as the Geddes Quadrangle, consisted of two blocks at right angles containing sensibly shaped rooms linked by spinal corridors. The style chosen was 'a domestic form of Classical design' which allowed the elevations 'to be expressive of the work carried on' inside. A 'play of line and light and shade' was aimed at, and the laboratories were built of red Dumfriesshire sandstone with cream dressings from Fife and Northumberland.[27] Inside the physics building the joinerwork, executed in dark stained wood, was exemplary: variously sized cupboards, benches and doors were carefully custom built, the latter with sliding apertures for optic experiments. The engineering laboratories finally cost £15 232. Today, the combination of site and buildings is still impressive (Plate 86).

In spite of the fact that many interesting projects were in hand in 1906, Anderson remained concerned that the arrangements for art education in Edinburgh were still temporary. His anger had been aroused in 1905 when he had heard that Edinburgh Corporation supported a campaign to erect a new National Gallery on Calton Hill, prompting a letter to the Scottish Office in Whitehall pointing out that Edinburgh's first priority should be the provision of a new and well-equipped art school. Sensing that a custom-built college was an unrealistic proposition at that stage, he suggested that temporary buildings should be erected in the High School Yards in order to ease the accommodation pressures at the Mound. At last, in June 1906 it was announced that Edinburgh City Council would be prepared to share the costs of a new art school with the Scotch Education Department. A provisional management committee for the new school was then set up, consisting of representatives of the Board of Manufactures, the Royal Scottish Academy, the Governors of Heriot-Watt College and the City Council. Shortly afterwards, a new building was commissioned to the designs of J.M. Dick Peddie, and on 1 April 1907 the newly formed school was handed over. That same day the Board of Manufactures ceased to exist.

Shortly afterwards, a 'Memorial' from the Edinburgh Architectural Association urged that the School of Applied Art's successful system of architectural teaching should be maintained in the new school. A similar letter arrived a little later from Rowand Anderson. He need not have been concerned; as agreed in 1903, Anderson was duly invited to join the board of the new art college, enabling him to ensure personally that his teaching methodology would be perpetuated. To his dismay, however, the sub-committee responsible for disposing of the Board of Manufactures' assets deprived the new Art College of the National Art Survey drawings. The committee members, the Lord Provost of Edinburgh and J.R. Findlay Junior, felt that the Survey was a national asset of such value that it should be deposited with the Portrait Gallery, a decision intended, paradoxically, as a tribute to Anderson and as a means to acquiring greater resources for its completion.[28] This was abhorrent to him. He had made it plain as early as 1894 that one of the School of Applied Art's aims was to develop from Scotland's distinctive historical heritage a national archi-tecture capable of meeting 'the wants and necessities of the present day'. The National Art Survey was crucial to this aim. In October 1908 the Secretary of the new College of Art wrote to the Portrait Gallery asking for permission for students to consult the Survey drawings, a request reluctantly granted. In the meantime the Survey continued from its new base, with two bursars operating for six months each. Anderson next requested that prints of the drawings be made. It would take Findlay and his colleagues at the Portrait Gallery three years to answer this request.

Notwithstanding these frustrations, it is clear that, during these years, Anderson was enjoying himself socially, and engaging in cultural pursuits in a way that had perhaps not been possible before. There were fewer commissions, reflecting the economic climate of the times, but still enough to ensure a prosperous practice. The partnership with Paul seems to have worked well. Predictably, Anderson made the majority of the design

Plate 87. Interior, 'Allermuir' (Royal Incorporation of Architects in Scotland).

decisions, except on those commissions initiated by Paul, who also ran the office. Anderson's confidence in Paul was great, and his partner seems to have happily concurred in these arrangements. Surviving photographs of the interior and exterior of 'Allermuir' from this period reveal that Anderson had accumulated a large collection of Blue China, to which he was still adding, going as far afield as Paris to attend sales. The photographs show an unremarkable but comfortable interior, suggestive of domestic contentment, and obviously the home of a well-to-do man of eclectic historicist tastes (Plate 87). Anderson was also keen on gardening. In a letter to Patrick Geddes of 1903, he had warned against 'cold and stiff formalities' in gardens, a policy he had himself adopted by combining formal and informal elements.[29] The garden also enabled Anderson to practice golf, an activity for which he had seldom found time in earlier years. In keeping with this more leisurely lifestyle, he had also acquired a motor car and chauffeur.

From the latter part of the old century onwards Anderson had been building up his book collection, adding volumes on Edinburgh's architecture and history, on ceramics and garden design, and, more prosaically, some books on investment and a series of language primers.[30] These took their place beside the novels of Poe, Daudet, Diderot and Lafontaine, and a predictably eclectic selection of architectural works which included Billings' *Antiquities*. Also occupying a large amount of shelf space at 'Allermuir' were Anderson's copies of the Scottish Ecclesiological Society's *Transactions*. This body had originally started out as the Aberdeen Ecclesiological Society, under the influence of Professor James Cooper. The Aberdeen Society had in 1887 elected Anderson an Honorary Vice-President, recognising both his pioneering role in the design of high quality, ecclesiologically correct churches and his pure and conservative restorations. On 17 March 1909 Anderson conducted the Society around Govan Old Parish Church, where his designs for an extended chancel had just been executed at Stirling Maxwell's expense.

Anderson enjoyed his successes, keeping a scrap book in which he placed newspaper reports on his buildings. Added to these were letters from patrons such as Bute and J.R. Findlay, obituaries and other memorabilia. 'Allermuir' was a hospitable place. In June 1910 Anderson conducted the combined Glasgow and Edinburgh Architectural Associations around St Cuthbert's church and the parish church, and then 'Allermuir' itself. The company was entertained to tea in the back garden by Lady Anderson. It was apparent that this northern Scottish lady, whose formidable reputation still persists in Colinton, supported her husband throughout his career in all he did. She seems to have been the perfect foil for Anderson.

Another social outlet came in the wake of his knighthood, when Anderson became a member of the Royal Company of Archers, the King's Bodyguard for Scotland. While the Archers still performed ceremonial duties at Holyrood and in other parts of the city, membership was tantamount to admission into an elite social club where the nation's peers, baronets and knights rubbed shoulders. Anderson loved the Archers, and was later described as 'one of the Royal Company's most devoted sons'.[31] He was particularly fond of the shooting activities, in which he took some part. These events involved good food and good company. Sir John McDonald was already a member when he joined, and Lord Elgin an office bearer. He also seems to have struck up a friendship there with Sir Henry Cook, an eminent solicitor. Anderson made his mark at Archer's Hall, a symmetrical classical box designed in the late eighteenth century by Alexander Laing. At around the time of his joining, he extended it at one end, destroying its symmetry and expressing its internal layout by inserting a Venetian window. On one occasion, Anderson had sent Charles Henshaw, a metal worker, to inspect a Louis Quatorze chandelier hanging in a castle in the neighbourhood of Compiegne.[32] It was reproduced for Archer's Hall at a cost of £700.

In 1912, at the age of seventy-eight, Anderson again found time to present a paper to the Antiquaries. He had visited the King's Library at the British Museum in a quest for material on Edinburgh Castle, unearthing a plan by Slezer from 1675 and a bird's eye view of the castle, which he cleverly dated between 1689 and 1707. A third drawing, made by William Adam, was found. Using this and other data Anderson was able to throw light on the chronology of various phases of the castle's building, point out unexecuted works, and to expose the inauthenticity of the postern gate on the castle's east side.[33]

At the beginning of 1912, having heard that money had been subscribed to complete the choir at Paisley Abbey, Anderson wrote to Stirling Maxwell reminding him that he had already drawn up plans for the work, and expressing the hope that he would be asked to act as architect. Stirling Maxwell then wrote to Paisley, suggesting that Anderson was the logical choice. A reply from Paisley indicated quite forcibly that the authorities there had 'no wish to repeat the experience'. The writer, the Rev. McLean, had already 'secured a threatening letter from him which is quite sufficient to show we have made a fortunate escape'. Besides, he pointed out, Anderson was now an old man, and since the work would take six to eight years, it was doubtful that he would be able to complete it.[34] The Paisley authorities had already selected Peter Macgregor Chalmers, whom, they felt, was taking the place Anderson had once occupied as Scotland's leading restorer. With tenacity and loyalty, Stirling Maxwell wrote back to McLean declining convenorship of the Building Committee, and stating that Anderson's designs were 'immeasurably better' than those of Chalmers. McLean, no respecter of persons, wrote back rather intemperately that in his opinion the reverse was the case. In spite of enlisting the support of other heritors, and even the Office of Works, the Paisley Committee refused to be persuaded and thus the final phase of the restoration began without Stirling Maxwell and was completed without Anderson.

As well as being hurt by developments at Paisley, Anderson was becoming increasingly anxious about the National Art Survey drawings. The Survey was still continuing from its new base, and the finished drawings were being added to the Portrait Gallery collection. Attempts were made to involve the main Scottish art schools in 1910 and 1911, but, in spite of funding being made available by the Education Department, nothing was done except at Glasgow where the erection of scaffolding in the cathedral in 1912 enabled two Glasgow students to draw parts of its upper reaches. After this, no other college participated.[35] On 11 March 1913, Anderson resigned from the Board of Edinburgh College of Art 'to make way for younger men', perhaps influenced by the comments about his age coming from Paisley. In the meantime, the existing drawings were being traced under the supervision of Henry F. Kerr, this being the National Gallery Board's response to the College of Art's request that the drawings should be printed to allow easy access by students. At the outbreak of the Great War the Survey was discontinued, and the drawings and tracings were put into storage. By this point a great many antiquities had been surveyed, and, although the protectionist attitude of the Gallery Board had prevented students from using the drawings as freely as Anderson would have liked, there was nevertheless a strong appreciation of the collection's worth, and there had also been some talk of publication.

When the war broke out Anderson was in poor health. Over the previous decade he had put on weight and had suffered intermittent illness, no doubt exacerbated by the reversals experienced with his pet projects. Early in 1911 he had gifted some of his best Blue China to Holyrood Palace, and this had been followed by gifts of cisterns in the spring of 1914. On 8 September that year, in order to avoid its undignified, posthumous disposal in salerooms, he offered to give the Palace his entire collection.[36] The gift was also intended as a gesture of loyalty to the King and at the same time fulfilled what he saw as a genuine need to brighten up some of Holyrood's corners. In the course of meetings about the china with W.T. Oldrieve of the Office of Works, he also made arrangements for the freshening up of the tablets he had designed in memory of Mary of Lorraine and Kirkcaldy of Grange at Edinburgh Castle. The lettering was recut and the stones washed.[37] The onset of the war had naturally reduced the amount of work passing through the practice, and the honour and challenge associated with the consolidation of the remains at Sweetheart Abbey, a commission in progress since 1910, had by the war years worn off.[38] Quite clearly, Anderson's great spirit had sunk to the lowest depths, and by 1916 he was again in the grip of serious illness.

In 1916 the Royal Institute of British Architects awarded Anderson its Royal Gold Medal, and with it there came a great uplift in his morale and sense of self-worth. There had been pressure for some time to honour him in this way. As early as 1912 the Glasgow Institute of Architects had voiced their unanimous support for his nomination, and when his name came up again in 1916 the RIBA Council were also unanimous.[39] He was, however, too ill to attend the presentation personally, sending Alexander Lorne Campbell to read out his address. The Lord Provost of Edinburgh, Sir Robert Inches, a friend from the earliest days of the School of Applied Art, accepted the medal on his behalf. Anderson's address expressed his gratitude and honour at being the first home-based Scotsman to receive the medal, especially since, unlike other awards, it was reputedly based on merit.[40] After commenting on the interaction between Scots and English architecture since the time of the Union, Anderson next outlined his reasons for starting the School of Applied Art and the National Art Survey, taking cognizance of the fact that the Gold Medal had in part been awarded because of his educational efforts.

In doing so, he again took the opportunity to explain his architectural philosophy; what was taught in the School of Applied Art was the primacy of function, visible in the careful analysis of old Scottish architecture, and hence the importance of the National Art Survey. But the message was not just for Scottish consumption. There was, he argued, evidence of a growing adherence to these principles throughout Britain, to the extent that 'we can now look forward to our buildings becoming more and more characteristic of the age and purposes to which they are devoted'. The honour, he concluded, was 'well worth a lifetime of earnest labour and thought'. Sir John Burnet, by then Vice-President of the Royal Institute, proposed a vote of thanks to the Provost of Edinburgh, taking the opportunity to state that

> we are all indebted . . . to those men who, like Sir Rowand Anderson, have made the needs of each building a subject of earnest research, and keeping clearly before them the fitness of the structure for its purpose, have been content to express it with that breadth and simplicity, free from all conscious effort to produce effect, which characterises the masterpieces of all time.[41]

Finally, Sir Robert Inches responded with an affectionate tribute to his old friend, making special mention of the fact that Anderson some years previously had personally designed ceremonial halberds for Edinburgh, a token of his deep love for his native city.

Anderson, as if injected with fire, soon shook off his illness to engage in his next great project. On 6 October 1916 Lorne Campbell, acting on Anderson's behalf, approached John Watson and William Whitie of the Institute of Glasgow Architects about the formation of a national institute.[42] The demise of the Architectural Institute of Scotland had occurred in the early 1870s; it had simply petered out. In the middle 1850s accusations of dominance by Edinburgh architects had appeared in the letters columns of the *Building Chronicle*, and John Honeyman had indicated that this had been a source of difficulty in a speech made in 1882. What was more, the Institute had not encouraged the younger men, and in Edinburgh this had actually led to the formation of the Edinburgh Architectural Association, which soon eclipsed the senior body. However the lack of a national association was keenly felt, in spite of the growing influence of the Royal Institute, which had increasingly attracted young architects. It offered an examination system, plus membership of an increasingly powerful professional body, its main drawback being the absence of a specifically Scottish perspective.

On 19 October John Watson, William Whitie and A.N. Paterson, representing the Glasgow Institute, met Lorne Campbell and T.F. McLennan, representing the Edinburgh Architectural Association, at a meeting in Edinburgh chaired by Anderson. Thereafter Whitie drafted a constitution, and on 30 November a resolution creating the Institute was passed. Dundee and Aberdeen had been approached in the interim, and all parties gave the proposal 'a most cordial and enthusiastic reception'. A year later, Inverness joined the Institute. The federal basis of the new body was calculated to overcome some of the problems of its predecessor. It was to have five chapters, each having its own independent existence and localised activities. The new Institute would, in contrast, represent the 'voice of Scotland', and at the same time organise its own periodic events and specialist committees. Essentially, this meant the addition of an extra national tier above the local associations. The relationship between the new body and the RIBA was clarified at an early stage. A.N. Paterson voiced the view of many when he insisted that the new body should not in any way impair the RIBA's 'natural predominance' as the central authority for the United Kingdom; this was agreed.[43]

Acknowledgement of the Royal Institute's supremacy had not come easily to Anderson. In the 1880s he had expressed doubts about its relevance to Scottish architecture. Together with other eminent architects, he had in 1892 signed the petition sent to the RIBA during the 'profession or art' controversy, questioning the appropriateness of the Institute's technically biased examinations to a profession involved in the aesthetic realm.[44] Having been assured, together with the others, that the Institute was not seeking to create a 'closed profession', his attitudes gradually relaxed, and in 1903 he had been elected a Fellow. His application had been supported by John Belcher, then in highly successful practice with J.J. Joass, as well as T.E. Collcutt and Aston Webb, who was then President. Acceptance of the Institute's Royal Gold Medal was in itself a full and final token of his acquiescence.

It soon became clear that Anderson's initiative, which had come with a gift of £5000 to the new Institute, was not entirely free of ulterior motives. In November 1916, prior to its formal creation, Anderson had managed to persuade the secretaries of the participating architectural associations to sign a letter to the Secretary of State. This alleged that the National Art Survey drawings had virtually been stolen from Edinburgh College of Art, to whom legal title belonged, and that they were a closed book to architects and public alike.[45] A reminder, advising the Secretary of State that the signatory bodies had now become the Institute of Scottish Architects, was sent when no reply had been received by May 1917. A minute of advice to the Secretary of State informed him that Anderson's gift of £5000 to the Institute was conditional on the Institute fighting for the National Art Survey drawings, an exaggeration but not entirely groundless. The Secretary of State's reply denied that there was any defect in the National Gallery Board's title to the drawings, and that he would pursue the question of publication when the war was ended. Anderson was not wholly satisfied, but the activities of the new Institute called for his immediate attention.

In spite of his protestations that 'someone younger and more active' should be chosen, he was unanimously elected president of the new body when its first annual conference took place at 117 George Street, Edinburgh on 8 June 1917. In his presidential speech he referred to the 'remarkable unanimity of feeling' among Scottish architects which had brought the Institute about, and their particular concern for the 'improvement of working class housing'. He also stressed the necessity to provide proper architectural education for the young. A congratulatory telegram arrived from the RIBA. Late in 1917 a National Art Survey Committee was set up in the new Institute. It met the National Gallery Board in December 1917, by which time agreement had been reached that the Survey should be published. By this point it was clear to Anderson that this was the best solution that could be achieved, and he therefore provided a thousand pounds to the Institute, who then contributed it as a subsidy for the Survey's publication. This was matched by the provision of a further thousand pounds over five years by the National Gallery Board.[46]

Anderson's last years were taken up with the business of the new Institute and the impending publication of the first batch of National Art Survey drawings. He had been active at the Institute's meetings and at subcommittee meetings throughout 1917, but illness restrained his activities in 1918, although developments were regularly reported to him. By 1918 the new Institute had 390 members and was growing fast. From the start it had been supported by the finest of Scotland's architects. Sir J.J. Burnet succeeded Anderson as President. He had been interested in the Institute since its earliest days and had sent up suggestions on its constitution from London. Anderson's absence in 1918 did not inhibit its healthy growth. Committees were formed to look after such matters as the welfare of demobilised architects after the war and to monitor developments in the provision of working class housing in the post-war period. Mainstream business included the establishment of standard scales of fees and the acquisition of a royal charter. By 1919, Anderson was back in harness; at this juncture the RIBA had expressed their opposition to the Scottish Institute's pursuit of a charter, since it was felt this would conflict with RIBA's position as the leading professional body for architects in the United Kingdom.[47] At the request of the Committee, Burnet negotiated informally with the Royal Institute's President, and after several meetings and exchanges of correspondence in 1920 the Royal

Institute declared itself partly satisfied. The new Institute was to become a Chapter of the Royal Institute in place of the local associations.

Anderson attended his final meeting of the Institute on 20 April 1920. By 7 May 1920 he had prepared his last will and testament. At a meeting of the Institute on 16 June that year, it was reported that Anderson was again ill, whereupon the Institute sent a telegram to Colinton with the Committee's hopes for a speedy recovery. On 30 July, as a token of the genuine reverence in which he was held, A.N. Paterson proposed that a bronze bust of Anderson should be commissioned by the Institute from Pittendreigh McGillivray. This was unanimously agreed to, and McGillivray began the work. The sculptor found that his sitter was intermittently unwell, and had occasionally to cancel or abandon sittings. Anderson had a nurse in full-time attendance and was receiving frequent visits from his friend and medical adviser, Dr Scotland of Colinton.

On 4 October 1920, at the request of Sir David Hunter Blair, Anderson wrote an appendix to his biography of the Marquess of Bute. It was, as usual, a model of lucidity as well as an insight into a unique relationship of thirty years' duration, a relationship quite remarkable in view of the two strong and diverse personalities involved. The disagreements, of which there had undoubtedly been a number, made no lasting difference to the friendship. Indeed, Anderson had visited Bute with increasing regularity during the final decade of his life. The architect in his tribute took the opportunity to recall Bute's great patience over architectural decisions, carefully denying the rumours of financial extravagance that had followed his great patron. Anderson next hinted at the disagreements, stating that Bute 'by no means always bowed the knee to authority', a salient example being his rejection of pure Gothic railings for the gallery at Mount Stuart. Anderson was despatched to copy the rails surrounding Charlemagne's tomb at Aix la Chapelle instead, and had been forced to admit that the end result was extremely good. The appendix was addressed from 16 Rutland Square. In a sense, Anderson had never retired.[48]

On 21 January 1921 Lady Anderson died. At their meeting that month the Institute of Scottish Architects sent a 'memorial' to Anderson assuring him of 'their continued esteem and devotion' on his bereavement. At the same meeting it was announced that the Royal Institute's objections to the Royal Charter could be overcome if the Scottish Institute was prepared to refer to it in its draft Royal Charter as 'the parent body'. This was acceptable. On 1 June 1921, shortly after he had strongly approved of McGillivray's fine bust in clay and had seen the first offprints from the National Art Survey drawings, Anderson died at 'Allermuir', aged eighty-seven.

On 6 June his funeral service took place at St James' Church,

Plate 88. Rowand Anderson's gravestone, Warriston Cemetery, Edinburgh (Author).

Inverleith. The large and distinguished attendance of mourners included Sir John Burnet, Sir Robert Lorimer and Sir John R. Findlay. Sir Henry Cook represented the Royal Company of Archers. His pall bearers were Sir Alfred Ewing, Principal of Edinburgh University, Sir J. Lawton Wingate, President of the Royal Scottish Academy, W.T. Oldrieve, representing the RIBA, and Alexander N. Paterson, President of the Institute of Scottish Architects. His ashes were interred in a casket of oak, his favourite wood, at Warriston Cemetery, beside the mortal remains of his beloved wife and daughter. The grave is marked by a small but beautiful stone erected for Annie Ross Anderson nearly fifty years earlier (Plate 88).

POSTSCRIPT

Rowand Anderson's personal fortune amounted to just under £70 000, which, at today's prices, would have made him a millionaire a number of times over. In life, Anderson had been extremely careful with money, as well as selectively generous; and so it was in death. His will was fastidiously drawn up in order to ensure that his intentions were carried out to the letter. His remaining relations, a few cousins living at a distance, were the first beneficiaries. His generosity also extended to a former secretary, his chauffeur, a godson in Canada, and his doctor, nurse and household staff at 'Allermuir'. Next, legacies were given to local hospitals, and to various other charities for the relief of the poor and the prevention of cruelty to children and animals. A sum of money was left to St Cuthbert's Church and to the local parish church for providing coal and food to the poor. Five hundred pounds were left to the Society of Antiquaries, and the same amount was left, significantly, to the pension fund of the Royal Scottish Academy. Three thousand pounds were left for the purchase of a plot of ground and the erection of a cottage to house a district nurse for Colinton. This building was to be called the 'Lady Rowand Anderson Memorial Cottage'. A sum of money was left to the Company of Archers to provide for 'match dinners'.

Among the special bequests designed to dispose of the contents of 'Allermuir', his French silver, Archer's uniforms and 'shooting graith' were given to the Archers, the latter to form part of a historic collection. Some antique guns, a Moorish dagger and some china were given to the Marquess of Bute. His Highland clothing and kilts were to be given to some friends in Dumfries for distribution among their sons, including a godson. Above all, Anderson was generous to the Institute of Scottish Architects. He bequeathed them his library, medals, diplomas and illuminated addresses, together with items of furniture and tableware. These were to be placed in his town house at 15 Rutland Square, which was given to the Institute as its new headquarters.

In the sixth clause of his will Anderson effected a masterstroke, sufficient in its own right to ensure that his name will never be forgotten by the Scottish architectural profession. He left the residue of his estate to the new Institute subject to the proviso that it secured a Royal Charter within two years of his death, an act which he knew was dear to their hearts and well within their grasp. This was duly done, a fact of which the Institute's chief benefactor would have been immensely proud.[49]

8

A Great Scot

Anderson's obituary notices were appropriately long and detailed, and on the whole, surprisingly accurate and objective. The *Builder* began its tribute as follows:

> On the death of Sir Rowand Anderson on June 1 at the advanced age of 87 years, there passed the greatest power in the architecture of Scotland of the past half century. His greatness is to be measured not only by his personal achievements but also by the stimulus he imparted to and the influence he exercised on the generation younger than himself. Not only did he re-assert the high standard of design which former Scottish masters of the art both practised and proclaimed, but he insisted upon the principles of simple and direct construction and the maintenance of high craftsmanship which are always associated with purity of design.[1]

While enumerating Anderson's major works, the writer made special mention of the 'dignity and stateliness' of his Edinburgh schools. These schools, together with his earlier church work, were 'full of knowledge and understanding of the [Gothic] style' and 'marked a new era' in its practice in Scotland.

His work at Edinburgh University Medical School was a demonstration of his 'immense capacity' and displayed 'an equally scholarly knowledge' of the Italian Renaissance style. His restorations were carried out with 'loving care and reverence'. He was also 'extremely felicitous in his decorative monuments', indeed, the writer felt that Anderson's greatest gift was 'the big mind, civic and monumental in character', and he believed that the Medical School was his 'chef d'oeuvre', with the McEwan Hall ranking 'among the noblest in the kingdom'. Reflecting the obvious fact that no architect, however gifted, can excel in every branch of design, the writer next faulted Anderson for lacking 'that touch of kindliness so essential to the maker of homes'. This criticism is particularly apt in relation to his smaller houses, especially those on the Braid Estate or at Barnshot Road in Colinton, where fine proportion, elegant detail and lofty effects do not always come off. In larger buildings these features elevate, while in smaller buildings they intimidate. On balance, though, the *Builder* judged that Anderson's achievement was of the highest order, an appraisal that still seems sound today.

His obituarist was, however, also critical of the Gothic style selected for the National Portrait Gallery and Museum of Antiquities, which, he felt, had resulted in the window tracery excluding part of the light, a factor not wholly compensated for by the 'stately and impressive exterior'. Here the writer is on less sure ground, since larger windows in the same style would have admitted as much light as windows in another style; in any case, developments in electric lighting technology would soon remove what problems there might have been. An insight into Anderson's use of assistants was also provided:

> With no gift of draughtsmanship himself, he had the marvellous power of compelling others to express his ideas. He knew precisely what he wanted and never failed to get it, sometimes without putting his own pencil to paper. Nevertheless, his work was as entirely his own and as completely the expression of his power and personality as though he had drawn every line with his own hand.[2]

While the gist of this statement is perfectly accurate, it is based on an underassessment of Anderson's drafting skills, which are quite apparent from his book of continental tour drawings. The writer might, of course, have been alluding to his comparative inability to produce 'artistic' impressions of buildings with the panache of, say, Norman Shaw, Nesfield, or even Billings. Over against this, such work was largely irrelevant to Anderson's architectural approach. Less controversially, Anderson's obituarist continued with an account of his educational activities and his involvement in the creation of the Institute of Scottish Architects, concluding that the Royal Institute of British Architects had 'all too tardily recognised his commanding position and outstanding ability as an architect', with the award of the Royal Gold Medal in 1916.

In keeping with its late recognition of Anderson, the RIBA's tribute, contained in its *Journal*, was based on second-hand information and studded with inaccuracies. It wrongly stated that his birthplace was Forres, and that his only training in construction and design was obtained 'in the ranks of the Royal Engineers when quartered at Edinburgh Castle'. The account did however redeem itself, when after citing a number of his successful buildings it observed that

> the personal note which characterises all his works . . . is that of largeness and nobility of treatment, studied proportion in mass, combined with refinement and elegance in detail. His planning in like manner, is direct, simple, balanced, throughout the work is that of the head rather than the heart.[3]

The final phrase sums up extremely well the feelings of beauty, reason and control aroused in the spectator as he or she stands before one of Anderson's best buildings. These works emit a sense of classical calm and completeness, far removed from, but no less worthy than, the expressive power of F.T. Pilkington or the originality of C.R. Mackintosh. Its source was Anderson's character, restrained, sober and practical, quintessentially Scottish, content to express function in preference to aesthetic display. Having captured the essence of Anderson's architecture, the obituary concluded with appropriate tribute to his committee and educational work.

In contrast with the RIBA's remote assessment, Alexander N. Paterson's *Appreciation* was based on his close personal acquaintance with Anderson. In his presidential address to the annual convention of the Institute of Scottish Architects on 21 June 1921, he began that

> it has commonly been remarked of Sir Rowand Anderson that his force of character, breadth of view, and determination of spirit, together with his powerful constitution would have made him great in whatever sphere his work had lain.[4]

Paterson saw Anderson as 'first of all a great Scot', who

> preferred to return [from London] to his native country, and throughout his long life remained a stout protagonist of things Scottish, of the interest and beauty of its national architecture, and the importance to the student of a thorough knowledge of its early examples in relation to the work, however divergent in requirements, of the present day.[5]

He next noted that while Anderson was organising and directing the School of Applied Art, 'he was still in the full flood of his career, as, by general admission, the premier architect of Scotland'. Mention of these factors alone was inadequate, however.

> As a great Scot we honour him, as a great educationist also, but most of all as a great architect. It is needless for me, in a gathering of Scottish architects, to enumerate the many buildings erected to his design and restored under his direction.[6]

Having been involved from the very beginning in the Institute of Scottish Architects, Paterson next outlined its genesis, making Anderson's vital role in it clear:

> To others the idea [of a Scottish Institute] had been present, but a leader and capital were wanted; a leader under whom mutual distrust and difficulties would be forgotten, capital essential to the working of a central institute without crippling the resources and energies of the local societies.[7]

It was Paterson's privilege, in concluding his remarks, to be able to announce Anderson's generous bequests to the Institute, which he felt 'is itself his memorial'. It was nevertheless his hope that a monument might be set up in recognition of his many attainments.

While Anderson's obituarists astutely assessed his architectural achieve-ments and the importance of his educational and committee work, the constraints of time, space and chronological proximity prevented them from dwelling in detail on the influence he exerted on other architects and on Scottish architecture generally. His wide influence throughout the late Victorian period is indisputable. The great thrust of his teaching, that an undue emphasis on pictorial values was harming architecture, had helped turn the tide of public opinion away from the excesses of the Scots Baronial and cognate styles, and was instrumental in producing the re-fined and sophisticated purpose-built structures erected in many Scottish cities over that period. By the Edwardian period, 'free' styles had emerged, and it might be concluded that the arrival of the Arts and Crafts and Art Nouveau styles, together with the technologies of steel and ferro-concrete framing, meant that his teaching was played out. This was far from the case. In the area of restoration alone, his work would set the standard for decades to come, especially at Dunblane, widely regarded as the finest of its kind. In the work of many architects, and in many other ways, his influence lived on well beyond his lifetime.

Burnet himself had in 1916 paid homage to Anderson's influence, strongly implying that his own freely and logically planned buildings owed more to the thinking of men like Anderson than to the rigid axial symmetry still taught in the Ecole des Beaux Arts long after he had left it. A specific example of possible influence is the Barony Church, Glasgow, designed by Burnet with his partner J.J. Campbell. Its wide nave and pierced chancel arch may well owe something to Anderson's Gerona-like layout at Govan Old Parish Church and, indeed, it is beyond dispute that Anderson's ecclesiologically inspired churches were in large measure responsible for a shift towards archaeological accuracy in Scottish church architecture generally.

On the secular front, the last decade of the nineteenth century and the first two decades of the twentieth witnessed a revival of the Scots archi-tecture of the sixteenth and seventeenth centuries. A series of buildings, stripped of the excesses of the earlier Baronial revival, started to appear in the wake of Anderson's productions at 'Allermuir', Pollokshaws, Govan and Glencoe. This was brought about by a number of factors: the Bryce students were advanced in years and declining in influence, and Mac-Gibbon and Ross had published *The Castellated and Domestic Architecture of Scotland* between 1887 and 1892, mainly for antiquarian reasons. The Edinburgh Architectural Association's sketchbooks, pushed on by Ander-son, were in the process of publication, and from the middle 1890s, the National Art Survey was being made and regularly exhibited. In 1891 no less a figure than Charles Rennie Mackintosh noted in a highly poetic paper on 'Scottish Baronial Architecture' that

from some recent buildings which have been erected it is clearly

> evident that this style is coming to life again and I only hope that it
> will not be strangled in its infancy by indiscriminate unsympathetic
> people who will copy its ancient examples without beginning to make
> them conform to modern requirements.[8]

It was not. An achievement for which Anderson could claim major
responsibility.

Proof may be found in the 1908 publication entitled *Domestic Architecture
in Scotland*, a volume containing sixty-six captioned illustrations of 'Scottish Domestic Work of Recent Years'. As well as showing how widespread
the style had become, the book was full of examples by prominent
Anderson ex-students, former assistants or associates including Robert
Lorimer, Ramsay Traquair, Washington Browne, Alexander N. Paterson,
Sydney Mitchell and Wilson, John James Burnet, Lorne Campbell and
James Jerdan. Their designs point directly to his influence, not only in
their restrained seventeenth century Scottish styling, but in their use of
coloured stones and slates. The work of provincial architects such as Alex
Cullen or Thoms and Wilkie was also illustrated, and suggests the same
inspiration.[9]

As late as 1922, the Edinburgh Architectural Association published
Details of Scottish Domestic Architecture, with a text by James Gillespie, ex-
National Art Survey bursar and Anderson pupil. The book was dedicated
to Anderson, who had both conceived the volume and aided its publication with advice and finance. Its preface amounted to a summary of
Anderson's hopes for the development of a national architecture; after
pointing out that Billings' work lacked measurements, plans or details,
and that MacGibbon and Ross had provided few measured drawings, the
view was expressed that the features illustrated would be 'rich in
suggestions for present day architects'. These included drawings of
gateways, doors, porches, oriels, dormers, balconies, corbelling, turrets,
chimneys, stairs, fireplaces and furniture, and it was felt that 'a careful
study of these details will not only lead to a fuller appreciation and
knowledge of our native art, but help to foster the Scottish tradition in
modern work'. Gillespie, recognising that the use of the plates by modern
architects was 'not so simple', hoped that the 'spirit of the old work may
be caught, and only such features used as may be adapted to modern
conditions'.

Details is evidence of the strength of the new Scots architecture: at the
time of its publication, the movement was entering its fourth decade. It
is also evidence of Anderson's increasing desire to foster it, one of the consuming passions of his final years. Typically, it was also a failsafe device
to ensure that at least part of the National Survey would be published.
Many of the drawings in *Details* came from this source. In the event,
Anderson need not have been concerned. The first volume of the Survey

ARGYLL LODGING, STIRLING.

ELEVATION OF N. SIDE OF COURTYARD

EAST ELEVATION

CENTRE PART OF WEST ELEVATION TO COURTYARD

SECTION

Plate 89. Argyll Lodging, Stirling, measured drawings (*National Art Survey*, Vol. II).

was published in 1921, a second in 1923, a third in 1925, and the fourth and last in 1933 (Plates 89–91). The full extent of Anderson's success in encouraging a national architecture has not yet been researched, but the evidence in many a Scots town suggests that it was considerable, especially in the years up to and immediately succeeding the Great War. Houses and small civic buildings, seventeenth century Scots in style and sometimes touched by Arts and Crafts influence, abound.

Anderson's influence on the major figures trained in his office was, of course, of paramount importance for Scottish architecture. Sir Robert

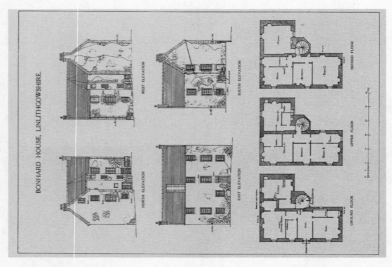

Plate 90. Bonhard House, Linlithgow, measured drawings (*National Art Survey*, Vol. II).

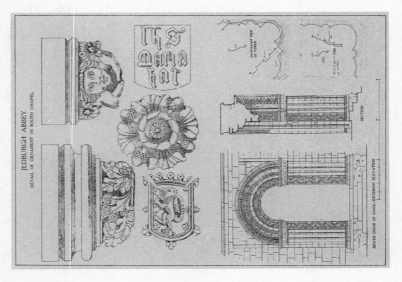

Plate 91. Jedburgh Abbey, measured drawings (*National Art Survey*, Vol. III).

Plate 92. Ardkinglas, Argyll, by Sir Robert Lorimer (National Monuments Record of Scotland).

Lorimer (1864–1929) served his apprenticeship in the 1880s, subsequently became chief assistant, leaving for an eighteen-month spell in Bodley's London office before returning (via Maclaren) to Edinburgh in order to set up in practice in 1893. Leslie Graham Thomson, writing Lorimer's obituary in 1929, affirmed that 'he paid homage to the "fitness for purpose" ideal', and that his greatest service to architecture was 'the rescuing of a noble national style from the oblivion into which the exaggerations of a Bryce and Burn had cast it', two of Anderson's central tenets.[10] Thomson also acknowledged that 'while a pupil in Sir R. Rowand Anderson's office he must have found time for an intensive study of old Scots buildings', an interest extended when Lorimer took over from the late David MacGibbon as a member of the Joint Committee of the School of Applied Art. Lorimer also became co-editor of the second folio of the National Art Survey in 1923, and was active in the early years of the Institute of Scottish Architects. These common interests are crucial to an understanding of the visual affinity between Anderson's work and buildings by Lorimer such as Ardkinglas, Formakin, or Briglands (Plate 92). There are obvious differences: Lorimer's large buildings are softer, take more liberties with rounded forms and in their details, and distort historical precedent just sufficiently to be describable as Arts and Crafts work. In large measure, too, Lorimer's distinguished restorations and late

Plate 93. Well Court, Edinburgh, by Arthur George Sydney Mitchell (National Monuments Record of Scotland).

Gothic work at St Giles for example, owe much to his experience at Dunblane and his exposure to Anderson's church work.

Arthur George Sydney Mitchell (1856–1930), an architect whose large and fine oeuvre has not yet received the recognition it deserves, joined the Anderson office as a pupil c. 1878, commencing practice in 1883. At Well Court, Edinburgh (1883–6), Mitchell's debt to Anderson is obvious (Plate 93). The seventeenth century styling, red roof tiles and the use of Corsehill stone are derived directly from his master. So too is Dr Guthrie's Boys' School, Lasswade Road, Edinburgh, where the vigorous Gothic of Anderson's Edinburgh and Fife schools is freely borrowed. While faithful to Anderson's functional planning in this latter commission, Mitchell is somewhat less rational and austere than Anderson at Well Court. The proliferation of dormers with tiny catslide roofs is a clear indication that Mitchell's approach is more visual and sculpturesque. Mitchell's reluctance to wholly embrace the spirit of the Anderson office may be judged from the fact that his own house, the Pleasance, Gullane, was in an English style. Nevertheless, stylistically Mitchell owes Anderson an immense debt, strongly discernible in the many restrained classical houses he erected in Edinburgh and its environs, and in the fine churches erected in the same city.

Robert Weir Schultz (1861–1951) completed his training in the Anderson office in 1884, moving to London for a spell with Shaw and then Ernest George and Peto. Schultz was not interested in the hurly burly of a large practice, and early on his two consuming interests came to the surface: Byzantine archaeology and a preoccupation with the Arts and Crafts movement. From 1891 onwards, the architect was able to combine both interests in the smallish commissions he undertook for the Third and Fourth Marquesses of Bute, the most well known of which is perhaps St Andrew's Chapel in Bentley's Westminster Cathedral. Schultz was also responsible for the small Archepiscopal chapel at Morningside, Edinburgh, where his scholarly detailing and interest in the formal qualities of building materials are shown to good effect. The Gothic revival, with its emphasis on the study of 'old work', has been identified as the main source of the Arts and Crafts movement, and it is therefore no surprise that Anderson's office was a springboard for several architects later distinguished for their work in this idiom, namely Frank Troup and F.W. Bidlake.

A much closer follower was Arthur Forman Balfour Paul (1875–1938), whose ready absorption of the Anderson aesthetic was referred to in Chapter Seven. His complete understanding of Anderson's Scots Jacobean work is again visible in the Lady Anderson Memorial Cottage at Thorburn Road in Colinton (Plate 94). This building, carried out under the terms of Anderson's will, is clearly a tribute to his former partner, and incorporates all his favourite Scots Jacobean touches, gable chimneys, asymmetrical crow-stepped gables, slit windows and reinforcing arches, all correctly and functionally deployed. Later works reveal more compatability of spirit. At Edinburgh University's Chemistry Block (King's Buildings), built from 1922 to 1924, Paul produced a quietly dignified Wrenaissance building in red brick with red sandstone dressings. Its homely if slightly lugubrious aspect shows Paul to have been a competent, but not great, architect, a conclusion which might also be drawn from a study of his Kimmerghame House at Fettes College, a building in the Gothic style noticeably lacking in the incisive quality typical of Anderson's best work.

The Watson brothers, John (1853–1924) and George Mackie (1859–

Plate 94. Lady Anderson Memorial Cottage, Colinton, by Arthur Forman Balfour Paul (Author).

1948), both faithfully followed the Anderson aesthetic in practices which were much less successful than some of those mentioned above. John, partner of Charles McArthy, of whom no details survive, had sketched 'old work' with Anderson in the 1870s. The partners produced a number of buildings deriving directly from the Anderson style, including a good double villa at 26–28 Polwarth Road, Edinburgh (1896), closely related to Anderson's design for 13 Braid Road (1890). At Blackhall Primary School, Edinburgh (1907), Anderson's motifs and planning rationale are employed with unspectacular results. Similarly at Falkirk Public Library, a competition win, good planning, red sandstone and Gothic details produce a building that works well but does not greatly impress. John Watson was Head of Architecture at Edinburgh College of Art from 1908 to 1914, keeping Anderson's teaching methodology alive during these years. He was also President of the Edinburgh Architectural Association in 1908–9. George Mackie Watson joined the Anderson Office as a pupil in 1876, and, by virtue of his drafting talents, had become 'head man' in 1884, commencing practice in 1899, after which he continued for a number of years as architectural teacher in the School of Applied Art. Watson had the misfortune to win a number of architectural competitions where his designs were not carried out. He was, however, successful in the competition for St Serf's, Goldenacre, where his church was completed less its tower, which would have been closely based on Anderson's late Gothic designs for St Paul's, Greenock, or Morningside. The potential of a good design was not, therefore, realised.

Son of Phoebe Traquair the painter, student at the School of Applied

Art and prize-winning National Art Survey Bursar, Ramsay Traquair designed several interesting buildings in Edinburgh before emigrating to Canada. Most relevant from the point of view of the Anderson influence is Mackenzie House, belonging to Edinburgh Academy and located in Kinnear Road. This fine building seems to embody all that Anderson hoped for in the revival of national architecture, without being slavishly copyist. Glimpses of the Anderson influence also appear in the work of John Kinross, an architect of high reputation but small output. In 1886 Kinross had erected a house at No. 1 Cluny Gardens on the Braid Estate which might easily be mistaken for Anderson's work. Its general sense of elegance and the lofty look achieved with the help of Renaissance motifs combine with red sandstone construction to excellent effect. At 31–35 Mortonhall Road and 24 Oswald Road, Edinburgh, Kinross also designed (c. 1888) four asymmetrically planned, crow-stepped and dormered detached houses, one of which was for himself. These appear to derive from 'Allermuir'.

Judged even by this preliminary assessment of Anderson's influence, it is clear that, like most of his other achievements, it is without parallel in Scottish architecture.

* * *

It is fitting to conclude by examining what remains of this magnificent heritage. Anderson's architectural theories, in essence derived from the High Victorian functionalists, were eventually overtaken in Scotland in the third and fourth decades of the present century by the anti-historical functionalism of Gropius and Le Corbusier. The development of a national style as he had conceived it was also curtailed by two world wars and the economic depressions sandwiched in between. The majority of Anderson's buildings still, however, remain for all to see, and his beloved National Art Survey forms the backbone of the drawings collection at the National Monuments Record of Scotland. At Edinburgh College of Art, too, the architectural education he instituted as far back as 1892 still continues, albeit in a form he would not recognise. It is, though, in the Royal Incorporation of Architects in Scotland, the body that, more than any other man, he had helped create, that his influence is still most tangibly felt. At its headquarters, next door to the architectural practice that still bears his name, his bronze bust and portrait preside over meetings held in rooms furnished with his books and personal effects, and where something of his powerful, patriarchal personality can yet be sensed. The Royal Incorporation is as active and successful today as at any time since its foundation, and remains conscious of the obligation, contained in its first Charter, 'To foster the study of the National Architecture of Scotland and to encourage its development', a cause that, more than any other, had been dear to Robert Rowand Anderson's heart.

Notes and References

CHAPTER 1

1. Scottish Record Office (SRO), Register of Sasines 7105 and PR 1496.58. James Anderson and his wife disposed of a cottage, gig house and grounds on the Drum Estate in 1837.
2. Merchants' Hall, Edinburgh, George Watson's Hospital Roll Book, 1841.
3. Alexander Heron, *The Rise and Progress of the Company of Merchants of the City of Edinburgh, 1681–1902* (Edinburgh, 1903), 84.
4. William Adam, *Vitruvius Scoticus*, ed. James Simpson (Edinburgh, 1980), 151.
5. Merchants' Hall, Edinburgh, George Watson's Hospital Governors' Minute Books, 1841–9.
6. Merchants' Hall, Edinburgh, George Watson's Hospital Cash Books, 1849–53.
7. SRO Trustees' Academy, Lists of Students, 1848–56, NG1/51/1.
8. *Scotsman*, 1850–1, passim.

CHAPTER 2

1. Inventory of pictures belonging to Lessels, contained in Dowell's (Auctioneers) List, 4 March 1884, 391.
2. *Scotsman*, 13 November 1883, 5.
3. National Monuments Record of Scotland (NMRS), copy drawings BWD 91/2 and BWD 91/3.
4. NMRS, copy drawings BWD 56/2 and BWD 1741.
5. R. Brydall, *Art in Scotland* (Edinburgh and London, 1889), 146–7.
6. Library of the Edinburgh Architectural Association, *History and Reminiscences of the Edinburgh Architectural Association* (Typescript), G.S. Aitken, 1913, 9–10.
7. V. Fiddes and A. Rowan, *Mr. David Bryce*, Exhibition Catalogue (Edinburgh, 1976), passim.
8. Esme Gordon, *The Royal Scottish Academy of Painting, Sculpture and Architecture* (Edinburgh, 1976), 89.
9. *Transactions of the Architectural Institute of Scotland* Session 1850–1, 141–58.
10. Ibid.
11. *Trans. Arch. Inst. Scot.*, Session 1852–3, 29.
12. Ibid., 34.
13. *Trans. Arch. Inst. Scot.*, Session 1853–4, 58.
14. Ibid.
15. Ibid, 59.
16. *Trans. Arch. Inst. Scot.*, Session 1859–60, 54–62.
17. Ibid, 62.

18. *Building Chronicle*, February 1855, 153.
19. *Building Chronicle*, June 1854, 14.
20. James L. Caw, *Scottish Painting 1620–1908* (Edinburgh, 1908), 226.
21. *Building Chronicle*, May 1854, 4–5.
22. Ibid.
23. Ibid.
24. *Building Chronicle*, April 1857, 181.
25. *Building Chronicle*, January 1856, 6–7.
26. W. Moir Bryce, *History of the Old Greyfrairs Church, Edinburgh* (Edinburgh and London, 1912), 147.
27. *Building Chronicle*, May 1857, 195.

CHAPTER 3

1. Gavin Stamp and Colin Amery, *Victorian Buildings of London 1837–1887* (London, 1982), 69–71.
2. Basil H. Jackson (ed.), *Recollections of Thomas Graham Jackson 1835–1924* (London, New York, Toronto, 1950), 51–61.
3. David Cole, *The Work of Sir Gilbert Scott* (London, 1980), Appendix 2.
4. Ibid., Appendix 4.
5. Jackson, *Recollections*, 52–3.
6. *Scotsman*, 3 June 1921, 6.
7. *Ecclesiologist*, Vol. XXII (1864), 279.
8. *Slater's (late Pigot & Co's) Royal National Commercial Directory and Topography of Scotland, 1860*, 133.
9. Royal Scottish Academy, *Complete List of the Exhibited Works 1826–1916* (Bath, 1975), 16–18.
10. *Trans. Arch. Inst. Scot.*, Session 1859–60, 6.
11. *Oliver and Boyd's Edinburgh Almanac*, 1861 Edition, 716; 1862 Edition, 685; 1863 Edition, 729; 1864 Edition, 698; 1865 Edition, 705; 1866 Edition, 714; 1867 Edition, 737.
12. NMRS drawings EDD/8/42 and 43.
13. Sir Francis Mudie, David Walker and Iain MacIvor, *Broughty Castle and the Defence of the Tay* (Dundee, 1979).
14. St James' Church, Leith, loose papers and letters on the building of the church.
15. Ibid.
16. James Grant, *Cassell's Old and New Edinburgh* (London, Paris, New York; N/D), Vol. I, 79–80.
17. Memorial Committee Minutes, Blair Castle.
18. SRO Register of Marriages 1863, 60, No. 4.
19. Marion Lochhead, *Episcopal Scotland in the Nineteenth Century* (London, 1966), 144.
20. See Dean Ramsay, *Reminiscences of Scottish Life and Character* (Edinburgh, 1863).
21. Lochhead, *Episcopal Scotland*, 99.
22. *Building Chronicle*, May 1854, 10.
23. *Trans. Arch. Inst. Scot.*, Session 1850–1, 43.
24. Ibid., Session 1856–7, 19.
25. Peter F. Anson, *Fashions in Church Furnishing 1840–1940* (London, 1965), 102–4.
26. *Ecclesiologist*, Vol.XX (1869), 383–4.
27. *The First Hundred Years, Christ Church, Falkirk, 1864–1964*, centenary booklet.
28. *Edinburgh Evening Courant*, 9 May 1863.
29. Ibid., 14 April 1864.
30. St Michael and All Saints Episcopal Church, Building Committee Minute Book.

31. In the possession of the present incumbent.
32. Specification, kept with vestry minutes at the church.
33. St John's Church, Alloa, vestry minutes, 20 October 1866.
34. Rowand Anderson's Scrapbook, Property of the Royal Incorporation of Architects in Scotland, 22–3.
35. Ibid.
36. *Ecclesiologist*, Vol.XXVIII (1867), 247–8.
37. SRO Mar and Kellie Muniments, GD124/9/134/4.
38. St James' Church, Cupar, vestry minutes.
39. Correspondence kept at St Andrew's Church, St Andrews. Letter from Anderson to Skinner, 19/1/67.
40. RA Scrapbook, 124.
41. Edinburgh Collection, Edinburgh City Library. *Opening Address, New School of Applied Art, Edinburgh*, R. Rowand Anderson LLD, 21 October 1892, 9–10.

CHAPTER 4

1. Edinburgh University, Anderson Office Drawings Catalogue, p.36 No. 72.
2. Ibid., p.36, No. 42.
3. Scottish Episcopal Church Year Book, 1960–61, 147.
4. *Builder*, 30 July 1870, 612–3.
5. Office Drawings Catalogue p.36, No.199.
6. Ibid., p.36, No.49.
7. St Vigean's restoration correspondence, kept by the Session Clerk.
8. Ibid.
9. Ibid.
10. Ibid.
11. Ibid.
12. Ibid.
13. *Proceedings of the Society of Antiquaries of Scotland*, 13 January 1873, 63–4.
14. Anderson's sketch book, copied with the permission of the late Sir William Kininmonth.
15. Office Drawings Catalogue p.37, Nos 174 and 199.
16. *Royal Institute of British Architects, Journal*, 24 June 1916, 270.
17. Mount Stuart Manuscripts, letter from Daniel Richmond to Lord Bute, 19 June 1873.
18. *Builder*, 5 October 1872, 778; *Scotsman*, 22 November 1873.
19. John Gifford, Colin McWilliam and David Walker, *The Buildings of Scotland – Edinburgh* (Harmondsworth, 1984), 336–7, 423–5.
20. Office Drawings Catalogue p.37, No.199.
21. Edinburgh University Library, letter from Anderson to Skene, 1 September 1874 (Laing Collection, L.a.IV.17.).
22. Ibid.
23. Edinburgh School Board Letter Book, Edinburgh City Library, Q YL353/G39598, passim.
24. Office Drawings Catalogue p.37, No.67.
25. loc. cit. p.37, No.74.
26. *Report of Progress of the First School Board of the Burgh of Kirkcaldy* (Kirkcaldy, 1876) 4, 5.
27. Fife Regional Archives, Kirkcaldy School Board Minutes, 22 May 1875.
28. The Book of the Old Edinburgh Club, Vol. XXXIV, part 2, 1979, 95–104. *Edinburgh University's Extension Scheme of 1874*, by Peter Savage.
29. Anderson's pocket book of notes, taken on his trip, copied with the permission of the late Sir William Kininmonth.
30. RA Scrapbook, 2.
31. Ibid.

32. Ibid.
33. Savage, *Extension Scheme*, 101.
34. SRO Newspaper Cutting BR/GSW 4/5–529.
35. SRO Caledonian Railway Board Minutes, 1 May 1877, BR/CAL/1–23.
36. SRO Newspaper Cutting, BR/GSW 4/5–529.
37. Mount Stuart Manuscripts, letter from Frederick Pitman to Henry Stuart, 11 March 1878.
38. Office Drawings Catologue, 38, No.110, Drawings 5 and 6.
39. Mount Stuart Manuscripts, letter from Lord Bute to Lady Bute, 2 October 1879.
40. RA Scrapbook, 42.
41. Office Drawings Catalogue, p.37, No.205.
42. SRO, Letter G. Wilson/Lord Lothian, GD 40/9/480.
43. Anderson's diary for 1879, copied with the permission of the late Sir William Kininmonth.
44. *Transactions of the Edinburgh Architectural Association*, 14 April 1909, 79.
45. Ex. inf. Rev. D. R. Cole, Colinton.

CHAPTER 5

1. MacPherson's Fellowship Nomination Papers, Royal Institute of British Architects.
2. Watson's Licentiateship Nomination Papers, Royal Institute of British Architects.
3. *R.I.B.A. Journal*, Vol.46 (1938/9), 904.
4. Building Committee Report, evaluating Anderson's work at St James, Stonehaven, 1878, in possession of the church secretary.
5. Office Drawings Catalogue, p.38, No.111.
6. *Builder*, 24 April 1881, 504; 7 January 1882, 24.
7. SRO, Board Minutes BR/CAL/1–26, 8 November 1880.
8. SRO, Newspaper Cutting BR/GSW 4/5–529.
9. Ibid.
10. SRO, Note on Costs BR/CAL/4–30.
11. SRO, Newspaper Cutting BR/GSW 4–20.
12. Office Drawings Catalogue, p.39, No.246.
13. *Builder*, 23 April 1881, 503; 7 January 1882, 24.
14. RA Scrapbook, 220.
15. Office Drawings Catalogue, p.39, partnership name and address.
16. Ibid., p.39, No.185.
17. RA Scrapbook, 40.
18. Ibid.
19. Ibid.
20. Gordon, *The Royal Scottish Academy*, 155.
21. Peter Savage, *Lorimer and the Edinburgh Craft Designers* (Edinburgh, 1980), 4.
22. Aitken, *Reminiscences of Edinburgh Arch. Ass.*, 14.
23. NMRS, Ian G. Lindsay Collection IN/3796.
24. *British Architect*, 4 July 1884, 7.
25. Office Drawings Catalogue, p.39, No.223.
26. *Newcastle Journal*, 19 June 1884.
27. Murray and Nora Lunan, *Brief History of the Church in Glencorse* (Glencorse, 1985), 7–8.
28. NMRS, Photographs of Biel Drawings ECO/191, 102 and 104. SRO Letter from Anderson to Miss Constance Hamilton GD 205/47.
29. John C. MacFarlane, *An Outline History of Govan Old Parish Church* (Glasgow 1965), 49, 50.
    T.B. Stewart Thomson, *A Guide to Govan Old Parish Church* (Glasgow 1963), 9.

30. Strathclyde Regional Archives, Glasgow, Architect's Account, 21 November 1889, CH2/1277/66.
31. Ibid.
32. SRA, Building Fund Letter Book 7 and 14, December 1885. CH2/1277/61.
33. NMRS, Copy letter.
34. Dumfries House, letter from Lord Bute to G.E. Sneyd, 3 June 1885.
35. Mount Stuart Manuscripts, letter Lord Bute to Lady Bute, 20 March 1882.
36. Mount Stuart Manuscripts, letter Lord Bute to Lady Bute, 1 October 1884.
37. Mount Stuart Manuscripts, letter Lord Bute to Lady Bute, 18 June 1882.
38. RA Scrapbook, 81.
39. Ibid.
40. *Builder*, 3 January, 1885, 49.
41. Helen Smailes, *A Portrait Gallery for Scotland* (Edinburgh, 1985), 27–8.
42. SRO, Building Committee Minutes, NGI/55/2. For example, that of 13 May 1885.
43. *Builder*, 14 August 1886, 225–6; 30 April 1887, 632.
44. *Builder*, 10 October 1885, 492.
45. Office Drawings Catalogue, p.40, No.167.
46. RA Scrapbook, 70.
47. SRO, letter Anderson/C.N. Hamilton GD 205/47.
48. SRO, Report from Ross to Lord Lothian, GD 40/9/494/1.
49. SRO, Anderson's report, GD 40/9/494/3.
50. Ibid.
51. Stamp and Amery, *Victorian Buildings of London*, 168.
52. *Builder*, 23 July 1887, 132–3.
53. RA Scrapbook, 109.
54. Ibid.
55. Ibid.

CHAPTER 6

1. *Transactions of the Edinburgh Architectural Association*, 8 March 1893, 104–10.
2. SRO, Dunblane Cathedral, Statement Regarding its Proposed Restoration, by Dr R. Rowand Anderson, Architect, 7 February 1889, NG1/62.
3. *Journal of the Society of Friends of Dunblane Cathedral*, Vol.I, 1931, 13–24.
4. SRO, NG1/62, loc. cit.
5. Ibid.
6. *Annual Report of the Society for the Protection of Ancient Buildings*, July 1888, 23–4.
7. SRO, Letter from Thackeray Turner to the Chief Commissioner of Works, 9 May 1889. NG1/62.
8. Ian G. Lindsay, *The Cathedrals of Scotland* (Edinburgh, 1926), 68–9.
9. *Transactions Edin. Arch. Assoc.*, loc. cit.
10. *Journal of the Society of Friends of Dunblane Cathedral*, loc. cit.
11. Ibid., Vol.IV, Part 2, 1943, 20–1.
12. *Transactions Edin. Arch. Assoc.*, March 1893, 104–10.
13. Ibid.
14. *Transactions of the National Association for the Advancement of Art and its Application to Industry, Edinburgh Meeting, 1889* (London, 1890), 141–2.
15. Ibid., 142–3.
16. Ibid., 145.
17. Ibid., 146.
18. Ibid., 148–9.
19. Ibid., 152.
20. Ibid., 186.
21. Ibid., 187.

22. Ibid., 150.
23. RA Scrapbook, 8.
24. Gordon, *The Royal Scottish Academy*, 159–61.
25. Ibid.
26. RA Scrapbook, 8.
27. Gordon, *The Royal Scottish Academy*, 164–8.
28. RA Scrapbook, 308.
29. Ibid.
30. Ibid.
31. Office Drawings Catalogue, pp.6–7, Section 2.1.
32. RA Scrapbook, 308.
33. Savage, *Extension Scheme*, 102.
34. Typescript History of St Cuthberts Church, N.D. R.C. Mathams.
35. Brydall, *Art in Scotland*, 152–3.
36. SRO, Letter book of the School of Applied Art, 5 September 1892–21 January 1897, NG1/56/1.
37. *Opening Address, New School of Applied Art*, by R. Rowand Anderson.
38. School of Applied Art, Letter book, passim.
39. Library, University of St Andrews. Circular entitled 'Dining Hall for Students at the University of St. Andrews'; University Court Minutes 9 June 1892, 28 October 1892, 1 February 1893.
40. RA Scrapbook, loose cutting on Tangier.
41. RA Scrapbook, loose letter from Pericardis to Anderson.
42. Typescript notes on the history of Tangier kept at the Tangier Office of the British Embassy.
43. Ibid.
44. Office Drawings Catalogue, p.41, No.231.
45. Typescript notes, Tangier.
46. Mount Stuart Manuscripts, letter G. Mullan to Lord Bute, 23 February 1894.
47. Office Drawings Catalogue, p.38, No.110.
48. RA Scrapbook, 149.
49. Beckles Willson, *The Life of Lord Strathcona and Mount Royal* (London, New York, Toronto, Melbourne, 1915).
50. *Journal of the Society of Friends of Dunblane Cathedral*, Vol.IV Part II, 1943, 20–1.
51. *The Journal of Glasgow Chamber of Commerce*, January 1971, 127–9.
52. RA Scrapbook, 321 and loose note.
53. RA Scrapbook, 39.
54. A.R. Howell, *Paisley Abbey, Its History, Architecture and Art* (Paisley, N.D.), 47.
55. Ibid.

CHAPTER 7

1. *R.I.B.A. Journal*, Vol.40 1932/33, 641.
2. *Builder*, 19 October 1901, 340.
3. Library, University of St Andrews, University Court Minutes, 24 January 1889, 25 July 1899.
4. Ibid.
5. Juliet Kinchin, *Pollok House — A History of the House and Gardens* (Glasgow 1983), 11.
6. Charles McKean, *Stirling and the Trossachs*, (Edinburgh, 1985), 78.
7. Office Drawings Catalogue, p.42, No.63.
8. *Builder*, 13 April 1901, 359–61; 3 August 1901, 95–6.
9. *Academy Architecture 1903 — Edinburgh*, Plates 63 and 65.
10. *Journal of the Society of Friends of Dunblane Cathedral*, Vol.IV, Part II 1943, 21.
11. Preface to the 1901 edition of the *Baronial and Ecclesiastical Antiquities of Scotland* (Edinburgh 1901).

12. RA Scrapbook, loose cutting.
13. Ex. inf. Dr Peter Savage.
14. RA Scrapbook, 14.
15. School of Applied Art Minute Book (Edinburgh College of Art Library), passim.
16. Edinburgh College of Art Library. Extracts, by Glenn Craig, from George Heriot's Trust Minutes, 31 December 1903, 5–17.
17. Ibid.
18. Ibid.
19. *Journal of the Society of Friends of Dunblane Cathedral*, Vol.IV, Part II 1943, 21.
20. SRO, Letter from Anderson to McKechnie 10 April 1902. HR 778 15/1.
21. SRO, Heritors Records, 18 December 1902. 158/2.
22. Ibid., 12 February 1904.
23. *Dunfermline Journal*, 19 May 1906, 5.
24. SRO, Heritors Records 27 July 1908, 158/2.
25. Office Drawings Catalogue, p.43, No.168.
26. Dundee University Library. College Council Minutes, 10 December 1906.
27. Dundee University Library. Report from Anderson, 31 January 1907. Recs A/331/2.
28. Ian Gow, 'Sir Rowand Anderson's National Art Survey of Scotland', *Architectural History*, Vol. 27, 1984.
29. National Library, Edinburgh. Letter Anderson to Geddes, MS 10535 189.
30. Card Index to Anderson's book collection, kept by the Royal Incorporation of Architects in Scotland.
31. Ian Hay, *The Royal Company of Archers 1676–1951* (Edinburgh and London, 1951), 184–5.
32. Ibid.
33. *Proceedings of the Society of Antiquaries of Scotland*, 12 December 1912, 17–28.
34. Strathclyde Regional Archives, Stirling Maxwell Papers, TPM 122/27.
35. Gow, op. cit.
36. Album, with pictures of the items gifted and accompanying letter, in the Library of the Edinburgh Architectural Association.
37. SRO, file on Anderson's gifts, MW2/62.
38. Wentworth Huyshe, *Dervogilla, Lady of Galloway and her Abbey of the Sweet Heart* (London 1913), 71–2.
39. John Keppie, *The Story of the Glasgow Institute of Architects* (Glasgow, 1921), 49.
40. *R.I.B.A. Journal*, Third Series Vol.XXIII, 265–73.
41. Loc. cit., 271.
42. Minute Book, Institute of Scottish Architects (kept by the RIAS), 19 October 1916, 2 November 1916.
43. Ibid., 28 December 1916.
44. Barrington Kaye, *The Development of the Architectural Profession in Britain* (London, 1960), 138–9.
45. Minute Book, Institute of Scottish Architects, 1 March 1917.
46. Gow, op. cit.
47. Minute Book, Institute of Scottish Architects, 27 March 1919.
48. Sir David Hunter Blair, *John Patrick, Third Marquess of Bute, K.T. (1847–1900)* (London, 1921), 241–4.
49. Rowand Anderson's Will. Copy kept by the NMRS.

CHAPTER 8

1. *Builder*, 10 June 1921, 739.
2. Ibid.
3. *R.I.B.A. Journal*, Vol.28, 1920/21, 457–8.

4. *R.I.B.A. Journal*, 30 July 1921, 511–12.
5. Ibid.
6. Ibid.
7. Ibid.
8. Hunterian Art Gallery, University of Glasgow, *Scotch Baronial Architecture* by Charles Rennie Mackintosh. Mackintosh Collection [F(C)].
9. James Nicoll (ed.), *Domestic Architecture in Scotland* (Aberdeen, 1908).
10. *R.I.A.S. Quarterly*, No.31, 1929, 63–76.

Bibliography

PUBLISHED SOURCES

Anderson, R., *Examples of the Municipal, Commercial and Street Architecture of France and Italy from the 12th to the 15th Century* (London, Edinburgh, Glasgow, 1868).

Anson, P.F., *Fashions in Church Furnishing 1840–1940* (London, 1965).

Armstrong, E.A., *Axel Hermann Haig and His Work* (London, 1905).

Barclay, J.B., *The S.S.C. Story 1784–1984* (Edinburgh, 1984).

Barty, A.B., 'The Restoration of Dunblane Cathedral', *Journal of the Society of Friends of Dunblane Cathedral*, Vol.I (1931), 13–23.

Brydall, R., *Art in Scotland* (Edinburgh and London, 1889).

Building Chronicle for the years 1854–1857.

Caw, J.L., *Scottish Painting 1620–1908* (Bath, 1975, first pub. 1908).

Centenary Booklet, 1867–1967, *St. Michael and All Saints Episcopal Church, Edinburgh* (Edinburgh, 1967).

Cole, D., *The Work of Sir Gilbert Scott* (London, 1980).

Crum, F.M., *Alexander Crum of Thornliebank, 1828–1893, a Memoir* (Glasgow, 1954).

Dictionary of National Biography, William Forbes Skene, Vol. XVIII, 339–40 (Oxford, 1937–8).

Dowell's List, 4 March, 1884, 391. Inventory of John Lessels' pictures, for auction.

Drummond, A.I., *Edward Irving and his Circle* (London, 1937).

Dumfermline Journal, 13 September 1890, p.3; 19 May 1906, p.5.

Eastlake, C.L., (ed. J.M. Crook) *History of the Gothic Revival* (Leicester, 1978, first pub. 1872).

Ecclesiologist, Vol. XX, 1869, 383–4; Vol. XXVIII, 1867, 247–8.

Edinburgh Architectural Association Sketchbook 1875–6 (Edinburgh, 1876).

Edinburgh and Leith Post Office Directory (Edinburgh, 1860–8).

The Education (Scotland) Act, 1872, Paras 8 and 9.

Ferguson, W., *Scotland — 1689 to the Present* (Edinburgh, 1968).

Fiddes, V. and Rowan, A., *Mr. David Bryce*, Exhibition Catalogue (Edinburgh, 1976).

The First Hundred Years — Christ Church, Falkirk, 1864–1964 (Falkirk, 1964).

Gifford, J., McWilliam C. and Walker, D., *The Buildings of Scotland — Edinburgh* (Harmondsworth, 1984).

Gillespie, J., *Details of Scottish Domestic Architecture* (Edinburgh, 1922).

Gordon, A., 5th Marquess of Aberdeen, *The Guide to Haddo House* (Edinburgh, 1981).

Gordon, E., *The Royal Scottish Academy of Painting, Sculpture and Architecture* (Edinburgh, 1976).

Gow, I., 'Sir Rowand Anderson's National Art Survey of Scotland'. *Architectural History*, Vol. 27, 1984.

Graham, J.G. and Christie, A., *The Chapel of St. Anthony the Eremite at Murthly, Perthshire* (Edinburgh, 1850).

Grant, J., *Cassell's Old and New Edinburgh* (London, Paris, New York, c.1883).

Hay, I., *The Royal Company of Archers 1676–1951* (Edinburgh and London, 1951).

Hitchcock, H.R., *Architecture — Nineteenth and Twentieth Centuries — Pelican History of Art* (Harmondsworth, 4th Edition, 1977).

Howell, A.R., *Paisley Abbey, Its History, Architecture and Art* (Paisley, N/D).

Hunter Blair, Sir David, *John Patrick, Third Marquess of Bute, K.T. (1847–1900)* (London, 1921).

Huyshe, W., *Dervogilla, Lady of Galloway And Her Abbey of the Sweet Heart* (London, 1913).

Jackson, B.H., *Recollections of Thomas Graham Jackson* (London, New York, Toronto, 1950).

Jackson, N., *F.W. Troup, Architect, 1859–1941* (London, 1985).

Journal of Glasgow Chamber of Commerce, 'Sir William Pearce', January 1971, 127–9.

Journal of the Royal Institute of British Architects, 'Royal Gold Medal Presentation to Sir Rowand Anderson'. 29 June 1916, 265–73. 'Sir Rowand Anderson', 30 July 1921, 511–12.

Juridical Review, 'Sir John H.A. McDonald', Vol.35, 1923, 109.

Kaye, B., *The Development of the Architectural Profession in Britain* (London, 1960).

Keppie, J., *The Story of the Glasgow Institute of Architects* (Glasgow, 1921).

Kinchin, J., *Pollok House — A History of the House and Gardens* (Glasgow, 1983).

Lindsay, I.G., *The Cathedrals of Scotland* (Edinburgh, 1926).

Livingston, P.K., *St. Brycedale Church, Kirkcaldy* (Kirkcaldy, 1957).

Lochhead M., *Episcopal Scotland in the Nineteenth Century* (London, 1966).

Lunan, M. and Lunan, N., *A Brief History of the Church in Glencorse* (Glencorse, 1985).

McBain, J.M., *Eminent Arbroathians* (Arbroath, 1897).

MacFarlane, J.C., *An Outline History of Govan Old Parish Church* (Glasgow, 1965).

MacGibbon, D. and Ross, T., *The Castellated and Domestic Architecture of Scotland*, Vol. V (Edinburgh, 1971) Facsimile of edition published 1887–92.

MacGibbon, D. and Ross. T., *The Ecclesiastical Architecture of Scotland*, Vol. II (Edinburgh, 1896).

McKean, C., *Stirling and the Trossachs* (Edinburgh, 1985).

McKean, C., *Edinburgh — An Illustrated Architectural Guide* (Edinburgh, 3rd Edition, 1983).

McKean, C. and Walker, D., *Dundee — An Illustrated Introduction* (Edinburgh, 1984).

McLelland, R., *The Church and Parish of Inchinnan* (Paisley, 1905).

Mackmurdo, A.H., *Wren's City Churches* (Orpington, 1883).

McWilliam, C., *The Buildings of Scotland — Lothian* (Harmondsworth, 1978).

Maltby, S. MacDonald, S. and Cunningham, C., *Alfred Waterhouse, 1830–1905* (London Booklet to accompany exhibition at the RIBA Heinz Gallery, 1893).

Miller, N.H., *The Company of Merchants of the City of Edinburgh* (Edinburgh, 1981).

Moir Bryce, W., *History of the Old Greyfriars Church, Edinburgh* (Edinburgh and London, 1912).

Mudie, Sir Francis, Walker, D. and McIvor, I., *Broughty Castle and the Defence of the Tay* (Dundee, 1979).

Muthesius, S., *The High Victorian Movement in Architecture* (London, 1972).

Nicoll, J., *Domestic Architecture in Scotland* (Aberdeen, 1908).

Oliver and Boyd's Edinburgh Almanac, (Edinburgh, 1830–1900 editions).

Pevsner, N., *Studies in Art, Architecture and Design, Volume II, Victorian and After* (London, 1968).

Proceedings of the Royal Society of Edinburgh, Anderson's Obituary, 1921, p.198.

Proceedings of the Society of Antiquaries of Scotland for the years 1870–1921.

Pugin, A.W., *The True Principles of Pointed or Christian Architecture* (London, 1841).

The Royal Scottish Academy, *Complete List of the Exhibited Works, 1826–1916* (Bath, 1975).

The Royal Scottish Academy, 94th Annual Report, 1921, Obituary R.R. Anderson, 13–16.

The Royal Incorporation of Architects in Scotland, *Quarterly*, 1922–1930.

St Aubyn, G., *Edward VII, Prince and King* (London, 1979).

Saint, A., *Richard Norman Shaw* (Yale, 1976).

Savage, P., 'Edinburgh University's Extension Scheme of 1874', *The Book of the Old Edinburgh Club*, Vol. XXXIV, Part 2, 1979, 95–104.

Savage, P., *Lorimer and the Edinburgh Craft Designers* (Edinburgh, 1980).

Scott, G.G. (Ed.), *Personal and Professional Recollections by the late Sir George Gilbert Scott, R.A.* (London, 1879).

Scott, G.G., *Remarks on Secular and Domestic Architecture* (London, 1857).

Scottish Episcopal Church Year Book and Directory, (Edinburgh, 1960).

Scottish Guardian for the years 1865–1868.

Society for the Protection of Ancient Buildings, Annual Report, 1888, 23–4.

Southgate, D., *University Education in Dundee — A Centenary History* (Dundee, 1982).

Shepherd, J.H., *The Story of St. John's Church, Pittenweem* (Edinburgh, 1926).

Stamp, G. and Amery, C., *Victorian Buildings of London 1837–1887* (London, 1980).

Stewart Thomson, T.B., *A Guide to Govan Old Parish Church* (Glasgow, 1965).

Smailes, H., *A Portrait Gallery for Scotland* (Edinburgh, 1985).

Stirling Maxwell, Sir John, *Shrines and Homes of Scotland* (London and Edinburgh, 1937).

Stirling Maxwell, Sir John, 'Sir Rowand Anderson', *Journal of the Society of Friends of Dunblane Cathedral* Vol. IV, Part II, 1943, 20–1.

Thompson, P., *William Butterfield* (London, 1971).

Thomson, A., 'An Enquiry as to the Appropriateness of the Gothic Style for the Proposed Buildings of Glasgow University, with some Remarks on Mr. Scott's Plans', *Proceedings of the Glasgow Architectural Society*, 1865–7 (III) 4–5.

Transactions of the Architectural Institute of Scotland for the years 1852–60.

Transactions of the Edinburgh Architectural Association for the years 1893–1909.

Transactions of the Franco Scottish Society for the year 1897.

Transactions of the National Association for the Advancement of Art and its Application to Industry, Edinburgh Meeting, 1889 (London, 1890).

Transactions of the Scottish Ecclesiological Society for the years 1889–1914.

Washington Browne, G., *Pugin Studentship Drawings, by G. Washington Browne, Architect* (Edinburgh, 1887).

Weatherley, L.R., *History of Holy Trinity Scottish Episcopal Church, Dunfermline* (Typescript, 1981).

Whitley, H.C., *Blinded Eagle — An Introduction to the Life and Teaching of Edward Irving* (London, 1954).

Who's Who in Architecture, 1914 (London, 1914).

Willson, B., *The Life of Lord Strathcona and Mount Royal (1820–1914)* (London, New York, Toronto and Melbourne, 1915).

Wordsworth, J., *The Episcopate of Charles Wordsworth 1853–1892* (London, 1899).

Also, the *Architect, British Architect, Builder, Building News* and *Scotsman* for the period 1840–1920, as applicable.

UNPUBLISHED SOURCES

Dundee University Library
Brechin Diocesan Archives MS/1/4/852, College Council Minutes, 1906–10, Recs A/331/2, Recs A/327/2

Edinburgh Architectural Association Library
History and Reminiscences of the Edinburgh Architectural Association, (Typescript), G.S. Aitken, 13 February, 1913. Photograph Album of the restored Mackenzie Tomb, Greyfriars. Photograph Album with pictures of Blue China gifted to Holyrood Palace.

Edinburgh College of Art Library
School of Applied Art Minute Books
Extracts (by Glenn Craig) of George Heriot's Trust Minutes, 31 December 1903, 5–17.

Edinburgh Room, Edinburgh Central Library
Copy Letter Book of Edinburgh School Board, Q. YL353/G39598.

Edinburgh University Library, Department of Ancient Manuscripts
The Edinburgh Collection of the Office Drawings of Rowand Anderson.
Laing Collection L.a. IV.17.
Building Committee Letter Book E 490120 Da 3.

Episcopal Church Records
Christ Church, Falkirk, Vestry Minutes.
All Saints, Brougham St Edinburgh, Building Committee Minute Book. Design drawings.
St John's Church, Alloa, Vestry Minutes.
St James' Church, Cupar, Vestry Minutes.
St James' Church, Leith, Correspondence and Vestry Minutes.
St Andrew's Church, St Andrews, Correspondence and Vestry Minutes.
St John's Church, Forfar, Correspondence and Vestry Minutes.
St Michael and All Angel's Church, Helensburgh, Vestry Minutes. Specification.
St Augustine's (formerly St Luke's) Church, Dumbarton, Vestry Minutes.
Holy Trinity Church Dunfermline, Vestry Minutes.

Falkirk Public Library
Stirling Castle, Its History and Its Architecture by Dr Rowand Anderson ACC No.R4731.

Fife Regional Archives, Glenrothes
Kirkcaldy School Board Minute Books.
Leslie School Board Minute Books.

Merchants' Hall, Edinburgh
George Watson's Hospital Roll Book.
George Watson's Hospital Governors' Minute Books.
George Watson's Hospital Cash Books.

Mount Stuart Manuscripts, Mount Stuart, Bute
Miscellaneous Letters.
Extracts from Lord Bute's Diary.
Plans of Galston R.C. Church.

National Monuments Record of Scotland
Rowand Anderson's Will.
Rowand Anderson's Scrapbook (property of the Royal Incorporation of Architects in Scotland).
Copy Drawings, BWD/56/2 and BWD 1741, BWD 91/2 and 3, EDD/8/42 and 3, EDD/257/7–22, ELO/191, 102, 103, 104, EDD/220/47, PTD/21/12, AND/7/1–6.
Mural Decorations in the Catholic Apostolic Church, 2205 (p) D5/E (p.).
News Clippings Book of the Edinburgh Architectural Association.
Architect's File (John Henderson).

Royal Incorporation of Architects in Scotland, Library
  Card Index of the volumes in Rowand Anderson's Library.
  Anderson's Photograph Album of English Church Interiors.
  Minute Books of the Institute of Scottish Architects, 1916–22.
Royal Institute of British Architects, Library and Drawings Collection
  Sketch book belonging to Rowand Anderson.
  Licentiateship, Associateship and Fellowship Nomination Forms.
St Andrews University Library
  University Court Minutes, 1899, 1892–3 and 1899–1900.
  Plaster Cast of Skull of Pedro de Luna.
  Letters from Rowand Anderson re Students' Union.
St Vigean's Parish Church, Arbroath
  Correspondence on the Restoration of the Church, 1870–4, together with related papers.
Scottish Record Office, Edinburgh

Trustees' Academy, Lists of Students	NG1/51/1
Trustees' Academy, Letter Book	NG1/51/3
Mar and Kellie Muniments	GD124/9/134/4
Letter R. Anderson/W.F. Skene	GD1/126/8/2
Letter G. Wilson/ Lord Lothian	GD40/9/480
British Rail Archives	BR/GSW/4/5–529
British Rail Archives	BR/CAL 1–23, 26
British Rail Archives	BR/CAL./4/12/38
Architect's Certificate	GD40/8/515
Braid Estate Plans	RHP 4469/1, 2
Braid Estate Plans	RH 2966
Letter Anderson/Constance Hamilton	GD205/47
(Ogilvy of Inverquarity Muniments)	
Portrait Gallery Building Committee Minutes	NG1/55/2
Report to Lord Lothian	GD40/9/494/1
Report to Lord Lothian	GD40/9/494/3
Dunblane Cathedral File	NG1/62
School of Applied Art Letter Books	NG1/56/1
Anderson's Gifts to Holyrood Palace	MW 2/62
Culross Abbey Heritors' Records	HR 158/2
Paisley Abbey Heritors' Records	HR 778/15

Strathclyde Regional Archives, Glasgow

Stirling Maxwell Papers	TPM/122/27
Letter R. Anderson/Sir John Stirling Maxwell	TPM/122/1/19
Govan Parish Church Records	CH2/1277/62–73
Govan Parish Church Letter Book	CH2/1277/61
Pearce Institute	UCS 2/138

Tangier Office of the British Embassy
  Typescript notes on the history of Tangier.
Rabat Office of the British Embassy
  Registers of British Citizens in Tangier, 1890–1910.
Hunterian Art Gallery, University of Glasgow
  Essay on *Scotch Baronial Architecture* by Charles Rennie Mackintosh, Mackintosh Collection.

Some of the above sources are privately owned and cannot be consulted without prior permission.

List of Plates

Plate 1. St Anthony's Chapel, Edinburgh, conjectural restoration. Prizewinning drawing by R. Anderson c. 1855 (Anderson Office Drawings, Edinburgh University).

Plate 2. Chancel arch, Duddingston Kirk. Prizewinning drawing by R. Anderson c. 1855 (Anderson Office Drawings, Edinburgh University).

Plate 3. St Margaret's Well, Restalrig. Measured Drawing by R. Anderson, 1855 (*Building Chronicle*, January 1856).

Plate 4. Maison du Grand Veneur, Cordes (R. Anderson, *The Domestic and Street Architecture of France and Italy*, 1868).

Plate 5. Place Champollion, Figeac (R. Anderson, *The Domestic and Street Architecture of France and Italy*, 1868).

Plate 6. Broughty Castle, Broughty Ferry (National Monuments Record of Scotland).

Plate 7. St James the Less Church, Leith (Grant's *Old and New Edinburgh*, Vol.III, 1883).

Plate 8. 78th Highlanders Memorial, Edinburgh Castle (Grant's *Old and New Edinburgh*, Vol. I, 1883).

Plate 9. Atholl Memorial, Logierait (Author).

Plate 10. Christ Church, Falkirk (Author).

Plate 11. All Saints Church, Edinburgh (Author).

Plate 12. Waddell's house, Portobello, contract drawings (Anderson Office Drawings, Edinburgh University).

Plate 13. St Michael and All Angels Church, Helensburgh (National Monuments Record of Scotland).

Plate 14. St John's Church, Alloa (Author).

Plate 15. St James' Church, Cupar (Author).

Plate 16. St Andrew's Church, St Andrews, c. 1900 (J.H. Scott).

Plate 17. St Andrew's Church, Kelso, design drawing (Anderson Office Drawings, Edinburgh University).

Plate 18. St Andrew's Church, Kelso (Author).

Plate 19. Houses at Inverleith, design drawing (Anderson Office Drawings, Edinburgh University).

Plate 20. St Augustine's (formerly St Luke's) Church, Dumbarton (Anderson Office Drawings, Edinburgh University).

Plate 21. St Vigean's Church, Arbroath (National Monuments Record of Scotland).

Plate 22. St Vigean's Church, Arbroath, interior (*Academy Architecture — Edinburgh, 1893*).

Plate 23. Working drawings in crypt, Roslin, illustrated by R. Anderson (*Proceedings of the Society of Antiquaries of Scotland, 1873*).

Plate 24. Frontage, Catholic Apostolic Church, Edinburgh (National Monuments Record of Scotland).

Plate 25. Interior, Catholic Apostolic Church, Edinburgh (National Monuments Record of Scotland).

Plate 26. St James' Church, Stonehaven (Author).

Plate 27. Fountainbridge School, Edinburgh. (National Monuments Record of Scotland).

Plate 28. Stockbridge School, Edinburgh (Author).

Plate 29. Kirkcaldy West School, design drawing (Anderson Office Drawings, Edinburgh University).

Plate 30. Wardrop and Reid's design for Edinburgh University Medical School (Anderson Office Drawings, Edinburgh University).

Plate 31. Elevation from Anderson's accepted scheme for Edinburgh University Medical School (Anderson Office Drawings, Edinburgh University).

Plate 32. Edinburgh University Medical School (Grant's *Old and New Edinburgh*, Vol. II, 1883).

Plate 33. West elevation, Edinburgh University Medical School (National Monuments Record of Scotland).

Plate 34. Main quadrangle, Edinburgh University Medical School (National Monuments Record of Scotland).

Plate 35. Central Station Buildings (later Central Hotel), Glasgow (National Monuments Record of Scotland).

Plate 36. Mount Stuart, 1880s (A.H. Millar, *Castles and Mansions of Renfrewshire and Buteshire*).

Plate 37. St Serf's Church, Dunimarle (Author).

Plate 38. Holy Trinity Church, Stirling (Author).

Plate 39. Pennycross School, Mull (Author).

Plate 40. Replacement door in south wall of nave, Jedburgh Abbey (Author).

Plate 41. Design for Brechin Diocesan Residence (Anderson Office Drawings, Edinburgh University).

Plate 42. Unbuilt design for Leven Episcopal Church (Anderson Office Drawings, Edinburgh University).

Plate 43. 'Allermuir', Colinton. (Royal Incorporation of Architects in Scotland).

Plate 44. St John's Church, Forfar (Author).

Plate 45. North Berwick Parish Church (Author).

Plate 46. Nos 4 and 6 Nile Grove, Edinburgh (Author).

Plate 47. Fettes College Sanatorium (now Malcolm House) (Author).

Plate 48. St George's West Church, Shandwick Place, Edinburgh (Author).

Plate 49. Main stair, Conservative Club, Edinburgh (National Monuments Record of Scotland).

Plate 50. St Augustine's Church, North Shields, contract drawing. (Anderson Office Drawings, Edinburgh University).

Plate 51. Glencorse Parish Church (Author).

Plate 52. Interior, Govan Old Parish Church (Scottish Civic Trust).

Appendix 1

LIST OF WORKS

There is no definitive list of Anderson's works. The list which follows has been compiled from two main sources, the Office Drawings Collection at Edinburgh University, and the list provided to the RIBA Journal in 1916 on the occasion of Anderson's Royal Gold Medal Award. The earliest date provided against each entry relates to Anderson's first known involvement with the commission. Works believed to have been by partners have been excluded.

Executed Works

 1. *1860–61 Broughty Castle — rebuilding*
 2. *1861–4 St James Episcopal Church, Leith — Clerk of Works*
 3. *1861 Monument to 78th Highlanders, Edinburgh Castle*
 4. *1863–4 Christ Church Episcopal Church, Falkirk*
 5. *1864–6 St Michael and All Saints Episcopal Church, Edinburgh (with later additions to 1897)*
 6. *1866 — House for Mr Waddell, Portobello*
 7. *1866–8 St Andrew's Episcopal Church, St Andrews*
 8. *1866–8 St James' Episcopal Church, Cupar*
 9. *1866–9 St John's Episcopal Church, Alloa*
10. *1866–8 St Michael and All Angels Episcopal Church, Helensburgh*
11. *1866 Monument to Sixth Duke of Atholl, Logierait*
12. *1867–9 St Andrew's Episcopal Church, Kelso*
13. *1868 Tenements, Balfour St, Edinburgh (demolished)*
14. *1869 St Mungo's Episcopal Church, Balerno*
15. *1869 St Patrick's Roman Catholic School, Cowgate, Edinburgh (demolished)*
16. *1870 Houses at Inverleith Terrace, Edinburgh*
17. *1871–3 St Luke's (now St Augustine's) Episcopal Church, Dumbarton*
18. *1871–2 St Vigean's Parish Church, Arbroath (Restoration)*
19. *1871–83 Catholic Apostolic Church, Edinburgh*
20. *1872–6 St Serf's Episcopal Church, Dunimarle, Culross*
21. *1873 Kellie Monument, St John's Episcopal Church, Alloa*
22. *1873 Robertson Memorial, St Andrew's Episcopal Church, Kelso*
23. *1873–7 St James' Episcopal Church, Stonehaven*
24. *1874–6 Iona, restoration of Abbey, Nunnery, Burial Grounds*
25. *1874 Lodge for Fettykill House, Leslie, Fife*
26. *1874–5 Holy Trinity Episcopal Church, Stirling*

27. *1874–6 West Fountainbridge, Causewayside and Stockbridge Schools (West Fountain-bridge and Causewayside demolished)*
28. *1874–6 Kirkcaldy West Primary School*
29. *1874–86 Edinburgh University Medical School*
30. *1875 Pennycross School, Mull*
31. *1875 Alterations to Iona and Balevulin Schools*
32. *1875 Jedburgh Abbey, restoration*
33. *1876–80 Leslie West Public School, Fife (demolished)*
34. *1876–84 St Augustine's Church, North Shields*
35. *1877 Double Villa at Colinton (11–13 Woodhall Road)*
36. *1877–84 Central Station Hotel, Glasgow (originally built as Caledonian Railway Offices)*
37. *1878 Yester House, East Lothian, alterations*
38. *1878–9 Double Villa, Milton Road, Kirkcaldy*
39. *1878 Newbattle Abbey, restoration of old tombstone*
40. *1878 Dean Ramsay Monument, Princes Street, Edinburgh*
41. *1878–86 Mount Stuart House, Rothesay (with further work to 1906)*
42. *1879–84 'Allermuir', Colinton*
43. *1879 Baberton Court, Juniper Green*
44. *1879–80 North Berwick Parish Church*
45. *1879–84 Conservative Club, Princes Street, Edinburgh*
46. *1879–81 St John's Episcopal Church, Forfar*
47. *1879 Villas at Nile Grove, Morningside (2)*
48. *1879–80 Fettes College Sanatorium and North Lodge*
49. *1879 Greenside Church, Edinburgh, alterations*
50. *1879 Tulliallan, repairs to Mortuary Chapel*
51. *1879–80 Montrose Asylum, additions*
52. *1879 St Bride's Church, Douglas, restoration*
53. *1879 Lady Flora Hastings Homes, Colinton*
54. *1879 Kelton Church, Kircudbright, alterations*
55. *1880–2 St John's Church, Canongate, Edinburgh*
56. *1881 'Torduff' (now 'Thirlestane'), Colinton*
57. *1881 4, 6, 8, Nile Grove, Edinburgh*
58. *1881–2 Tower, St George's West Free Church, Edinburgh*
59. *1881 Alterations to National Gallery steps, Edinburgh*
60. *1882–4 Normand Memorial Hall, Dysart*
61. *1882–8 Govan Old Parish Church, Glasgow*
62. *1882–7 S Sophia's Roman Catholic Church and Presbytery, Galston*
63. *1882 House for Mr Beatson, Colinton Road, Edinburgh (demolished)*
64. *1883 Lady Flora Hastings Homes, 1–11 Barnshot Road, Colinton*
65. *1883 St Mary's Parish Church, Hawick, rebuilding after fire*
66. *1883–5 Alterations and Additions to Carrington House, Fettes College*
67. *1883–7 Alterations to Beaufort Castle, Beauly (H.M. Wardrop, completed by Anderson)*
68. *1883 New East Window, St Machar's Cathedral, Aberdeen*
69. *1883 Moredun Crescent, Edinburgh (demolished)*
70. *1884 Moray Aisle Pulpit, St Giles*
71. *1884 Glencorse Parish Church (tower added 1890)*
72. *1884 Kirkliston Parish Church, addition to nave*
73. *1884–7 Biel House, E Lothian, alterations, extensions and Cottage (all but Cottage demolished)*
74. *1884 Stornoway Parish Church, alterations*

75. *1884–7 1–10 Hermitage Terrace, Edinburgh*
76. *1884–9 National Portrait Gallery and Museum of Antiquities, Edinburgh*
77. *1885–8 St James' Episcopal Church, Inverleith, Edinburgh*
78. *1885 Buccleuch Monument, Parliament Square, Edinburgh*
79. *1885–7 Ardgowan Estate Office, Greenock*
80. *1886 Crichton Mains Farmhouse, Midlothian*
81. *1886 Braeburn House, Currie (for Bruce)*
82. *1886 All Saints Episcopal, Inveraray*
83. *1886–7 Dome to complete Adam's Old College, University of Edinburgh*
84. *1886–8 Ballochmyle House, Ayrshire (H.M. Wardrop, completed by Anderson)*
85. *1887 Hamilton Parish Church Hall*
86. *1887 Queen's Hall, Charlestown, Fife*
87. *1887 Montrose Memorial, St Giles, Edinburgh*
88. *1887–8 Hoddam Castle, additions and alterations, (H.M. Wardrop, completed by Anderson*
89. *1887–9 St Cuthbert's Episcopal Church, Colinton (with further work to 1898)*
90. *1887–8 St Anne's Episcopal Church, Dunbar*
91. *1888 Old College, Edinburgh University, redressing basement as rusticated masonry*
92. *1888 Fencing at Comely Bank for Fettes College*
93. *1888 Tron Kirk, Royal Mile, Edinburgh, interior refurbishment (destroyed)*
94. *1888 Pitfirrane Castle, Dunfermline, alterations*
95. *1888–1908 Braid Estate, Edinburgh, miscellaneous terraced housing at Nile Grove, Cluny Ave, Braid Ave and Braid Rd*
96. *1888 Heatherlie Manse, Selkirk*
97. *1888–97 McEwan Hall, Edinburgh University*
98. *1889 Duddingston Parish Church, interior refurbishment (destroyed)*
99. *1889–97 St Andrew's Home, Joppa, alterations and Chapel (demolished)*
100. *1889 Hall, South Morningside Free Church, Edinburgh*
101. *1890–1 King's College Chapel, Aberdeen, refurbishment, restoration*
102. *1890–3 Dunblane Cathedral Restoration*
103. *1890 Alterations to front hall, Broomhall, Dunfermline*
104. *1890–1 Luscar House, Carnock, addition and alterations*
105. *1890 South Morningside Free Church, Edinburgh*
106. *1890 Dunfermline Abbey Church, new pulpit*
107. *1890 St Paul's Church, Greenock*
108. *1890–1 Holy Trinity Episcopal Church, Dunfermline*
109. *1891–1905 Freeland House, Forgandenny, additions and alterations*
110. *1891 Inglis Memorial, St Giles, Edinburgh*
111. *1891–3 University of St Andrews, conversion of buildings in North Street and Butt's Wynd into Students' Union*
112. *1891 Alterations at Royal Institution, Edinburgh*
113. *1892 Charleton House, Montrose, extensions and alterations*
114. *1892–1907 Pearce Institute, Govan, Glasgow*
115. *1892 Dunfermline Abbey, steps and gates, redecoration of Parish Church (latter removed)*
116. *1892 Glencorse House, Midlothian, alterations*
117. *1892 Ethie Castle, Forfar, alterations*
118. *1893–95 Baldacchino, Catholic Apostolic Church, Edinburgh, supervision of Mural Decoration*
119. *House for R.R. Anderson, Marshan, Tangier (demolished)*
120. *1893 Mackenzie Tomb, Greyfriars, Edinburgh (restoration)*
121. *1894 Inglis Memorial, St Giles Cathedral*

122. *1894 Crum Memorial Library, Thornliebank, Glasgow*
123. *1894 Falkirk Old Parish Church (extensions)*
124. *1894 St Margaret's Roman Catholic Church, Dunfermline (nave & aisles)*
125. *1895 Bush House, Roslin, additions and alterations*
126. *1896–7 Glencoe House and Lodge, Invercoe, Argyll*
127. *1895 'The Swallowgait', St Andrews*
128. *1895 Hopetoun House, Linlithgow, additions and alterations*
129. *1896 Brankston Grange, near Culross, additions*
130. *1896–8 Houses at Comely Bank Terrace, Edinburgh*
131. *1897–1902 Chapel, Mount Stuart, Rothesay*
132. *1897 Pollokshaws Burgh Buildings, Glasgow*
133. *1897–9 Rosslynlee Asylum, additions and alterations*
134. *1897 Eastwood Parish Church, Glasgow, redecoration and alterations*
135. *1897–9 9–21 Inverleith Gardens, Edinburgh*
136. *1898–1911 Keir House, Dunblane, additions*
137. *1898–1907 Paisley Abbey Restoration*
138. *1898 Double Villa at Gullane*
139. *1899 Bothwell Parish Church, restoration*
140. *1899–1904 Inchinnan Parish Church, Inchinnan (demolished)*
141. *1899 Colinton Bank House, alterations*
142. *1899–1900 Senate Room, University of St Andrews, refurbishment*
143. *1900 Pulpit and interior rearrangements, St Salvator's Church, St Andrews*
144. *1900 Drill Hall for 5th Volunteer Brigade, Royal Scots, Dalmeny Street, Leith*
145. *1901 Alterations to Merchiston Castle School, Edinburgh (demolished)*
146. *1901–8 Pollok House, Glasgow. Wings, alterations, garden works*
147. *1902 Balmoral, additions and alterations*
148. *1902 Archers Hall, Edinburgh, reconstruction and additions*
149. *1902–8 Culross Abbey Church, restoration*
150. *1903 Dunblane Cathedral Hall*
151. *1905 Edinburgh University, alterations to provide for new Engineering and Physics Laboratories*
152. *1905 Kincairn House, Dunblane, alterations*
153. *1906 Assembly Rooms and Music Hall, George Street, Edinburgh, additions and alterations*
154. *1906–10 Dundee University, new Physics and Engineering Laboratories*
155. *1908 Royal Infirmary Edinburgh, minor alterations*
156. *1909 Monument to Stirlings of Keir, Dunblane Cathedral*
157. *1911 Dollar Academy Science Laboratory*
158. *1911–14 Sweetheart Abbey, restoration*

Executed Works (Undated)

c. 1890 Keavil House, Dunfermline, additions
c. 1880 Hatton House, Midcalder, additions and alterations
c. 1900 Sumburgh House, Shetland, additions and alterations
Kelso Abbey, restoration
Memorial to Mary of Lorraine, Edinburgh Castle
Memorial to Kirkcaldy of Grange, Edinburgh Castle
Memorial to Earl of Moray, Edinburgh Castle
Monument to Oliphant of Aberdalgie, Stirling Castle
Monument to Earl of Wharncliffe, Newtyle Parish Church
Memorial to J.R. Findlay, National Portrait Gallery

State Halberds for Municipality of Edinburgh
1880s (?) Houses at Barnshot Road, Colinton (3)

Unexecuted Projects

1. *1865 Duncan Institute, Cupar, Competition Designs*
2. *1873 Paisley Abbey, Restoration of Cloisters*
3. *1874 Sillyholm School, Lanark*
4. *1876 Brechin Diocese Official Residence*
5. *1876 Kirkcaldy Free Church Competition Designs*
6. *1877 Leven Episcopal Church*
7. *1877 St Paul's Episcopal Church, Greenock, Competition Designs*
8. *1878 Old St Paul's Episcopal Church, Edinburgh*
9. *1885 Pitmedden House, Aberdeen, alterations*
10. *1886 Industrial Exhibition, Edinburgh, Competition Designs*
11. *1887 Imperial Institute, London, Competition Designs*
12. *1887 Holy Trinity Episcopal Church, Pitlochry, alterations*
13. *1889 Arbroath High School, Competition Designs*
14. *1892 Midlothian County Buildings, Competition Designs*
15. *1892 Bishop's House, Elgin, Restoration Proposals*
16. *1895 North British Hotel, Competition Designs*
17. *1897 House for Mr Craig, North Berwick*
18. *1901 Queen Victoria Memorial, Competition Designs*
19. *1904 Extensions to British Museum, Competition Designs*

Appendix 2

PUPILS AND ASSISTANTS

As the Anderson office records have not survived, the list which follows is necessarily incomplete.

Name	Details	
JOHN WATSON	Pupil	1870–5
	Assistant	1875–82
ARCHIBALD MACPHERSON	Assistant	1873–6
GEORGE MACKIE WATSON	Pupil	1876–80
	Assistant	1880–4
	Principal Assistant	1884–99
ARTHUR GEORGE SYDNEY MITCHELL	Pupil	c. 1878–83
THOMAS ROGERS KITSELL	Pupil	1878–83
	Assistant	1883–7
ROBERT WEIR SCHULTZ	Pupil	c. 1879–84
VICTOR HORSBURGH	Pupil	c. 1882–7
ROBERT STODART LORIMER	Pupil	1885–9
	Assistant	1889–90
JAMES JERDAN	Assistant	c. 1885–90
WILLIAM HENRY BIDLAKE	Assistant	1887
FRANCIS WILLIAM TROUP	Assistant	1887
ALFRED LIGHTLY MACGIBBON	Pupil	c. 1890–5
JOHN JAMES JOASS	Assistant	1890–3
FRANCIS WILLIAM DEAS	Pupil	1890–6
ARTHUR FORMAN BALFOUR PAUL	Pupil	c. 1892–7
	Assistant	c. 1897–9
JAMES MCLACHLAN	Pupil	1892–c. 1897
HENRY THOMAS WRIGHT	Pupil	c. 1892–7
	Assistant	c. 1897–1900
J. HERVEY RUTHERFORD	Pupil	1893–8

DAVID MCCARTHY	Pupil	c. 1900–5(?)
JAMES FORBES SMITH	Assistant	1900–3
JAMES DAVIDSON CAIRNS	Assistant	c. 1901–5
BURNET ORPHOOT	Pupil	1902
JAMES GILLESPIE	Assistant	1903–11
THOMAS L. TAYLOR	Pupil	1905

Index